Catch the Falling Flag

Also by Richard J. Whalen

The Founding Father
The Story of Joseph P. Kennedy

A City Destroying Itself
An Angry View of New York

Catch the Falling Flag

A Republican's Challenge to His Party

Richard J. Whalen

HOUGHTON MIFFLIN COMPANY BOSTON

1972

Portions of this book
have appeared, in different form,
in *Harper's* magazine.

First Printing c

For Christopher, Laura and Michael

Preface

IN THE LATE SUMMER of 1967, Richard Nixon asked me to help him become President of the United States. I agreed to help because I am a moderate conservative, at home near the center of the Republican party, committed to the belief that government should serve the individual and preserve the community, performing the limited tasks government can perform honestly and well — and because I supposed that Nixon also believed such things.

I served him as an adviser and writer, one of the "bright young men" he liked to talk about, and was given such assignments as working out his position on Vietnam. It took me most of a year to discover why Nixon wanted to be President and what he would actually do with the office if he gained it. By that time, he had won the Republican nomination and seemed assured of winning the election. Nevertheless, I resigned from his staff.

This is a narrative of my experience as a nonpolitician on the inside of the greatest enterprise in American politics, the quadrennial struggle for the presidency. It is also a critical appraisal, from a privileged outsider's vantage point, of the performance of the Nixon administration. My purpose is not polemical — antipathy toward Nixon on the part of anyone who can write an English sentence is scarcely novel in present-day America. Rather, my purpose is personal and ideological. As a citizen, I participated in events worth recording that I am in a position to record. As a Republican, I am moved to challenge the Nixon administration's self-deception —

that our party can govern successfully with borrowed ideas and without any guiding ideals.

To the best of my knowledge, the expanding literature on the contemporary presidency contains no book quite like this one. The reason is obvious: anyone who helps elect a President usually has a strong interest in seeing him re-elected. This portrait of Nixon as candidate and President is offered without concern for the partisan consequences. My only loyalty is to the survival of America in freedom, and we are weaker and less free today than we were when Nixon entered the White House.

Wherever possible, I have identified who said what. It has often been impossible to identify sources, however, because they have asked to be protected against the certain reprisals that their open cooperation would invite. It betrays no confidence to disclose that among those who have read the manuscript, in whole or in part, and whose invaluable assistance is gratefully acknowledged, are several who know the President well. Sadly, Nixon's worst enemies have nothing to say about him so damaging as the observations of hurt, puzzled friends.

Although much of this book was written while I was affiliated with Georgetown University's Center for Strategic and International Studies, the institution, of course, bears no responsibility for my views. Among the friends who lent support and assistance during the writing, George and Anne Allen are owed a debt of gratitude.

In a very special sense, this book could not have been written without my wife, Joan Giuffré Whalen. She made many structural suggestions, typed and helped revise drafts of the manuscript, and suggested the title. Her greatest contribution, arising from patience, good humor, and courage, was to assist in countless ways the author's search for the elusive character named "I," whom she knew better than he did.

Contents

PART ONE

In Pursuit
A Personal History

I

1. Toward nine o'clock one evening in the early fall of 1970, Len Garment and I were crossing Executive Avenue, returning to his office from the White House Mess, when he pointed to a figure, about a hundred feet away, descending the steps of the Executive Office Building. It was the President, whom I had not seen or spoken with in more than two years. Now he passed in the gloom, flanked by Secret Service agents.

"How do you get along with the Old Man these days?" asked Garment, Special Consultant to the President on youth, civil rights, and culture and a close colleague in the 1968 campaign.

It was both a natural question, in view of my resignation from the campaign staff in August 1968, and a nuanced query stemming from the peculiar circumstances of the Nixon White House. Garment had given up a lucrative partnership in the old Nixon law firm and gone "inside" because he rarely saw the President — only to discover that most of the supposed insiders saw him infrequently, too. Anyone who had opened an avenue of personal contact with Nixon, however narrow, stirred Garment's interest and curiosity.

I started to say I didn't get along with the President, but that wasn't quite accurate. "On things where the country is in trouble, we correspond," I said, "and I do what I can."

When the late Senator Winston Prouty of Vermont informed the President in the spring of 1969 that he would support him on the proposed Safeguard antiballistic missile system, and sought assistance in preparing a speech explaining his changed position, I went,

at the request of the White House, to an out-of-the-way basement
office in the Capitol and assisted the senator. A week later, as the
gallery stirred, Senator Prouty cast the surprise vote by which the
ABM — and presidential decision-making authority in national defense — survived. When someone was needed to edit the *Report* of
the President's Commission on an All-Volunteer Armed Force, I
was drafted.

Garment understood what I meant. Along with the Cabinet
members and other administration officials, he had received from
the White House a copy of my May 1969 speech at Bohemian
Grove on the U.S.-Soviet nuclear balance, with a presidential memorandum commending "this excellent analysis." The last link between Nixon and me, then, was the same as the first — concern for
America's security.

In June 1967 I wrote an article for *Fortune*, "The Shifting Equation of Nuclear Defense," which reported on the growing Soviet
threat to the U.S.'s deterrent posture and the foundation of the Pax
Atomica. The facts were as ill-concealed as they were alarming.
The article disclosed the accelerating build-up of giant SS–9 Soviet offensive missiles, described the ominous implications of the
then classified multiple independently targetable re-entry vehicle
(MIRV), and discussed, in layman's language, the possibilities for
missile defense opened up by the X-ray effect, caused by exploding
nuclear warheads above the earth's atmosphere. If the Soviet drive
continued, the article forecast, the U.S. would have to consider the
drastic step of defending its supposedly "invulnerable" land-based
Minutemen missiles. When the article appeared, the telephone
began ringing.

One of those who called was Ray Price, an acquaintance from
New York and former editor of the editorial page of the defunct
Herald Tribune. He had a new job, he said, and his new boss, Rich-
ard Nixon, had liked the article, too.

"Nixon?" I demanded. "What are you doing working for that
loser?" Price, a liberal Republican, had close ties to that wing of
the party through his former employers, John Hay Whitney and

Walter Thayer. He had put eloquent conviction into the 1964 editorial endorsing Lyndon Johnson over Barry Goldwater, and since had written speeches for Senator Charles Percy. Price took my surprise in stride. Obviously I wasn't the first to react in this fashion. He said that Nixon wasn't at all like his public reputation — at least not anymore — and that I could find out for myself by meeting him. In fact, Nixon wanted to talk with me. I reminded Ray that he once had tried to recruit me as his replacement on the dying *Trib.* We left it at that.

Soon afterward, another liberal Republican, former Kansas congressman Robert Ellsworth, invited me to breakfast. (Washington, unlike Manhattan, transacts business at 7 A.M.) Ellsworth, bright-eyed and crisp, got to the point before we finished our juice. He had met Nixon accidentally on a plane some months earlier and had come away with an entirely new impression of the man; they had corresponded and wound up taking a trip to the Soviet Union together. Ellsworth's favorable impression had grown into a commitment. Would I be willing to "visit" with Nixon and talk about his plans for 1968? His staff, now little more than a nucleus, needed someone to "pull together research." I told Ellsworth that I had written a hostile review of Nixon's *Six Crises*, anticipating the verdict of California's voters on his bid for the governorship in 1962, and had no reason to change my mind. What was so different about him now that he had moved to Manhattan and a $250,000-a-year law practice in Wall Street? Ellsworth echoed Price: judge for yourself. As we parted, I promised to think about it.

The more I did, the more I wondered about Nixon's ability to enlist skeptics. Price had been toying with a novel and Ellsworth contemplating an uncertain future after an ill-timed race for the Senate. Both were available for adventure. Still, they were not "Nixon men," vintage 1960, and he had convinced them. My antipathy was quite different from that of the long-memoried liberals who hated what Nixon had stood for two decades ago. I was irked by his chronic failure to stand unequivocally. The man who suspected Alger Hiss and defeated Helen Gahagan Douglas was not the same man who turned mush-mouthed in the presence of John Kennedy. "Throughout his career," I had written of Nixon, "he has tried to synthesize sincerity, when all he had to do was unlock himself and let it out."

In 1967, the country ached for purposeful leadership; failing that, for almost any alternative to Lyndon Johnson. During the summer months, Negro rioting and looting erupted in more than a hundred U.S. cities, with the bloodiest clashes in Newark (26 dead, 1200 injured) and Detroit (43 dead, 2000 injured). The President's response — a virtual confession that the tormented country had escaped his control — was to appoint a committee to look into the disorders. Johnson was caught in war at home and abroad, yet stubbornly refused to face up to the imperatives: declare his objectives plainly to Congress and the people and ask for the taxes and sacrifices to pursue them. While he and Soviet Premier Kosygin traded grandfathers' stories in Glassboro, New Jersey, America's land war in Southeast Asia against a Soviet-backed foe dragged on hopelessly. Our dubious allies in Saigon were perfectly content to rule perched on our bayonets, which meant the war could continue indefinitely.

A Republican who told the American people the truth of their situation might conceivably beat Johnson and lift the country and our party toward renewal. But which Republican? George Romney looked splendidly forceful in his shirt-sleeves as he evangelized about rebuilding the cities. But his "brainwashing" remark after the obligatory candidate's tour of Vietnam underlined his total inexperience in foreign affairs. Ronald Reagan, hero of Late Show westerns, was an ideal television candidate, a fresh, "nonpolitical" citizen in politics, but he had never spent a day on duty in Washington. Nelson Rockefeller, able and seasoned, had unique appeal to Democrats and Independents, but they could not cast ballots at G.O.P. conventions. The mention of Rockefeller sent party regulars, especially matronly committeewomen, into fits of rage. Charles Percy, John Lindsay — the dark horses — were impossible long shots.

Which left only Nixon. Loyal in the 1964 debacle, effective as a campaigner in the congressional races in 1966 when the Republicans gained forty-six House seats, he was a known quantity among the party faithful, a "centrist" who split the difference between the warring ideological camps. Nixon's chances for the nomination, coolly appraised, were much better than they appeared at first glance — *if* he could dispel the loser's image. When Ellsworth telephoned again, I told him to arrange the meeting he had proposed. Perhaps Nixon saw not only the presidency, gleaming like Everest, a personal challenge, but also the uses of that office in calming and redirecting our society.

2. The turmoil of the late 1960s exposed an emptiness within America. In part, we saw the bankruptcy of our official ideology. The world refused to stay within the categories of genteel, respectable liberalism. Middle-class Negroes ignored their statistical well-being and looted; the adored and pampered college young rose in revolt against their benefactors; North Vietnamese commissars scorned a rational "limited" war and poured out rivers of their countrymen's blood to humiliate the capitalist aggressor. Fresh perceptions and new policies — on race, class, civil order, and peace-keeping — were needed.

To declare what we were fighting for in the jungles and paddies of Asia raised, especially for the educated young who came of age in the sixties, the question of what we were living for in the United States. The politicians were unable to answer because the question was social and cultural before it was political. It cast up for angry debate the unspoken assumptions underlying "the American way of life," and it opened to assault the institutions resting on those long unexamined and undermined assumptions.

We faced pseudo-revolt in the streets and on the campuses — and a very real revolution inside people's heads. The young and the blacks, clamoring for the attention of a society from which they claimed to be alienated, indulged in more or less violent play-acting. The most culpable were the stage managers, the leftist intel-

lectuals who did little physically yet rationalized and justified violence. Meanwhile, the real revolution was brewing in all the quiet,
neglected places like Queens, New York, among middle-class
Americans whose belief in God, country, and the American Way
was taken for granted.

I had grown up with these people, the Irish, German, and Italian
Catholics of Richmond Hill, the East European Jews of Rego Park
and Flushing, the New Yorkers the *New York Times* seldom noticed.
The collapse of liberalism and the savage leftist insurgency it produced exposed these people to the prospect — as they saw it — of
anarchy. The liberal state coerced them while comforting their
enemies. The liberal media censured them (when they were noticed at all) while lavishing concern on rebellious and violent minorities. Those who had imagined that they stood near the center
in the American scheme of things, and who believed that their
work, self-reliance, and responsibility earned them a measure of esteem, felt themselves pushed and crowded and cornered. Under
pressure from above and below, they were becoming truly alienated: they turned away. They were withdrawing trust from established leaders, institutions, and codes, abandoning the old assumptions and retreating beyond suspicion into open hatred of those
unlike themselves. All this was dangerous — and not at all surprising to me.

The fifties were my time of intellectual awakening. During the
years between Korea and John Kennedy, the country in which I
had been reared, the war-winning, true-believing, God-fearing
America of patriotic myth, remained outwardly intact, yet disinte-
grated within. My heroes in the early fifties were upright national-
ists and moralists like MacArthur and Taft. I was one of a small
band of dissenters, more antiliberal than "conservative," as we
called ourselves, who formed the Robert A. Taft Club on the campus of formidably liberal Queens College. By the end of the fifties,
my heroes seemed as much antiques as the round-screen Dumont
television set stored in the basement, the machine that had helped
topple them. The sixties saw the ascendancy of electronic media

politics and the New Culture. And the people who still believed saw themselves mocked. Under the reign of the clever and the beautiful, who patronized rebellion in all its forms, the disintegration of the old America speeded up.

In our society and under our system, the true pillars of order historically have been nonpolitical. Mother Benigna, the aged but indomitable principal of Our Lady of Perpetual Help School, with her ever-present yardstick, did much more to raise the level of citizenship in South Queens than any President of the United States. But stern nuns and parents went out of fashion in the late 1960s, even in the provincial backwaters. The family, the churches, and practically every other institution outside government were steadily drained of legitimacy and authority. This was the outcome of the disintegrating process and the primary cause of the cultural civil war.

The orgy of grief following John Kennedy's murder, the hysterical rush to enthrone a Leader and a Consensus — these were symptoms of sickness. It passed chiefly from middle-aged liberals to the susceptible young, from those empty of belief to those demanding to be filled up with a purpose for living — *any* purpose promising escape from a life sentence of boredom. Children brought up in ignorance of the values, goals, and self-discipline required for citizenship in a free society descended on the colleges to obtain, under authority they rejected, passports to careers they didn't want. Not surprisingly, the colleges exploded.

The true American establishment — parenthood — collapsed quietly and by stages throughout the sixties. Poverty in the lower classes and barrenness in the upper caused parents to default on the responsibility only they could discharge. The people in the middle, the last to lose authority over their children, yet feeling it slip away under the impact of the cultural insurgency, reacted in helpless fury. Even as they grew more distrustful of a system that rewarded the undeserving and cheated them, they looked to the state and its police power to uphold "law and order," by which they meant their own crumbling authority. They began to look in the direction of the Republican party and "conservatism" — for someone and something to take the place of vanished Mother Benigna, her yardstick and her certainties.

From being an unsilent member of my college generation, I had gone on to be an outspoken conservative journalist. But the whiggish doctrines I championed as an editorial writer on *The Wall Street Journal*, and the managerial pragmatism of the editorials I later wrote for *Fortune*, were irrelevant in a crisis less political than moral. I had come to see my native New York as a city destroying itself, and when the opportunity arose, I left. I took up the invitation of Admiral Arleigh Burke, former Chief of Naval Operations, to study and write at his small research center in Washington, the Center for Strategic and International Studies at Georgetown University. By the time I went to visit Nixon, I was no longer the combative ideologue of a decade earlier, but a writer searching for what was worth conserving in the midst of upheaval.

3.   On a gray, chilly Sunday afternoon in early September 1967, I took the three o'clock shuttle to New York and presented myself in the lobby of Nixon's apartment on East 61st Street. A doorman with a delightful brogue whisked me upstairs and a white-jacketed butler ushered me into the Nixon duplex. In the gold and white living room, Nixon stood talking with Bill Safire, a member of Nixon's circle since his vice-presidential days and now a Manhattan public-relations man. "I enjoyed *The Founding Father*," said Safire as he left.

Nixon, with an air of cordiality, led the way into his small study and offered a drink. There wasn't any bourbon, so I drank Canadian Club. My host sat in an armchair, and I perched on the edge of a long velvet-covered couch in front of a window overlooking Fifth Avenue and Central Park. As we talked, the late afternoon sun streamed through the window. Nixon rose to adjust the shutters, and shadows filled the room.

He praised my *Fortune* article, referred knowledgeably to such points as the Soviet lead in testing for the effects of high-yield weap-

ons, and expressed concern over the future of the "blue chip" —
U.S. nuclear superiority. I produced an inscribed copy of my book
on New York — "a city only outsiders can appreciate." He flipped
the pages, noting with approval that it wouldn't take long to read.
This led into talk about his speech-writing procedure. He wrote, he
said, in longhand on yellow legal pads, several painful drafts, and
needed a week for 2500 to 3000 words. After he was satisfied, he
committed the speech to memory, then discarded the draft. He
didn't recite the speech, but "saw" the text unreeling before his
mind's eye.

Nixon seemed easy to talk with. He would ask a question and listen closely to the answer. Sometimes he would interject a phrase,
then reconsider and correct himself in midsentence, revealing a feeling for the shade and weight of words. His quick intelligence was
apparent: he was with you or ahead of you or taking an interesting
tangent.

We talked at length about each of the possible candidates. He
wanted to know anything I knew, what I thought of each. He was
detached in his comments — acute but dispassionate in discussing
the strengths and weaknesses of the other men stalking the prize he
wanted so badly.

Romney: He'd gone beyond his depth, talked too much and too
often, leaving an impression of confusion. He appeared to be
finished after the "brainwashing" lapse. But he owed nobody anything and just might stay in the race, win or lose, right up to the
convention.

Rockefeller: Nixon spoke of him with a mixture of dislike and respect. He had experience and impressive qualifications. He had
carefully stayed out of the line of fire on Vietnam, taking the line
that he was governor of New York, without access to the information available to the President. But he would not enter the primaries and could not be nominated. Goldwater would lead his people
out of the convention.

Percy: He was bright and agile, but little-known and inexperienced. His manner was not imposing.

Reagan: The people around him wanted him to run. He hadn't made up his mind. So far as Nixon could tell, the Goldwater forces were not flocking to him. If he didn't enter the primaries (except for California and Oregon), he would be asking the convention to take him on image and faith. Goldwater had told Reagan bluntly that the Democrats would destroy him on the issue of experience. Reagan, like Rockefeller, was an attractive but unreal candidate, whose chance might come only if Nixon faltered.

Of his own chances, Nixon said with detachment that he must win impressively all the way to the convention, building momentum as he shed the "loser" label. If he stumbled, and he might in "cranky" New Hampshire, he was through, although he left open the question whether he would withdraw.

He recognized that a new tide of isolationism was running in the country as the result of the Vietnam war. He conceded that there was a shift in Republican sentiment away from all-out support of the war and admitted the practical wisdom of maneuver. He listened closely as I argued against the continued bombing of North Vietnam. I said the U.S. should mine Haiphong harbor and establish a naval "quarantine" of the coast, which, I suggested, should be coupled with a strong stand against the Soviets. He agreed emphatically that the Soviets, contrary to the administration's line, had no interest in seeing the war ended quickly.

Nixon seemed attracted to the idea of a two-prong maneuver — away from the administration's hard line on Vietnam, toward a firmer stand on the intentions of the Soviets, particularly in the Mediterranean and the Middle East. His reactions indicated that he was not as inflexible on Vietnam as recent articles in the press made him appear ("There are things you don't say in interviews"), but he wanted to work out carefully in advance the details of any demonstration of flexibility. He agreed that such a demonstration would help him with the unenthusiastic party professionals. But would it hurt him with the conservatives? "I am a conservative," he said, "at least as I define it."

We talked for a time about liberals and conservatives, about the enmity he aroused in the Alger Hiss case. "That was twenty years ago — they never forget, do they?" Nor would they ever forgive him, I suggested, for being a representative of the new American middle classes. The left-liberal intellectuals and journalists despised middle-class, "bourgeois" values and the "square" culture. Nothing that Nixon could say or do would appease them. He threatened their status as an antidemocratic elite in much the way that Lyndon Johnson did, and he could expect the same vindictive assaults that Johnson was experiencing. Beyond his political objective, I suggested, lay a cultural objective: the building of the foundation of a new intellectual establishment that would restore and conserve values under attack from the radical left.

Our talk next turned to the missed opportunities of the Eisenhower years. Nixon spoke of Eisenhower without his usual reverence and recalled the pain he suffered from Ike's famous press conference gaffe. Asked to identify a decision Nixon took part in, Eisenhower, who was on the way out of the room, said to howls of laughter from the press: "If you give me a week, I might think of one." Said Nixon: "He called me right after that hit the fan. He was being facetious, he didn't mean it the way it sounded." But nothing was done by the President or his staff to repair the damage to Nixon's credibility.

Nixon said earnestly that he wanted new blood and fresh ideas — not the tired, stale speeches he got from the Eisenhower holdovers in 1960 — and praised the "grace notes" in Ray Price's work. This led him into a discussion of the baleful effects of the traditional influence of big business in the Republican party. Businessmen, approaching politics as a necessary ordeal, fell naturally into lifeless, cut-and-dried formulations. They were afraid of unfamiliar ideas. And yet they had strong opinions on everything, said Nixon. "Just because they know something about their business, they think they know all about Vietnam. I get it all the time."

Nixon wanted a small research and writing staff — "no more than six" — *young* men who were skilled "generalists." (I noticed that he had picked up some of the jargon of business.) Romney had a staff of twenty. "I'll take my two researchers any time." Nixon, who had been over the road before, didn't need as large a staff as a newcomer. But, regardless of the number of men around him, would he delegate responsibilities? He hadn't in 1960. This time, he assured me, he would let his staff run him. "That's why I want to pick it so carefully."

People with ideas, Nixon noted, were able to publicize them by assisting a political figure like him — a plain invitation. "Of course, you can have your say in magazines, and reach a national audience. But, when you're with a man going for the presidency, you have a chance not only to get your ideas across, but maybe to see them put into practice. That's a big difference." I agreed, and changed the subject.

I told Nixon that I hoped he would show the side of him that didn't come across in 1960. He was perhaps the best-disciplined political technician of our time. Could he discipline himself to *relax*? He drew out my thoughts on the media, listening intently, almost *too* intently, so that I could almost hear the wheels whirring in his head. My only advice was: be *natural*. Could he turn it on and off, becoming politician-actor as our entertainment-oriented politics demanded? He was interested in thoughts on setting, lighting, audiences, length of speeches — the technical details of the image-politics in which he once lost so narrowly. ("I hurt my damned knee before the first nineteen sixty debate," he recalled. "I was as sick as a dog.") He liked the half-serious suggestion I tossed out that perhaps he might rerun portions of the tapes of the second and third 1960 debates, in which he compared favorably to Kennedy. He recalled once again Kennedy's margin: only 119,000 out of 68,000,000 votes. "Of course they stole the election — and Johnson will do anything to win the next one, too."

Nixon conceded that his defeat in California, which he blamed on the Birchers, was compounded by his televised display of temper at the post-midnight "last press conference." It was "a great mistake," and it might haunt him. Still, he believed that he would be able to "get under Johnson's skin" and provoke him into losing his temper. "He didn't have to face that last time — Barry was running against himself."

Well past the three-hour mark in our conversation, Nixon took me by surprise by suggesting that I consider becoming his "press man." He was enthusiastic. "You have a good voice, you'd look well on TV, and you'd get along with the reporters. It would be a lot of fun — and a lot of work. You're on call at all hours, but you're always in on everything — the press man is always there — and you'd get quite a book out of it. You always have to consider self-interest. You'd get the book and the experience of being on the inside of a national campaign, which adds an extra dimension to you. You're at just the right age, too. Think about it and get back to me as soon as possible."

At 9:20 P.M., I broke off the visit — if Nixon had no thought for dinner, I did — and dashed for the airport.

4. I spent a bouncing flight back to Washington sorting out my reactions. The pathological Nixon-haters in the press, by denying his humanity, ironically gave him an advantage in personal encounters. Compared with Herblock's Nixon, the Nixon I had met seemed pleasant and engaging. Trivial discoveries about him — he swore expertly — assumed encouraging significance. There was no trace of the arrogant self-importance often found in politicians. He made no pretense, as some vain public figures did, of being drawn into politics reluctantly. He lived for it and took pleasure in analyzing himself and the other players. Of course, this kind of tactical analysis also afforded Nixon a measure of protection, for it steered conversation away from ends and made the listener feel that he was learning more than he actually was. One hesitated to ask Nixon, naively, just *why* he wanted to be President.

Staring out the window into the dark, I wondered how many times in the course of a career extending over more than twenty years Nixon had found it necessary to devote Sundays to meeting with useful strangers like me. All those years, while men of conventional ambition were playing golf or washing their cars or taking naps, Nixon had been soliciting support and services that would inch him closer to his goal. There had been no sign of anyone else in the twelve-room apartment. I wondered what his wife and the girls did with themselves while Nixon received Sunday callers.

His suggestion that I become his "press man" sat oddly with me, like an invitation to join the wedding party of a casual acquaintance. Jack Kennedy's campaigns were run by the Irish Mafia that had come together like a hedgerow brotherhood over the years, and he was surrounded by a swarm of friends, classmates, and shipmates. Lyndon Johnson could call on staff, cronies, and henchmen who went back with him to Texas and the New Deal years. As far as I knew, aside from his long-time secretary, Rose Mary Woods, Nixon was without retainers.

I marveled that he would offer to let me in on "everything" when we had never worked together for a day. His reputation as a solitary man, who in 1960 hoarded authority from his staff to the point, it was said, of whittling his own pencils, seemed to exclude the possibility of such an instant grant of confidence. But perhaps his undoubted capacity for self-analysis had prompted self-correction. He had had years to ponder the lessons of defeat. Apparently, his proposal was part of a compromise he was determined to make with his sense of self-sufficiency in the future. He would gather around him functional people whom he scarcely knew, and whom he did not *want* to know, except as instruments performing required tasks.

I realized I was beginning to take his proposition seriously. The point about reaching the people with ideas was a hard-sell job description, and yet perhaps this time he meant it. He would be running free of the Eisenhower record and incoherent Modern Republicanism. Nixon had said: "I am a conservative, at least as I define it."

Price had told me that, after talking with Nixon, he did some reading and listening for a week before making up his mind. As the plane touched down at National Airport, I decided to follow the same course. Fortunately, Washington was the place where people had — or thought they had — answers to every question.

The following day I had lunch with three friends, two from New York publishing houses and the third a Washingtonian, Garth Hite, then publisher of *The New Republic*. I told them of my interview with Nixon and his offer, drawing the expected response from the Manhattan liberals. Hite said little, but sent a note that afternoon. "I don't know how you could refuse a challenge like that . . . There's one thing that was left unsaid at the luncheon table: Dick Nixon *is* qualified and he might damned well *win!* The world moves too fast these days to be hung up on the past."

A couple of days later, I saw columnist Robert Novak, just back from a swing through California. He reported a sharp turn against Vietnam even among conservative and publicly hawkish Republicans. John McCone, former CIA Director and a pillar of the G.O.P. establishment, had declared to him that the U.S. must get out of Vietnam. What about the loss of U.S. prestige? It would be severe, McCone admitted, but the only thing worse would be for the U.S. to stay. Nixon's chances, Novak concluded, probably would depend on how well he gauged this growing mood within the party and the population.

Later, I spoke with Arthur Krock, as stout a supporter as Nixon had in the press. He puffed on his cigar, then delivered his oracular judgment. Nixon would be nominated and defeated. "He's clearly the best-qualified Republican, but that isn't enough. Like other qualified men, he had the misfortune to run at the wrong time. By all means work for him, behind the scenes for a while anyway, until you know him better, and then write the book — an anatomy of defeat. It could be very good."

Next I went to Capitol Hill and visited, among others, the man acknowledged to be the smartest Republican politician in Washington, Congressman Melvin Laird, powerful Chairman of the House Republican caucus. We talked about the potentially pivotal primary in his home state of Wisconsin. Two of Laird's aides, William Baroody, Jr., and Carl Wallace, believed Reagan would enter it, but the congressman disagreed. The key date, said Laird, was February 26. By that deadline, two weeks in advance of the first presi-

dential primary in New Hampshire, Reagan would have to ask the
Wisconsin primary commission to remove his name from the ballot
by declaring that he was not a candidate at that time or his name
would be entered automatically. "Wisconsin," said Laird, "just
won't vote for a man who doesn't come into the state and campaign
— and Reagan has said he won't campaign."

The great imponderable in Wisconsin and elsewhere was Alabama's former governor George Wallace. Demonstrations and
marches for open housing in Milwaukee were stirring an explosive
backlash among white voters. Although Wallace had taken one
third of the votes in the Democratic 1964 primary, he would fade,
Laird predicted, as other candidates, including Nixon, began campaigning and offering alternatives. What would Nixon say on racial disorders and the urban crisis generally? I had to confess that I
had no idea. Up to that time, he had said nothing publicly. These
professionals clearly regarded Nixon as one of them, but I detected
not the faintest spark of excitement about him and the likely quality of his leadership.

A few days later, Nixon telephoned and asked if I would accom-
pany him to the West Coast in early October. I proposed instead
that I remain in the background for some time, as an adviser and
writer, adding that this was the suggestion of our mutual friend, Arthur Krock. Nixon was somewhat puzzled and said of Krock:
"He's never been inside a campaign, so he doesn't know what it's
really like." But he said that he needed advice and had a specific
question. Should he make another visit to Vietnam? I replied that
it depended on what he used the trip for. If he returned only to re-
iterate his support of the war and the administration, the trip was
pointless and probably counterproductive. I told him that he
should go only if he had made up his mind in advance to adopt a
new position. He seemed to agree. (In the end, he did not go to Vietnam again.) "Flexibility is the first principle of politics," he said
in closing. "I want you on any basis and whenever you want to
come."

II

1. By MID-SEPTEMBER 1967 the unannounced Nixon candidacy was more than a year and a half into the ritual of emergence. The "spontaneous" stirring of grassroots support that summer had been followed by the opening of Washington headquarters of the Nixon for President Committee. The Committee occupied a former bank (the vault was used for storing pamphlets, buttons, and bumper stickers), only a block west of the White House on Pennsylvania Avenue and conveniently across the street from the local offices of the Nixon law firm. Dr. Gaylord ("Parky") Parkinson, a Californian whose bedside manner had restored a semblance of unity to that state's riven G.O.P., carried the title of chairman but was little more than a figurehead. The actual headquarters of the Nixon campaign, remote from the eyes of the press and public, was the lower Manhattan offices of Nixon, Mudge, Rose, Guthrie, Alexander & Mitchell.

When I joined the campaign, Parkinson had just resigned and returned to California, where his wife was seriously ill. That put a civilized gloss on certain brutal facts. Ellsworth, acting on Nixon's orders, had purged the Washington office, down to the secretaries and switchboard operators. Another figurehead had been installed as chairman, Oklahoma's former governor Henry Bellmon, but he intended to leave early in 1968 to run for the Senate. Ellsworth, as executive director, was effectively in charge of the visible campaign.

Working with him was a young lawyer from the Nixon firm, John Sears, who had begun writing speeches and performing chores

for the candidate in the spring of 1966. Sears had been educated at
Notre Dame and Georgetown Law School, but his precocious skill
as a delegate-hunter and organizer was inbred. A generation earlier, he and I and the several other Irish Catholics who figured
prominently in the preconvention campaign almost certainly would
have been Democrats, faithful to the party of our fathers. Now we
hoped for an ideologically congenial home in the party of the small-
town, middle-class Protestants. Sears combined his practical talents
with a subtle grasp of the issues rending the country and a sense of
moral urgency on the necessity for facing them. We took an immediate liking to each other.

Ellsworth and Sears candidly instructed me in the division of
power between the visible and invisible Nixon apparatuses. The
Washington headquarters was like a Hollywood set — all posters
and pretty girls and red, white, and blue bunting. There wasn't a
speck of real authority on the premises. That was to be gained only
through direct access to the candidate, and they advised me to get
up to New York as quickly as possible.

First, they suggested, I should pay a protocol visit on the senior
Nixon policy adviser in Washington, Bryce Harlow. Late in September, I spent two hours with Harlow in the K Street offices of
Procter & Gamble, whose Washington interests he watched over. A
native of Oklahoma in his early fifties, he spoke softly and precisely,
the force in his words coming from his piercing blue eyes. He had
an encyclopedic knowledge of national politics acquired during
three decades in the capital. He had served Eisenhower for eight
years as a speech-writer and congressional lobbyist and helped
Nixon in 1960. He had no illusions about the man or his prospects.

He believed that Nixon would win the nomination handily, but
frankly doubted that he stood much chance against Johnson. In the
early 1950s, Harlow had served on the staff of the Senate Armed
Services Committee, and from that vantage point, he began to form
a respectful estimate of Johnson's qualities as an in-fighter and sure-
footed survivor. He anticipated the moves that Johnson would
make early in 1968. As Harlow saw it, the President would: "Get a

Vietnam peace campaign going. Move McNamara over from the Pentagon to head the War on Poverty. Fire Sargent Shriver and Orville Freeman. Make a flock of law-and-order speeches. Offer the greatest array of promises for the cities that anybody has ever seen. He can't deliver on them? So what? He can blame Congress. The whole performance will make the point loud and clear that Johnson may be down, but he's a long way from being out."

The source of Harlow's pessimism concerning Nixon's chances was impersonal. The "grotesque disproportion" between the power of the incumbent, no matter how badly he had failed, and the inherent weakness of the opposition lengthened the odds against Nixon. Johnson could win most surely, in Harlow's judgment, by "daring to be President" — by declaring the national interest in plain language and doing what plainly served it. Of course, he allowed, this demanded a disinterested suspension of partisanship that would be quite out of character for Johnson. Could he be both himself *and* President?

I came away convinced that Nixon could be President only if he beat Johnson to the attack and kept the initiative.

2. A couple of days later, I took a late afternoon flight to New York and arrived at the Nixon law offices just as the rush hour in the financial district was thinning out. The twenty-seventh floor was a maze of construction. Workmen were putting up partitions to accommodate the expansion of the firm, now one of the ten largest in the country. I found Ray Price tucked away in a littered corner office at the end of a corridor. An intense, thoughtful thirty-seven-year-old who managed a pipe gracefully, often quiet to the point of communicating entirely by nods and frowns, he made me welcome and explained that his current project was a "thematic" book for the campaign. He brightened as I reported Nixon's praise of his recent ghostwriting, including an article, "Asia After Vietnam," for *Foreign Affairs*. He assured me that "the Boss," contrary to past habit, wanted and would use staff-written material. It was simply a matter of gaining his confidence through performance.

(No one had asked me, and so I had not mentioned it, but I had never ghostwritten a line in my life.)

We were soon joined by Leonard Garment, an engaging man in his early forties. He wore a slightly perplexed and harried expression. Restless, quick-moving, and faster-talking, he did not look like a veteran of Wall Street litigation. Instead, he looked more the old part that every article on the new Nixon staff would note with amazement — that of part-time sideman (tenor sax, clarinet) in the Woody Herman and Henry Jerome orchestras during the years when he was pushing to the top of his class at Brooklyn Law School. An aura of show biz still clung to him and crept into his conversation, along with the jargon of his new concerns — polling, media, and advertising. The outgoing Garment was the organization's chief talent scout, recruiter, and promoter, as well as self-appointed liaison man between Nixon and alien worlds. It was Garment who sat up all night on his kitchen floor rapping with people like Dick Gregory.

The organization of the "issues and policy development area" was easily explained because there wasn't any. "Everything's in flux, very free-form and ad hoc," said Garment. Carefully chosen advisers were busy alongside volunteers whose services could not be refused. Projects overlapped, confusion reigned, and Garment stood in the middle of it, enjoying himself in the role of impresario. For example, he was supervising the preparation of a white paper on urban problems by a very senior Republican "task force," which deliberated in ignorance of position papers being written elsewhere in the same building on the same problems by one of Garment's prize recruits — Dr. Martin Anderson. A brilliant, thirty-one-year-old assistant professor of economics at Columbia, Anderson had turned his doctoral dissertation on urban renewal into a devastating book, *The Federal Bulldozer*. While we talked, Anderson joined us for a few minutes. With his owlish horn-rimmed glasses and unruly forelock, he looked improbably youthful and strictly professorial. Yet he would prove, during the campaign and afterward, a remarkably effective political operator, whose ideas somehow got through the maze. ("You have to understand, Dick," he remarked to me one day some months later. "Academics are born connivers.")

Over dinner that evening, Garment and Price expressed concern over "the Reagan thing," which threatened Nixon at his weakest point — his lack of charisma. Nixon would have to achieve through "substance," Garment said, the effect that Reagan's "style" won for him. It would be the responsibility of the policy advisers to carve out positions and the responsibility of the media group —including Garment, Harry Treleaven (on leave from a vice presidency at J. Walter Thompson), and Frank Shakespeare, a CBS vice president giving part-time assistance — to devise formats for communicating these positions in ways that made the most of Nixon's unexciting personality. Ideally, the candidate would be made to appear as his media men saw him: mature, responsible, and compassionate.

The next afternoon, I met the "senior" member of the new Nixon staff in point of service, twenty-nine-year-old Patrick J. Buchanan, who had come to the candidate from the editorial page of the St. Louis *Globe-Democrat* in January 1966. Another Irish Catholic, trained at Georgetown University and Columbia Journalism School, he wore his right-wing views as a proud badge of identity. Price, the liberal, and Buchanan, the conservative, nicely balanced one another, as Nixon intended they should. Neither they nor I knew as yet how I would fit into this arrangement of ideologies and personalities. Ellsworth had counseled me to "take charge" on my arrival in New York, as though I had a directive from Nixon to do so. The other members of the staff, unaware of "RN's" wishes, would fall into line, he said, and Nixon would give his approval after the fact.

That was shrewd Nixonology, but too devious for me. Buchanan had an air of barely contained explosive energy and a brusque manner. Looking closer, however, I saw that he was also a bit uncertain of his place and unsure whether he should defend it. We would get along best, and I would accomplish my purposes, it seemed to me, if I did what I could to assure him that I had no designs on his place. He sat literally at the Boss's right hand, in a small room crowded with file cabinets just outside Nixon's office. Buchanan screened and underlined reading material for Nixon, maintaining black looseleaf briefing books on scores of issues, and he also collated the flow of opinion polls and political intelligence. While I stood talking with Buchanan, Nixon strode by and asked me to "stick my head in the door" before I left for Washington.

I spent an hour and a half with Nixon. His office looked like a trophy room, overcrowded with mementos of his vice-presidential travels. Behind his desk were arrayed, in double file, signed photographs of crowned heads and statesmen, whose names he frequently dropped. A large book about the Quakers sat a bit obviously on a small table next to his desk. Much more than his apartment, this office was Nixon's carefully set stage for winning over the skeptical.

He asked what I thought of his team, then answered his own question. "They're all very bright and independent. It's not like nineteen sixty at all. Of course, we don't have anybody with the political savvy of Bob Finch, but Bob Ellsworth is coming along — and he's a great issues man, too. Boy, can he get tough! Almost *too* tough, the way he fired those Parkinson people."

Nixon remained fascinated — and pleased — by the reaction to Romney's "brainwashing" remark. "I've never seen anything like it in all my years in politics. One moment he's the front runner, the next he's down. Words are so very, very important." He said that Senator John Tower, the Texas conservative, had come by for a visit and told of Reagan's growing popularity. But Tower was bothered when Reagan called for escalation of the bombing of North Vietnam. "That's a bad word," Tower told Nixon. "He should have called for *increased* bombing."

Nixon was interrupted by a long-winded telephone call concerning a dinner he would address. He put the receiver down with a look of exasperation. "Why do they all have to give all the details to The Man? Why can't they talk to the man who talks to The Man?"

Nixon would make a speech in a few days at Stanford University, and he asked me, apologetically, to try a draft. "I know it's short notice — you should have at least a week — but do the best you can." I was impressed with his practiced ease as he took up in rapid sequence the theme, tone, length, and content of the speech.

He would speak at the Hoover Institution, before a conference on the fiftieth anniversary of the Bolshevik revolution. "I don't want it to be the typical anti-Communist harangue — you know, there's Nixon again. Try to *lift* it. I want to take a *sophisticated* hard line. I'd like to be very fair and objective about their achievements — in fifty years, they've come from a cellar conspiracy to control of half the world. But I also want to underline the horrible costs of their methods and system." He handed me a copy of his speech the previous summer at Bohemian Grove, telling me to take it as a model for outlining the changes in the Communist world and the changing U.S. policy toward the Soviet Union.

He speculated on the "news peg" the speech should contain. Recalling our discussion of the shifting nuclear balance, he said: "Perhaps it's time to open up a high-level dialogue with McNamara. His line on the ABM — the so-called Chinese threat — is pretty sad. Let's get the Soviets into the picture. Put it roughly in these terms: Perhaps it is now possible to live in peace with the Soviet Union, to build at least our end of the bridges to the east and all the rest. *But* we can't lose our nuclear deterrent, the umbrella over the non-Communist world. If you took the United States out, the rest of the world would live in terror."

He wanted only a general reference to Vietnam in the text — "something like, 'We must halt the export of revolution.'" But no more than that for the present. Clearly the rise of antiwar feeling among Republicans concerned him and complicated his strategy. Romney was in trouble because he seemed indecisive, not because he'd called the war "tragic." Reagan seemed to be taking a superhawk position, not excluding the use of nuclear weapons. But it was not such a jump, Nixon realized, from saying "get it over with quickly" to saying "get out and save the lives of American boys." Nixon had consistently supported the American commitment in Vietnam and backed each increase in U.S. military forces, all the while faulting such piecemeal application of power. He was in no position abruptly to turn against the war and the commitment even if he wanted to. Moreover, he was conscious of the danger that Johnson might be baiting a trap for the Republicans, which he would spring through a peace offensive or attacks on their weakness and confusion.

But Nixon was aware of the changing public mood — the *Foreign Affairs* article had noted it — and he recognized the need to say something that at least *sounded* new. "In three to five hundred words, what should my answer be when someone asks: How does your position on Vietnam differ from President Johnson's? What should be the Republican position on the war?"

I realized that he was thinking aloud and kept silent. "Militarily and diplomatically, we're stuck on dead center. The greatest danger of escalation into a big war is through a long, drawn-out war. Our national interest requires ending the war . . ." He paused. "I've been saying, 'an honorable end to the war,' but what the hell does that really mean? What about, 'The war must be ended promptly on a basis consistent with the strategic interests of the United States and the free Asian nations'?"

Now the pause was longer, indicating that he expected a reply. Personally, I wanted to see the war ended, period, because we were not serious about fighting it. Korea and its aftermath should have taught us something about the strains that undeclared and protracted limited war imposed on a democratic society. The formulation Nixon proposed was better than the old one, and I said so. But it echoed the Johnson-Rusk line and put him under an obligation to define America's "strategic interests" in Vietnam in a way that justified the pain and bloodshed. Johnson had been unable to do it.

The inevitable question Nixon faced was: How will you end the war? He took up retired Air Force general Lauris Norstad's proposal: the U.S. would halt the bombing of North Vietnam for thirty days, make an all-out diplomatic effort to get negotiations started, and then, if Hanoi balked, apply whatever level of military force, particularly bombing, proved necessary to end the war. "Now speak up," Nixon said, "if you don't agree."

I didn't agree. The plan struck me as awful. It was nothing more than a thirty-day ultimatum, backed by a threat that wasn't credible. With opposition to the bombing growing in the United States, I asked, why should Hanoi believe that we would suddenly hit them with everything? The trouble was we had made it clear long ago that we *wouldn't* hit them as hard as we could, which in terms of American power in Asia meant at least the implied threat of nuclear weapons. The whole Cold War truce line had been drawn and backed by our nuclear power. The Republican version of recent history claimed that only the threat of nuclear weapons had extricated the U.S. from the Korean War. But in this war, no such threat was remotely in sight.

"Would you have me urge the use of nuclear weapons?" Nixon asked.

No, I replied, but I had no *a priori* objection, nor did the Russians, nor would the Chinese when they got nuclear weapons. The United States was a world power not only because of its population and productive wealth, but also because of its technological superiority, especially nuclear superiority. If we refused or were afraid to assert that superiority symbolically, we were finished in Asia and a good many other places in the world. And the sooner we recognized it, the less dangerous our retreat would be.

This was scarcely sound Republican doctrine, yet Nixon seemed to relish the excursion into heresy.

"Well, if I were in there," he said, "I *would* use nuclear weapons." He explained at once that he did *not* mean that he would use them in Vietnam, only that he would be as willing as John Kennedy to threaten their use in appropriate circumstances.

We talked next about the 1962 Cuban missile crisis. Kennedy had rejected plans for air strikes against the missile sites in favor of a naval strategy, I recalled, because the sea was a flexible environment, permitting many degrees of commitment and offering the widest range of options. What was so terribly wrong about Vietnam was precisely the environment. We were fighting a man-for-man war in the jungles, at levels of attrition too low to defeat the enemy, but too high for us to sustain in view of our fuzzy objectives. Nixon said he had learned from General Wallace Greene, the outgoing Marine Commandant, that General Westmoreland had asked earlier in the year for an additional 200,000 troops — and even then he could not guarantee results within less than three years.* Westmoreland had received only another 45,000 men, enough to arouse the public further against Johnson, too few to make much difference on the ground in Vietnam.

Nixon picked up my earlier suggestion of a "quarantine" of North Vietnam's coast. In his Bohemian Grove speech, he pointed out that the Soviet Union supplied all the oil and most of the sophisticated equipment for Hanoi's war effort. Wouldn't "quarantine" risk confrontation with the Soviets? I reported on research I had done following our first conversation. In 1966, according to the Department of Defense, the Soviets had sent 122 merchant ships to North Vietnam, the Eastern Europeans 45, the Chinese 138 — and non-Communist nations, including some of our allies, 74. At the least, I said, the announcement of our future intention to impose a "quarantine" might reduce this traffic.

Of course, the risk of confrontation with the Soviets was real. I pointed out, however, that we already shadowed their ships closely by sea and air without incident. What's more, the present bombing of Haiphong was at least as dangerous as patrolling the harbor's approaches. It came down to this: where did Vietnam fit in a realistic, world-wide assessment of American "strategic interests"? Was it as important as, say, the Middle East? And how important was it to the Soviets? Perhaps if we gave the appearance of being serious, the Soviets would respect our seriousness — especially if we simultaneously began scaling down our effort in the paddies of South Viet-

* The inspiration for Westmoreland's request, a ranking Pentagon official told me two years later, was not the battlefield situation, but the political judgment of the army's Chief of Staff, General Earle Wheeler, that the time was ripe for boosting the army's size and budget.

nam. Perhaps they could get Hanoi to talk. Nixon, it developed, held out hope for inducing Soviet cooperation through economic and trade concessions, such as freer access to advanced U.S. technology in electronics, chemicals, and other fields.

Regardless how we went about it, our aim, I insisted, should be to disengage from a land war in Asia we never intended to fight, before it paralyzed our will to stand firm in other parts of the world where vital national interests were at stake. I read aloud from Nixon's *Foreign Affairs* article: "If another friendly country should be faced with an externally supported communist insurrection . . . there is serious question whether the American public or the American Congress would now support a unilateral American intervention, even at the request of the host government."

To stay in Vietnam was to guarantee the outcome Nixon forecast in his article. Vietnam, a war sprung from reckless globalism, was pushing us toward the other extreme of isolationism. The answer, it seemed to me, was to withdraw from Southeast Asia as quickly as we could, on the best terms we could obtain. A firm stance vis-à-vis the Soviets would cover that retreat and prepare public opinion for possible tests elsewhere.

Nixon listened closely. For the moment, all he needed was language that would give the press and public a sense of *movement*. Earlier, he made the point in connection with the Stanford text that he wanted to introduce "a hopeful note, an upsweep of optimism" toward the end of his speeches. Language that signaled flexibility would do this. But he admitted that he would have to say a great deal more later on.

While we talked, Nixon cocked his feet up on the desk and threw his head back against the chair, completely relaxed. I studied his face. His heavy brows and dark, deep-set eyes gave him a forbidding appearance even in repose.

3. Following Nixon's directions, I finished a draft of the Stanford speech in a couple of days and sent it off to New York. It care-

fully skirted the subject of Vietnam, except for a passage linking American frustration to Soviet involvement. "Our eagerness to reform the Russians, with or without their cooperation, often takes the form of putting our ideas in their heads . . . The strangest view attributed to Moscow by certain mind-readers in Washington alleges that the Soviets really want to help us reach a prompt and honorable settlement in Vietnam. On the contrary, the Soviets quite obviously want to keep us bogged down in Southeast Asia as long as possible . . ." Word came back through Buchanan that RN was pleased with this first collaboration. Before long, Governor Romney picked up the same theme in characteristic head-on fashion, declaring: "We are in direct conflict with Russia in Vietnam."

The fall of 1967 was a season of hesitant maneuver for the Republican opposition. If Johnson suddenly gained results from one of the secret "peace" initiatives that the capital gossip mill incessantly rumored, or if he could depict himself as a beleaguered "War President" beset by cynical opportunists while American boys died in Asia, then, Senate Minority Leader Everett M. Dirksen and other senior party strategists feared, the Republicans would be in deep trouble. The safest course seemed the one of least resistance: to leave the debate to Johnson and his array of Democratic critics.

This prescription for inertia, so congenial to the conventional Republican temperament, offered the voters a choice between a bad policy and no policy. Congressman Mel Laird, better attuned to public opinion and partisan opportunity than most Republicans, gave an important speech in September. He charged the President with making "a fundamental change" in U.S. policy in South Vietnam at the Manila conference in October 1966. The U.S. promise, announced at Manila, to withdraw within six months after the North Vietnamese left and the fighting subsided, Laird said, "would be tantamount to turning South Vietnam over to the Communists." Anything short of the earlier Johnson goal of a free and independent South Vietnam "cannot justify the sacrifices that have already been made by Americans, nor the further spilling of another drop of American blood, nor the expenditure of another

American dollar . . . If the choice is between turning South Vietnam over to the Communists in 1969 or right now in 1967, we might as well do it now and prevent further American casualties." Here, from a party leader shrewdly taking cover under hawkish language, was the beginning of Republican movement toward a policy of clear-cut opposition to the President.

Later in September, Kentucky's senator Thruston Morton, the former Republican party chairman, turned Romney's phrase around and accused the President of being "brainwashed by the military-industrial complex" into believing the United States could achieve a military victory in Vietnam. "I am convinced," Morton told a group of businessmen opposed to the war, "that unless we gradually and, if necessary, unilaterally reduce the scope of our military involvement, we may well destroy the very society we sought to save."

What struck me during this period was the waning confidence among informed men in Washington who had formerly been outspokenly in favor of the war. In their public remarks, senior military officers, active and retired, continued to do their duty, loyally supporting the Commander in Chief and the war effort as well as protecting their services' prestige. In conversation, however, stereotypes of the military as robotlike and uncritical fell apart. Men in uniform tended to be privately as pessimistic on American prospects in Vietnam as antiwar radicals, and much better equipped with factual arguments against Johnson's policies. The mistakes made in Vietnam were in part the result of the poor judgment and incompetence of military men. Nevertheless, the fact was that the professional military had had less to say about the launching and conduct of this war than any other in our history. The greater part of the blame belonged to the armchair strategists, who designed and managed the war down to the smallest detail. These civilians in E-ring offices in the Pentagon and cubicles in the White House basement, elbowing aside the generals, had seized the opportunity to test their theories of "conflict management" on a real battleground.

Early in October, as we had lunch together, Admiral George Anderson, recently retired Chief of Naval Operations, made these points:

1. Yes, an isolationist wave was running in the country, but it wasn't as worrisome as the defeatist wave engulfing the upper echelons of the administration and much of the media. Many influential men had already accepted defeat in Vietnam and were rationalizing the consequences — or thought they were.

2. Were we clear, even at this late date, about our *political* objectives in Vietnam? We could win every military engagement, yet lose the larger struggle.

3. Nixon, for now, could talk about our strategic interests, the future of Asia beyond Vietnam, and the role of our allies, especially Japan. In the short term, he could get away with faulting the conduct of the war. But ultimately he had to answer the central question of *how* to end the war on satisfactory terms.

The admiral said a high administration official had hinted broadly that Anderson's son, a naval officer stationed on a carrier off Vietnam and due home for leave at Christmas, might not have to return to his ship. By January, "peace" talks might begin.

How often we had heard that — and how willing we were each time to believe it.

4.   Toward the end of October, the press reported the formation of the Citizens Committee for Peace with Freedom in Vietnam, a prestigious, bipartisan group including former Presidents Truman and Eisenhower, several former Cabinet officials, and a number of World War II-era military men. The co-chairmen, General Omar N. Bradley and former Senator Paul H. Douglas, explained at a press conference that the committee had been organized to support "the office of the President." The newspaper photograph of Bradley, Douglas, and Mrs. Oswald B. Lord, white-haired senior citizens all, revealed what was wrong. These honorable, patriotic Americans were reaching out to public attitudes that were simply no longer there. The committee's manifesto echoed the language of the Cold War that even the most resolute anti-Communists no longer

used. America, said the committee's statement, is "shedding its blood and expending its treasure in a distant country for the simple privilege of withdrawing in peace as soon as that country is guaranteed the effective right of self-determination. We ask nothing for ourselves."

In a note to Nixon, I predicted a short, unsuccessful life for the committee. "Its statement is wholly out of key with the trend of opinion even among those who want the United States to stick it out in Vietnam. Why is it 'noble and worthy' to fight for South Vietnam, and not for Cuba and Hungary? Why did Eisenhower reject intervention in Indochina in 1954 if he feels so certain it is now the right course?" I warned that the slightest gesture of sympathy toward the committee on Nixon's part would confirm the suspicion of many Republicans that he was "set in cement" on Vietnam.

Nixon heeded the advice and did not endorse the committee, gaining a continued flexibility from his silence. But he could not keep silent indefinitely.

For several weeks, Price had been turning out paragraphs on the war that could be fitted into speeches at Nixon's discretion, but a full statement of his position proved elusive. Nixon's voluminous public record was undeniably hawkish. To be at once consistent and "flexible" was a tough assignment, and the prose stockpile in Price's bottom desk drawer grew steadily. Finally, in early November, some of the pieces came together in a 1000-word statement that Buchanan described in a note as "a skeletal outline of RN's position."

The statement justified Vietnam as the testing ground for "the future of peace and freedom in the Pacific" against the threat of the Communist-supported wars of liberation. "If a bunch of ragged guerrillas can defeat the powerful United States in Vietnam, isn't this the way to spread Communism in other parts of the world?" The statement repeated past criticisms of the administration and urged "policies which will end the war and win the peace as quickly as possible." These unspecified policies should convince the North Vietnamese that they could not win militarily in South Vietnam, or politically in South Vietnam and the United States. It directed a "loud and clear" message to Hanoi: "Regardless of what happens in the elections of 1968, a majority of Americans, Democrat and Republican, are united in this resolve — that there shall be no reward for Communist aggression in Vietnam." The war could be ended by "getting out," the statement conceded, describing this as an "increasingly popular viewpoint," but withdrawal was rejected on the ground that it would surely lead to another war elsewhere.

The statement was filled with such headline-seeking phrases as "end the war and win the peace." Certainly it was the time-honored prerogative of the opposition to offer slogans appealing to the widest possible spectrum of discontent. But I had misgivings about a statement that simultaneously indicted Johnson's lack of public candor ("an inexcusable failure") and encouraged optimistic illusions about our ability permanently to "deny" Hanoi the reward of its aggression. My reaction was requested and I gave it promptly.

MEMORANDUM

TO: DC*   November 10, 1967

FROM: RJW

The statement on Vietnam answers the need to say *something*, but let us not be captivated by our own rhetoric. I have thought long and hard, and have tried to come up with a statement that would square with the realities of the war and with our political necessities. Tactically, it may be the wisest course to line up behind the President. After all, he has absolute control over the war issue, and he could deny it to overeager and patently expedient Republicans by some stroke of diplomacy tomorrow morning. But this is a fairly remote possibility. The war is very likely to be with us come next November.

On that assumption, I must voice this serious reservation. As a

* "DC" was the code name assigned Nixon in mail communications, at once a touch of intrigue and hopeful prophecy.

"lesson" to the Communists on the unprofitability of future wars of national liberation, the struggle in Vietnam has failed completely. It has failed because it has gone on too long, grown too big, and drawn the United States into fighting the war the South Vietnamese should be fighting — the crucial "other war" for the loyalty of the Vietnamese people.

The American people are divided on this war, but I believe they are overwhelmingly agreed there will be no future Vietnams. (Reflect for a moment on the overwhelming opposition in Congress to the administration's proposed dispatch of aircraft to the Congo; think about what we are all hearing from John McCone and George Humphrey and their conservative kind.) I believe the United States is in a truly tragic position: we cannot lose the war militarily, but neither can we "win" it politically.

Try to imagine, as I have, the possible terms of a negotiated settlement, and it adds up to American withdrawal, leaving behind an ally incapable of overcoming its own vulnerability. If the war suddenly trails off, do we stay or go? If we go, the war will surely be revived — and the American people will *not* support reintervention. The Communists, far from being taught a lesson, are in fact profiting greatly from the lopsided American effort and from the spreading sense of futility and disillusionment among the American people that will forestall our intervention in future wars where our national interest is ambiguous.

I do not counsel saying anything so bleak, but I want you to *think* about saying it later on. It fits in with your criticism of the conduct of the war, which must be emphasized and enlarged upon in all future statements.

Nixon telephoned to say that he "appreciated" my point of view and that he would be thinking about the questions I had raised. "It's still very early, you know."

III

1. UNDER MY ARRANGEMENT with Nixon, I served as a part-time, $75-a-day consultant, and commuted to New York once or twice a week, delivering completed assignments and picking up new ones. When I made the trip on a Saturday, I took along for company my son Christopher, then nine years old, who was unimpressed with presidential politics but enthusiastic about jet airplanes. Chris, assuming the role of travel secretary, decided that we should patronize American Airlines because they served soft drinks, an amenity missing from the dreary Eastern shuttle, even though it might mean waiting an extra half-hour. In that leisurely period before the primary campaigning began, there was plenty of time to wait for a Coke.

While Chris sat in an empty office and scribbled on Nixon, Mudge stationery, I would make the rounds, chatting with Garment, Buchanan, Anderson, and Price. Visitors on other errands passed through these informal meetings — the pollster, Tully Plesser, delivering soundings from New Hampshire and Wisconsin; a P.R. man from Omaha preparing for the sure-thing Nebraska primary; Nixon operatives from the much chancier battlegrounds of Oregon and California; Treleaven and his crew of advertising men and film makers; fund-raisers, well-wishers, and people promoting pet schemes. I was struck by the importance of these professional specialists whom the public never heard about. The indispensable Hessians of American politics, they hired out their talents, if not to the highest bidder, then surely to the prince whose party, pay scale, and prospects combined most attractively.

In contrast, our small group was professional only in the sense that we received compensation for our services. In the complex business of President-making, we were rank amateurs, and our main task looked suspiciously like intellectual play — certainly we had fun at it. Our job seemed to be the improbable one of defining for ourselves, the prince, and the Hessians the cause in which we had enlisted. While the pros exchanged numbers, we debated ideas. To draw the connection between their activities and ours, we had to make a rather large act of faith. In spite of the evidence to the contrary, which Plesser and other pollsters delivered neatly bound, we had to assume that issues moved the voters.

A major source of concern in our brainstorming sessions was the discrepancy between Nixon's credentials for dealing with foreign affairs and his unimpressive domestic record. As America turned inward, the candidate whose interests ran so strongly to the outside world could seem out of step with his countrymen. In fact, he was out of step. By the standards of the Eisenhower era, he had been enlightened on civil rights and agreeable to doing something to ease the plight of the cities. But the Negro revolution and racial violence in the cities had all but destroyed the "moderate" position. The priorities of the fifties, which put Quemoy and Matsu ahead of Chicago, were anachronistic in the late sixties, yet Nixon held them sincerely and even fatalistically. If the cities outranked Vietnam in the voters' minds, he said more than once privately, he would probably be passed over for the nomination.

By the fall of 1967, fear of crime had reached epidemic proportions in the United States, especially white fear of crimes committed by Negroes. The Gallup poll disclosed that fully 83 percent of those responding believed that law and order had broken down completely. In such a psychological climate, public trust in, and respect for, self-government dissolved. If freedom produced seeming anarchy, a resounding majority was for limiting freedom as severely as necessary. Conservative Republicans, whose influence over the nominating process was decisive, liked the take-charge authority they heard in Ronald Reagan's voice. To protect our right flank, Buchanan drafted a blunt-spoken article for the *Reader's Digest*, putting Nixon squarely behind the domestic "peace-keeping" forces. But Reagan and George Wallace could beat us in any nay-saying contest. Nixon had to give the impression that he understood what was happening in frightened America, that he cared deeply about it, and that he saw ways of guiding our society between the twin perils of anarchy and repression. To do this, he would have to escape the psychological undertow of the fifties and enter the radically different atmosphere of the late sixties in a credible and dramatic fashion.

Garment had a thought. As we talked one day in October, he passed a manuscript across his desk. "That's Pat Moynihan's speech. Take a look at it. I think there's something in it for us."

Daniel Patrick Moynihan had spoken the previous month before the national board of Americans for Democratic Action and had caused a stir with his indictment of his fellow liberals. I noticed that the text bore the speaker's handwritten alterations. It was Moynihan's reading copy, forwarded to Garment in support of Moynihan's central theme: Liberals should recognize that "their essential interest is in the stability of the social order, and that given the present threats to that stability, it is necessary to seek out and make much more effective alliances with political conservatives who share that concern, and who recognize that unyielding rigidity is just as much a threat to the continuity of things as is an anarchic desire for change." He went on to advance two other propositions. Liberals "must divest themselves of the notion that the nation, especially the cities of the nation, can be run from agencies in Washington." And, more to the heart of the matter: Liberals "must somehow overcome the curious condescension which takes the form of sticking up for and explaining away anything, howsoever outrageous, which Negroes, individually and collectively, might do."

There was indeed something in this speech for Nixon. Moynihan wanted to place much greater reliance on private enterprise and the profit motive in rebuilding cities. He favored sharing federal revenues with states and localities. These bows toward Republican ideas pleased Mel Laird, who inserted Moynihan's remarks in the *Congressional Record*, declaring that the speech "and earlier correspondence with me demonstrates a refreshing willingness to dispense with the rhetoric of debate and deal with the issues." Nixon could be equally generous, but he could not stop at saying We-told-you-so and Me-too.

Nixon's re-entry problem and Moynihan's inviting call for a coalition posed again the perennial question: what were thoughtful conservative Republicans *for?*

On those occasions when a prominent liberal publicly agreed with them and admitted their ideas to respectability, conservative intellectuals displayed an almost pathetic gratitude. In this instance, William F. Buckley heralded Moynihan's speech as "a Magna Carta for American liberals," whom he hoped would now see the light. Suppose many of them did — what then? The light glowing from *National Review*'s window signaled antiliberalism and little more. The right did not offer a positive, coherent alternative to the left and was annoyed at the suggestion it should. American conservatism, though ideological, had few cultural institutions and outlets for intellectual expression. It was almost exclusively a *political* opposition movement within the Republican party, held together by shared moral attractions and aversions. Many of these were sound, but except for Buckley and a handful of other commentators, conservatives were inarticulate. They had a ready excuse based on a half-truth: liberals dominated the academy, the arts, the media, the foundations — the whole apparatus of ideas — and tended, sometimes ruthlessly, to exclude nonconformists. But this excuse ignored the rest of the truth: conservatives weren't much interested. They poured money and energy into politics, rather than cultural and intellectual enterprises.

As a result, conservatives depended on liberals to set the terms of debate. Liberals proposed and conservatives opposed. Perhaps this situation was inevitable, given the different temperaments of left and right. In any event, it was more agreeable than conservative intellectuals cared to admit. They were relieved of the necessity of making their own social analyses and developing their own programs. Throughout a generation and a half of liberal ascendancy, the fact that debate centered on the liberal program made for a certain stability and continuity within the system. Liberals won a great many arguments without winning too much ground all at once. Conservatives mustered enough bipartisan support on key votes in Congress so that liberal legislation was enacted at a moderate pace. Ideologues of the left and right, to be sure, were impatient with debate and compromise that excluded extremes, left basic assumptions undisturbed, and seldom "settled" anything once and for all. But the electoral majority in the middle of the road appeared satisfied with measured progress toward the Welfare State.

Simply by virtue of its post–New Deal ascendancy, liberalism had become the established public philosophy and "tradition." But this status was at odds with the rhetoric and self-image of liberalism. Liberals liked to regard themselves as they had been — idealistic advocates of a vigorous, fighting faith, champions of the unfortunate embattled by the forces of reaction. Militant right-wing fringe groups such as the John Birch Society were a godsend to middle-aged liberals, whose adrenals were set pumping once again by the specter of "fascism." When liberals detected an enemy on the right, they at once reconciled themselves to their true condition of power and influence, and to the duty of defending the existing social and political order. Behaving as an established elite, they guarded their accomplishments and upheld the legitimacy of their values and aspirations. They rallied around "the vital center" — Arthur Schlesinger, Jr.'s phrase — and called down the heavens on those "extremists" who dared to challenge liberal leaders and dispute liberal policies.

During the latter 1960s, however, liberals encountered opposition from a new and unexpected quarter — on their left. By definition, only fellow "progressives" assembled there. Left-wing extremism was the real thing, hurling bricks instead of words, and a great many liberals were intimidated. When campus radicals and black militants bit the hand that had spoon-fed them, liberals apologized and offered the other hand. When abysmally ignorant New Leftists, who made Birchers look like scholars, screamed obscene abuse of "the Establishment," liberals pleaded guilty. And when self-appointed black avengers leveled the mindless but morally devastating charge of "racism," liberals sank to their knees under the weight of other people's alleged sins.

To say that liberalism collapsed beneath the assault of leftist extremism was an understatement: its nerve failed and it came apart. Prominent liberals who had recently been lords in Kennedy's Camelot now begged leave to join the revolt against Johnson's imperialism. Of course, the failure of nerve was by no means universal. Many like Moynihan bravely resisted, but they formed at best a rear guard. Under cover of opposing an unpopular war and President, liberal opinion-leaders sought to abandon their mistakes, shed responsibility, and move fashionably leftward, until the "vital center" they once protected lay on their right, open to attack.

The cultural civil war that erupted in the late 1960s was curiously one-sided. For more than a generation, a truce had existed between the university-based "adversary culture" and the conventional culture. Episodes such as Senator Joseph R. McCarthy's anti-Communist crusading had only served to draw the dividing line more sharply. Now the campus radicals abruptly broke the truce. Those who lived in the conventional culture — an unselfconscious culture, shaped by custom and routine and impervious to innovative intellectual currents — did not at once understand the nature of the hostilities launched from the campuses and carried into the streets. But upper-middle-class liberals, who commonly owed their rise and status to higher education, understood well enough. As the society's cultural middlemen and intellectual retailers, they stood in the line of fire. Often, the battleground was as intimate as the family dinner table.

Just as older liberals with little to say invented a self-excusing

"generation gap," so vocal young extremists excused antisocial violence by calling their aggression "dissent." The notion that Vietnam and racial turmoil "caused" the cultural civil war was a fiction
put forward by academic leftists as part of their general claim of
moral superiority over the mass of ordinary citizens. Many of the
leftists who railed against Vietnam had long seethed with resentment against a society that undervalued them. The insurgency had
its roots in the breakneck expansion of higher education and in the
fantastic increase in the number of people, many of them indif-
ferently endowed, who saw themselves as belonging to an elite owed
privilege, influence, and power — above all, power. Bored, aimless
postadolescents, sent to college by their parents, found nourishment
for their grievances in lectures subversive of everything beyond the
campus. In the hothouse climate of the universities, the spectrum of
opinion deemed respectable ran from left-of-center to exotic extremism. Left-wing intellectuals could easily mobilize shock troops
against an America that neither they nor the young understood.
Especially they failed to understand that those who were assaulted
eventually would retaliate.

Moynihan's call for alliance, then, was not the simple proposition
it seemed. Conservatives were asked to cease opposing liberalism
and reinforce the loyalist rear guard. They were asked to bring
numbers to bear in a conflict less political than cultural. "It is pleasant to hear the New Left declare that the white liberal is the true
enemy because it is he who keeps the present system going by limiting its excesses," Moynihan had said, "but it is more the informed
conservatives who perform that function — the Robert Tafts of the
nation — and at the present juncture they are needed." This com-
mendation of my hero before such an unlikely forum was satisfying.
But the fifties were irrevocably gone, and so were the Robert Tafts
and Adlai Stevensons who had brought principled convictions to
the public questions of that time. Their era had closed with the ad-
vent of television and the triumph of "style."

A Taft would not have known what to make of the sort of excesses the late 1960s witnessed. His antagonists had fought within the system, on the familiar ground of politics, for tangible prizes and advantages. When they were beaten, they abided by the result, even as they worked to overturn it. In short, they acknowledged rules. The new cultural insurgency acknowledged no rules and recognized no limits. A native anti-Americanism, it attacked the foundations of the system and violated not particular laws but the concept of the law. Those patrician Midwesterners, Taft and Stevenson, would have been equally shocked by the uprising against their civilization and, even more, by the measure of tolerance and approval it gained. Radicalism springing from hatred of America among Americans would have seemed to them a pathological rather than a political phenomenon.

Latter-day liberals spread confusion by extending the presumed scope of politics. Any act, however irrational, was deemed to have sociopolitical significance. Crime was not simply crime, nor violence simply violence. Underlying every outbreak was supposed to be some intelligible motive, which could be isolated by social scientists and dealt with politically. The urban Negro who looted and the white student who smashed the dean's office were said to be acting out "frustrations," and these could be eased and perhaps removed by reordering the environment through government action. Liberals behaved as though government stood at the center of human affairs, displacing or replacing family, religion, customs, and codes.

Schlesinger, in his early Cold War phase of advocacy, had concisely expressed the liberal myth of limitlessly competent and morally effective government. "The history of government intervention," he wrote in *The Vital Center* in 1949, "is the history of the growing ineffectiveness of the private conscience as a means of social control. The only alternative is the growth of the public conscience, whose natural expression is the democratic government." Without realizing it, the radical young, the angry blacks, and their liberal apologists were rebelling against the failure of that myth.

The individual's surrender of power, responsibility, and conscience to overweening government had not brought the earthly paradise of happiness and fulfillment. Frustration persisted. Powerlessness bred rage. The putative keepers of the public conscience were remote and unresponsive bureaucrats. There were no godlike wise men in Washington to provide what was missing in mean and meaningless lives — there was only the Department of Health, Education, and Welfare. Politics could not penetrate the mystery and loneliness of the human soul.

Nevertheless, the possible alternative of anarchy commended the failing liberal order to the conservative. The opinion polls certified an incipient hysteria and the reality of the threat of anarchy in the public mind. Moynihan drew it in stark terms. He spoke of "the vast Negro underclass that has somehow grown up in our northern cities; a disorganized, angry, hurt group of persons easily given to self-destructive violence." He linked the black underclass to a new, triggering element: "radical, nihilist youth, not themselves members of this underclass, but identifying with it, able to communicate with it, and determined to use it as an instrument of a violent, apocalyptic confrontation with a white society they have determined to be irredeemably militaristic and racist." He detected a set of signs conveying a "painful, even hateful" warning: "We must prepare for the onset of terrorism." Its extent and success were uncertain, but its probability seemed so great that "it would be an act of irresponsibility or of cowardice not to face it."

Nixon, surely, could face it. Phrased as an issue, the possibility of racial catastrophe was probably enough to nominate and elect him. If terrorism loomed, repression was a sufficient program. The Moynihan speech offered a better, more decent program. It invited conservatives to pursue power without any larger purpose than shoring up things as they were, for as long as we could. It asked for alliance on the basis of liberal assumptions to produce not change, but continuity. The prerequisite for change, I told myself, was victory. If Nixon won, there would be time and opportunity afterward to act on a new perception of the root causes of society's disorder.

2.   Nixon planned to address the National Association of Manufacturers' 72nd Annual Congress of American Industry in early December. In a note to him, I suggested that he use this forum to define the "politics of stability" in his own terms. He readily agreed. Other thoughtful liberals were echoing and expanding on Moynihan's concerns. Columnist Joseph Kraft was among the first to call attention to the class conflict between whites that found expression in opposing attitudes toward the Negro. The memorandum outlining my approach to the NAM text was accompanied by a column in which Kraft admonished white upper-class liberals to show some sympathy for the claims of "a truly explosive element in American politics . . . the low- and middle-income white."

MEMORANDUM*

TO: DC   November 12, 1967

FROM: RJW

. . . While attention has been focused on the plight of the Negro, almost no concern has been shown for the equally legitimate frustration of the middle-income white.

The median family income in 1966 (latest figure available) was $7436, but the Bureau of Labor Statistics recently estimated that a typical city worker's family of four persons needs more than $9000 a year to live modestly but adequately, an increase of 50 percent over the last such estimate in 1959. In four out of ten families with incomes above $10,000, both husband and wife are working, and she brings home as much as 30 percent of the total income. Rising taxes and unchecked inflation put such families under relentless pressure. Small wonder they resent the solicitude heaped upon the

* To spare the reader, my sometimes lengthy memoranda are condensed here and elsewhere in the text. The major points have been preserved, but supporting data and secondary lines of argument are omitted where indicated. Candor compels me to acknowledge that the resulting loss to history is slight.

Negro and the implicit (and ironically racist) suggestion that the white American has it made.

The ordinary white American . . . lacks the wherewithal to purchase what I call "social insulation" — unlike well-heeled liberals who, for example, zealously promote integration of the public schools while they send their own children to expensive private schools. By refusing to see that profound social change *always* occurs gradually, they have pressed far ahead of the public consensus on which change must rest. The so-called white backlash represents the repudiation of promises made to the Negro for which middle-class whites feel no personal responsibility; and because they must live with the consequences of fulfilling those promises, their veto power is absolute.

It is time, I believe, to take the explosive issue of race out of the hands of the absolutists. Their unrealistic goals and target dates have guaranteed failure and a rising sense of outrage among whites and blacks alike. It is time to face the truth about race in America. It is not "ugly." It is, in fact, extraordinary: no other society has attempted to do so much, so quickly, and has succeeded so well.

What we are experiencing now is the natural reaction after a period of great activity. The rhythm of advance and consolidation in our society can be ignored, as it has been, but it cannot be broken short of revolutionary upheaval. We must draw back from the brink of such upheaval, asserting as forcefully as the situation requires the fundamental right of a society to survive on terms tolerable to the great majority.

This emphatically does not imply repression of the Negro. It implies the restoration of balance between the claims of the minority and the majority. . . .

The white middle class, up to this point, has generally retreated in silence from the consequences of the racial programs sponsored by the ultraliberals. The cities have been emptied, the suburbs filled up; in some areas, the public schools have been abandoned in favor of parochial schools. But the room for further retreat is extremely limited. "Open housing" is a flaming issue in suburbia;

plans to provide tax support for the parochial schools, which in some areas have become, in effect, the white public schools, are being thwarted. Meanwhile, the curtain of unreal promises and sham professions about the nature of the society has been torn down. White and black are face-to-face, and Kraft laments, as must all of us, "the absence of any mediating agent to blunt, obscure, fuzz over and mix up a naked confrontation of racial groups." In this, he tacitly concedes the irresistible power of the force of natural change, for men prudently seek ways of evading issues on which no basis has been prepared for mutually acceptable compromise. If we are to be denied further avenues of escape and evasion, we have no alternative but to take refuge in the truth.

As I have suggested, we can live with the truth — at least those of us, white and black, who wish to see our free society survive. One long-neglected aspect of the truth is that the white middle class is the foundation of our society, and its values are the basis of our civilization . . . If this simple statement appears to have racist overtones, it is because we have been conditioned to accept the false premises of the absolutists. In his untutored common sense, however, the ordinary white citizen resists these sophisticated and ultimately suicidal assumptions about whose values shall prevail. He has retreated before militant untruth, but when he begins to feel cornered, he will find his voice and speak out, unconcerned with the risk of being labeled a "bigot." Before that time comes, someone with courage must speak for him, someone who will, simultaneously, restore that citizen's sense of social esteem while appealing to his innate sense of fair play — and even more, to his deep and prudent desire to avoid racial confrontation through tolerable compromise. I suggest that DC is this spokesman, for he exemplifies, and proudly asserts, the rise of the American middle class and the triumph of its values in the creation of a society wherein talent and effort are rewarded in a contest open to all . . .

These small essays, here condensed, were directed as much to myself as to "DC," which was just as well, for I could not gauge long-
distance what effect, if any, they had on him. The Hessians did not
tax Nixon with such theorizing. His evident preoccupation was
with technique:

MEMORANDUM

TO: Dick Whalen   November 17, 1967

FROM: DC

Tom Dewey took the National Industrial Conference Board
speech and marked it up. He feels that the trouble with the speech
was there were too many "buts" in it — qualifying phrases. The
typical intellectual attempt to put all sides of an issue in it and that
at points it was just too intellectual for any audience, let alone that
one.

He also felt — and I think this is constructive criticism — that a
speech needs to have sweep and it must always sweep upwards and
when you put negatives in, particularly toward the end of a speech
it tends to drop the audience down as you try to lift them.

Would you look this over as a help in your writing?

Also I am sending you some speeches which I have written —
ones that are typical of my own style.

Guild Hall Speech
Acceptance Speech — 1960
Bohemian Grove Speech
Goldwater Introduction — 1964

(All of these have this characteristic of sweeping up)

———————

Tom Dewey? Sweeping up? My heart sank at the tone of these instructions. Nixon's dismissal of "the typical intellectual attempt" at

communication told in a phrase why Republican intellectuals were so few. Our politicians simply did not speak our language — and could not, as John Kennedy did, gracefully pretend.

The theme of the speech I drafted was war and the point of departure, Vietnam. But the text at once asserted the relative inconsequence of Southeast Asia and, indeed, of all the other places where America was committed. "None of these testing-places — not in Europe, not in Asia — can approach in importance the ground we are standing on. The ultimate testing-place of America is America itself." "If we do not see clearly and act quickly, recognizing the war-in-the-making within our own society, it will not matter what happens in Vietnam and elsewhere. We will have defeated ourselves." What America faced was not a "problem" or even a "crisis," but a form of conflict "entirely new, for which we have not yet found an acceptable name in our vocabulary." Just as American troops were trying to pacify hamlets in Vietnam, so special army teams were touring scores of American cities, making contingency plans for their pacification next summer. "A riot is a spontaneous outburst. A war is subject to advance planning."

Such warlike precautions in our cities reflected the changing nature of racial violence, which was assuming the character of guerrilla warfare under the direction of self-proclaimed black revolutionaries. "We are psychologically unprepared for the emergence of men who openly declare their hatred of society and their intention to destroy it." These educated, articulate members of the Negro middle class were guerrilla leaders in the classic pattern, men who had risen and who now were reaching out to the submerged mass of Negroes with a message of hatred and revenge. At the same time, rising street crime and racial tension were spreading a cancer-like fear through the white population. "Not for a century, not since the Civil War, has our nation been so divided, our citizens so apprehensive toward one another."

Now came the turn in the speech, pivoting in good Republican fashion on Lincoln's famous lines addressed to a war-wracked nation in the bleak winter of 1862. "The dogmas of the quiet past are inadequate to the stormy present . . . As our case is new, so we must think anew and act anew."

The dogmas of liberalism, sprung from a time "when men despaired of their individual efforts and turned to the government to protect them and order their lives," were plainly inadequate. "The Negro is not alone in feeling helpless and frustrated in our present society. Amid our boundless affluence, a new despair deepens. We are at once imprisoned and left adrift. We gain status from a rigid, bureaucratic system, but only at the sacrifice of our individuality."

The rule of law had been eroded for a generation by the practice of arbitrary social engineering, which justified the destruction of traditional values as necessary to the realization of utopian ideals. "Under the illusion of the government's unlimited power to remake society, endless promises have been made to the Negro, which encouraged him to believe that his burdens would be lifted and the obstacles to his progress removed immediately. Worse than not keeping a promise is making a promise that cannot be kept." The rule of law, supported by a broad public consensus, was the only sure guarantee of justice and progress for Negro Americans. "There can be no social justice for anyone in a society which labors under artificial burdens of mass guilt and mass innocence. What Americans, white and black, owe to each other is summed up in an old-fashioned word — *respect*. Respect for each other's rights under the laws that apply to them equally."

(In a passage edited from the overlong text, I quoted a Harlem clergyman who had formed an armed citizens' patrol to cope with what he described as "the tide of crime" in the ghetto streets. "The muggings and rapes and robberies around here have reached the point that the people must do something," said this anguished Negro victim of Negro violence. His, I wrote, was the voice of *the great, silent majority* of *black* Americans. My phrase would ultimately be used by Nixon in a quite different context.)

Against this background, Moynihan's propositions were quoted and his call for alliance accepted in defense of that "core of beliefs and institutions which is essential to our civilization." Shamelessly borrowing Schlesinger's phrase, I called this threatened core the "vital center." The balance of the text urged businessmen into the front line ("Too many . . . have adjusted too well to the system centered on Washington") and proposed specific actions they should take independently of the government on behalf of "the Negro who wants and expects to be as upwardly mobile as the next American." Incorporating language that Price had supplied ("The modern corporation is no longer just an economic unit. It is a social unit, an *action* unit"), the text moved on to the obligatory upsweep, urging American business to lead the way in transforming the nation's cities "from a hostile front to a hopeful frontier."

Upsweep aside, it was, compared with the sober products of his own pen, a most un-Nixon-like speech, and I wondered what would happen to it in New York. To my delight, Ellsworth reported that the Old Man was very pleased.

The speech was well received and made the front pages across the country. Columnists and editorial writers praised Nixon's forthright assessment of the racial-urban front without asking where he had been up to that time. So far, his re-entry was a success.

When the candidate called to offer congratulations, Chris picked up the telephone. "It's that Mr. Nixon again," he shouted. I grabbed the receiver and began to apologize. The laughter on the other end told me it wasn't necessary.

IV

1. AS ACTING PRESS SECRETARY, Buchanan was the first stop for reporters writing about the candidate; and as ranking newcomer, he was the prime source on the young men around Nixon. We had agreed that I should stay in the background for a while, but Pat was eager to promote the new team. He called one day and said: "I hope you don't mind, but I've surfaced you as a brain truster."

Now I found myself, for a change, on the defensive end of the interview game. With a little practice, I learned how to sound spontaneous on the telephone without exceeding dictation speed. While I sold Nixon to my callers, the situation also required me to sell myself. This, of course, was what Nixon intended, for he well knew the rule laid down by Niccolò Machiavelli, the original image-maker: "The first impression that one gets of a ruler and of his brains is from seeing the men that he has about him."

After twenty-two years spent under intense and often hostile journalistic scrutiny, Richard Nixon seemed far beyond the point of making first impressions and incapable of altering old ones. Yet the very familiarity of the man, the feeling within the press that he was a completely known (and unappealing) quantity, gave him an opportunity to achieve surprise by advertising the circle of bright new faces around him. Why were we helping the most durable figure in American politics this side of Harold Stassen? Back came our answer: we're riding with a winner this time. Suddenly, the press found something fresh to write about Nixon.

Of course, the articles mentioned many familiar names from Nixon's vice-presidential years and the 1960 and 1962 campaigns, but the emphasis fell where Nixon wished it — on the newcomers. We found ourselves admitted on his authority to first-degree insidership. For example, Ellsworth and Sears were publicized as Nixon's chief political emissaries. Scarcely anyone thought to ask what had become of his earliest and most controversial mentor, Murray Chotiner. (Chotiner was busy behind the scenes, where the press never saw or heard of him.) Safire had been helping Nixon with his speeches for years, but his name rarely appeared along with the rest of us. Quite apart from the services we rendered, Nixon valued our names, titles, and accomplishments. He invariably told interviewers that he had hand-picked his new "first-rate" staff, in contrast to the inherited "hacks" around him in 1960. When Nixon testified that we had his ear and confidence, a reporter was left to infer an implausible conclusion: that this group of talented strangers somehow reflected the candidate's private mind and intentions.

By directing the spotlight toward the fresh supporting cast, the star of the longest-running road show in American politics not only spruced up the latest production, but also assembled several credible character witnesses. We were at once ignorant and unscathed, innocent and enthusiastic. What most of us knew of Nixon's earlier campaigns was only what we had read in Theodore H. White's chronicle of the 1960 disaster; we could testify only in the present and future tenses. By certifying our supposed intimacy and influence, Nixon gave our testimonials impressive weight. Faced with questions from reporters, some of them friends and former colleagues, I could say honestly that I had never met the brooding loner described by White and other Nixon-watchers. The Nixon I knew — I did not dwell on our slight acquaintance — was open, attentive, and evidently willing to accept ideas. The fact that few, if any, of the newcomers fit the traditional mold of political job-seekers and hangers-on enhanced our credibility with the press. Almost without exception, we had something else interesting and rewarding to do. Consequently our answers to the big question — Why are *you* working for Nixon? — commanded attention.

Later in the campaign, television completely overshadowed the writing press. In these early stages, newspaper stories served several useful, short-run purposes: politicians were impressed, along with pollsters, network news executives, magazine editors, and, of course, ordinary readers. The print journalists, who would be shut out later, enjoyed easy access to Nixon and his new staff — and thereby received and conveyed a false impression of the coming campaign. To Republicans skeptical of backing a two-time loser, Nixon played through the press this message: *This isn't the same old Nixon; and he won't blow it again. Stay loose and uncommitted and see what he and his young men do in the primaries.* For several months before the New Hampshire primary, we were Exhibit A in the case for giving Nixon another chance.

Typical of the staff-centered publicity was a long article in *Newsday*, which the Nixon for President Committee reprinted and distributed by the thousands to the Republican faithful. It was written by Nick Thimmesch, with whom I'd worked at Time Inc., and it showed why he enjoyed a reputation for unusual fairness to Republicans. Though he noted past debacles and the recollections of forlorn, ignored staff men who had stumbled after Nixon to defeat eight years earlier, Thimmesch was willing to judge him anew at the value of the politically unknown faces around him. WHY ARE THESE MEN FOR NIXON? asked the headline of his article. The subhead summarized our credentials: *One is a best-selling author; another is an intellectual who played saxophone with Woody Herman's band; two others are ex-editors of editorial pages. And there are more, all sharp young men who have joined Richard M. Nixon's campaign staff because they share the belief that he is the best man to take over the White House.* A pair of photographs showed a beaming Nixon and his youthful entourage.

Nixon set the stage by heaping praise on his staff members, *praise that subtly reflected back on him.* "The first thing they have is brains. They have high intellectual quality, character and courage.

They're not for sale. These are guys that money can't buy . . ." *And he had attracted them.* "They like challenge. They want to be in the battle. They are individualists and debate with each other." *And he was where the action was, the center of this free play of ideas and debate.* "It is vitally important for a man in public life to bridge the generation gap. You talk to the new generation through these fellows." *And he was tuned in, listening to new voices.*

Next came our testimonials. Anderson: "Nixon is just as much an intellectual as the professors I knew at Dartmouth, MIT, and Columbia." Price: "I didn't expect him to be the warm, sensitive human being he is." Garment: "With Nixon it may be a coming-together of the man and the times as it was with Churchill . . ." Ellsworth: "Nixon is a very with-it individual." And my own: "I am impressed with his willingness to listen and give new direction . . . We need a lively, conservative Republican administration, which provides a sense of competition. The whole center of gravity in politics is shifting from left to right in the country. An honest conservative movement can keep the shift in line and prevent it from becoming anti-Negro and Know-Nothing. Nixon is the kind of man who can keep us on a sound course."

Quote unquote. Next witness. In truth, I didn't know at the time what kind of man Nixon was. I knew what kind of President I wanted to see in the White House. Like Garment's Churchillian hero and Anderson's egghead, my straight-talking conservative was a projection of personal hopes and desires. Only after I had given several such testimonials did I realize that Nixon knew us better than we knew him — or knew ourselves. He knew how to massage our egos and how to capitalize on the sense of self-importance that comes from being publicly labeled important. ("I learned a great deal about nuclear weaponry from Dick Whalen," Nixon confided to Thimmesch.)

Nixon's advertising of his articulate and quotable newcomers had a precedent. Like much else in his campaign, the gambit could be traced back to the man who had defeated him in 1960 — John F.

Kennedy. Nixon lifted us to the level of celebrities-by-association, satellites orbiting on an inside track around a political star of the first magnitude. Kennedy had done the same with his intellectuals, Schlesinger, Galbraith, and the rest, whose proclaimed brilliance added luster to his own nonintellectual personality. In this early print publicity, Nixon plied a special kind of politics of nostalgia. He did not recall his own past — with half the population under twenty-eight, the memory of the Hiss Case, the McCarthy years, and even the Eisenhower era was blurred or nonexistent. Rather, he recalled a past borrowed from the martyred and romanticized Kennedy. The most vivid public recollection of Nixon was as Kennedy's adversary in the televised debates at the outset of the sixties. Deliberately, he evoked the memory of that time of youth, excitement, and bold promise. We were *Nixon's* New Frontiersmen, Republican style: basically conservative but provably younger. Commenting on this "youth movement," the friendly columnist John Chamberlain noted that Nixon was "tapping members of a generation that look upon Arthur Schlesinger and John Kenneth Galbraith as old fuddy-duddies. This generation, insofar as its intellectuals are concerned, represents a reaction against what was deemed bright and 'liberal' around the Round Table at the Court of Camelot." Chamberlain assumed that Nixon, in his own fashion, would carry the imitation of Kennedy beyond publicity into practice.

A long-time friend of Nixon's, quoted in the Thimmesch article, understood what Nixon was up to. "It's good that he has a new crew around him with a fresh and young approach. Kennedy started this in 1960 when he evoked a response from young people. Robert Kennedy and Lindsay do the same. Nixon knows it's a big plus."

It was a big plus, obviously, to have others standing as a buffer between him and the press, ex-journalists who were the same age and who spoke the same language as their inquisitors. It was a big plus, also, to spread the illusion among the "word-men" (as Nixon called them) that prose mattered crucially. Nixon liked to tell reporters how he played nit-picking editor with his writers: why, he would fiddle for minutes with a single word. This was true, but not as revealing as some listeners supposed. For Nixon did not say what the word thus prayed over actually said. The staff-centered publicity raised an attractive, deceptive screen between the press and the actual Nixon campaign. In fact, the eager press deceived itself. Long after ideas had been devalued and the "youth movement" derailed, reporters continued to seek out the supposed "insiders" they had identified and, unwittingly, created.

2. In his encounters with reporters, Nixon always stressed the importance of the "issues." So did Buchanan in his frequent communiqués to the staff and supporters. Early in November, a *New York Times* story reported that Nixon planned a leisurely campaign and limited exposure in New Hampshire, which was indeed the plan. Buchanan fired off a memorandum intended to correct the *Times*' "false impression," declaring: "We anticipate a tough race in N.H. if we get into it. The people of New Hampshire are going to be interested in how many good ideas a man has, not in how many hands he shakes." This, of course, was Pat playing the role of agitprop commissar, telling the troops not to be worried by that indefatigable hand-grabber, George Romney, who campaigned all the harder as he sank in the polls. The coy hedging phrase — "if we get into it" — was the purest sham. The Nixon forces had been hard at work in New Hampshire since the early spring of 1967. Some of these unseen preparations put the high-sounding talk about "issues" into a different perspective. An issue, by definition, was anything Nixon decided to talk about. The intensely subjective scale of values governing the place of issues in the campaign was reflected in the design and use of a very costly, in-depth poll taken among more than five hundred New Hampshire Republicans — a very large sample in so small a state.

These Republicans were interviewed at length on a broad range of questions concerning issues, personalities, and candidate preferences, but the part that chiefly interested Nixon's strategists dealt with Nixon himself. What the voters thought of Vietnam, racial tensions, and the rest of the nation's troubles was secondary to their attitudes toward the man whose fate they would decide in March 1968. Their tape-recorded impressions of Nixon were transcribed and divided into "favorable" and "unfavorable" sections of the report, each running several pages. These summaries of *vox populi* passed from hand to hand in New York headquarters until they were dog-eared. Along with the others, I mulled ways to call attention to Nixon's strengths and conceal his weaknesses — especially the latter:

He's a loser. I don't think he's big enough for the job. Frankly, I don't think he stands too much of a chance. He tried it before and didn't get it. He's a very poor loser. He's always running for something but never getting there. The most unfavorable thing against him is the fact that I do not think he could win. I don't think he comes out strong enough for what he believes in. Should be honest with himself and quit running.

And so on and on. Almost every complaint was a variation on the damning theme: *Nixon's a loser.* Flipping through the pages of favorable judgments, containing praise of Nixon's intelligence, candor, experience, and grasp of world problems, brought little solace. The common complaint would remain true until Nixon won an election.

Garment practically memorized the transcript. His eye kept returning to a pair of sentences that he had underlined. *He's proven that he can take it. He's been slapped down and can come back.* "That's it, Dick," he told me. "Nixon's the Man Who Came Back."

The portrayal of Nixon as the game, gallant underdog was perhaps valid but superficial. Nixon could make one of the great comebacks in American political history, but politics was more than a win-or-lose sport. *Where* was Nixon coming from, and *why?* It seemed to me that the relevance of what he stood for, not his plucky resiliency, would determine whether he succeeded or failed, probably for the last time in his career. Churchill, Garment's favorite figure of comparison, wasn't loved because he was a loser coming back from oblivion; he was followed because he was a battler for England's survival. Something like America's survival as a recognizably great nation seemed at stake in 1968.

Garment wouldn't go that far — indeed, he didn't go very far with Nixon's views on most questions, for he was a liberal at heart and Nixon wasn't. What fascinated him was the sheer challenge of putting a two-time loser into the White House. The game was the thing. Garment had a gift of convenient vagueness, a way of sliding over disagreements. He assured me that the "specifics" of Nixon's position would "flow" from his general stance of poised command, all according to plan and schedule. Then he launched into an act he often staged for visiting journalists, spinning out his characterization of Nixon as the "existential" politician who defined himself and forged his destiny in each choice he made.

A man prepared to remake himself according to the tabulated opinions of others was not an abstraction sprung from the pages of Martin Buber, but a flesh-and-blood, fallible human being. Every attempt to depict Nixon as a larger-than-life symbol, whether hero or villain, ultimately failed before the fact that he was so *un*extraordinary. He interested me precisely because he seemed one of us, mirroring strengths and weaknesses unmistakably in the American grain. The last ordinary man to be President, Harry S Truman, also had proved to be a singularly effective leader. After Truman came the larger-than-life figures: the General, the Prince, and the Wheeler-Dealer, all of whom had failed to match plain-spoken Harry's success. Like Truman, Nixon had no mask, manner, or reputation to hide behind; no tall tale, legend, or mystique would divert public attention from his performance. He would have to stand up, as Truman had, and make the most of himself and his opportunity to enter history.

If he succeeded, he could accomplish something that might be

crucial to the future of our system and society. He might rescue a once self-reliant and self-confident people from the tide of
hopelessness carrying them and America toward a regime of
fear, dependence, and unfreedom. Larger-than-life Presidents
who played the monarch — distant, dazzling, deceitful — swelled
the tide by convincing us of our unimportance and impotence,
by causing us to regard ourselves, not as citizens, but as helpless
subjects to be manipulated by the powerful. Nixon, I supposed,
would not dare try to enthrone himself. He would be laughed
at. He would *have* to treat the rest of us as fellow citizens, and he
would have to tell and act on the truth. His chance for the personal victory he so desperately wanted, I believed, depended
on showing the people what lay beyond it: on saying plainly
what he would *do* as President. But neither Nixon nor his senior
advisers wanted to face, much less accept, the risks this view implied.

The campaign was being planned months ahead in terms of staff,
finance, media, scheduling, and travel arrangements, but we lived
from day to day in preparing Nixon's stand on issues. By November, the pollsters' tape recorders had moved on to Wisconsin, where
the second and potentially decisive primary would be held the following April, and the new transcripts were avidly read in New
York. At a panel interview in Milwaukee someone brought up Nixon's "loser" image and an anonymous Republican voiced disagree-
ment. I liked his answer so well that I marked it and sent it to Garment:

*I think the main thing going for him, as far as getting elected . . . is the fact
the people . . . are looking for an end to Vietnam. Whether they are for the
war or against it, they're looking for an end, whether we win or pull out. And
this might overcome his losing label.*

That seemed to me a much stronger theme. *Nixon's the One,* our
advertising trumpeted. And the reader asked: *The one to do what?*
Nixon was the only one who would not only lead us out of Vietnam
and domestic turmoil — he would also lead us back toward trust in

ourselves and our President by describing in advance the path he proposed to follow.

3.   Once the political writers had introduced the new Nixon cast, the next step was to mount a drama. We were divided into rival factions, according to how we supposedly lined up on the issues. The feedback from such publicity became an increasingly difficult problem within the organization, for John Mitchell and others believed that managed news was the only good news. *The Economist* of London did some damage by fancifully reporting the emergence of "a new group of youthful advisers to Mr. Nixon, calling themselves 'liberal.' Not really liberal in philosophy, but less tradition-bound than Mr. Nixon's older advisers, the Ellsworth-Whalen group is privately advising Mr. Nixon that he must alter his frame of reference radically."

The story in *The Economist*, along with similar publicity, conjured up in the vigilant Mitchell's mind a dangerous band of liberal plotters. The magazine described the supposed drift of our thinking in this fashion: "Primarily, they believe that Nixon should soften his line on Vietnam to the extent of saying that the war is now militarily unwinnable and that, consistent with its commitments to the Saigon regime, the United States must now accelerate its efforts to bring an end to the fighting. Once this is said and a clear distance thus opened between Mr. Nixon and Mr. Johnson on the Vietnam issue, these advisers believe that Mr. Nixon should immediately turn his attention to domestic affairs, and put his emphasis there." Not long afterward, Evans and Novak heightened the imaginary drama by reporting "a deep but hidden conflict" pitting, on the one hand, Ellsworth, Garment, and me, and, on the other, unnamed "old-line Nixonites." We were supposedly fighting to push Nixon toward nonideological problem-solving, the sort of "operational liberalism" the columnists detected in the NAM speech.

Such reports of issue-centered conflict within the Nixon camp only served to bring jealousies and resentments to the surface. Veteran Nixon men suspicious of the favored newcomers could more easily justify their hostility on the lofty ground of "issues" than on the petty terrain of personality. The actual internal debate revolved entirely around questions of timing and technique. The only programs seriously talked about were television programs: should Nixon go on Cronkite or wait a while?

The kind of idea that engrossed Nixon's attention was Buchanan's thesis: Nelson Rockefeller's rise in the polls was due to the *absence of television exposure*. If this were true, it raised the question whether Nixon really needed to seek access to the tube. TV commentators, magazine articles, and newspaper editorials were doing a much better job of selling Rockefeller than he could himself, Buchanan argued in a memo. "The conservatives hate the old Rocky. But the old Rocky must have died because no one sees him in the flesh any more. We do read about a different person now, whom the press tells us about, a fellow without ambition, a happy family man, the most popular Republican in the country." In Rockefeller's shunning of television, Buchanan saw lessons for Nixon. "We don't need TV to prove we are the most experienced, most qualified and most able; we don't need TV to get ourselves known; we don't need it to demonstrate we have the looks and the glibness. Do we need the damn thing at all and do we want it? Yes. But only to do the job we want it to do. We want it controlled . . ." Buchanan urged that Nixon try to control the subject matter during his television appearances. "To destroy the myth that RN is mean and that he places politics ahead of principles, RN ought to get on shows where he can kid himself, where he can talk about family, where he can crack jokes about past foibles. On other shows, he ought to talk about problems, dismiss questions about primaries . . . In short, use TV to convey the impression that RN isn't thinking about New Hampshire or Wisconsin, but about Harlem and Appalachia."

Invited to comment, I endorsed Buchanan's judgments, especially the warning that a one-minute, one-hundred-and-fifty-word comment on Vietnam was worse than meaningless. (As facile as Nixon was, he might use a word carelessly and pay as heavy a price as Romney had for his lapse.) Nixon encouraged a general free-for-all within the staff on the use of television and also asked for critiques of his performances. "Don't be polite," he told us. I took him at his word.

MEMORANDUM

TO: DC   November 20, 1967

FROM: RJW

. . . DC should be aware that he is pressing on TV, and when the interviewer is shaky, the pressing becomes painfully obvious. DC talks too much. He answers the question, and then he answers it again, and then analyzes the question, recasts it, and starts off on another set of answers . . . Too much gab makes the viewer confused and distrustful.

This is especially so if DC isn't looking into the camera (and the viewer's eye) when he talks . . . When he presses, DC not only talks too much, his left hand moves as though it had a will of its own.

Finally, although all sorts of things are said on TV these days, DC shouldn't deliberately jar the ear by telling us again and again how the press "shafted" him in 1960. The word is totally out of key, and the precise echo of an unfortunate incident recalls that incident all too vividly. If DC believes the press was *unfair,* let him say that — and leave that other word for the cozy backgrounders with the press.

But I had not joined Nixon's staff to play TV critic and tell him what was as obvious as his unconquerable five o'clock shadow. My assignment, as I understood it, was to tell him what I thought he should know and to suggest what he might do about it.

Dr. Jerome B. Wiesner, then provost of MIT and previously President Kennedy's science adviser, had written an article for *Look* op-

posing the construction of a U.S. antiballistic missile system, and
Nixon asked for my comments.

MEMORANDUM

TO: DC   November 28, 1967

FROM: RJW

. . . Wiesner's "case" against the ABM isn't very convincing.
Early this year in Cambridge, he told me: "If you're honest, you
can't say flatly that the Soviets *can't* do what some people say they
are doing. We just don't know." Putting aside this very sound ca-
veat, Wiesner, in *Look,* is full of unsupported certainties, e.g., "I do
not believe that a really effective antimissile system is remotely possible for either the U.S. or the Russians."

It doesn't matter what Wiesner thinks. It does matter what the
Russians think of their ABM system, for it introduces a dangerous
element of uncertainty into the equation of deterrence. Our best informed officials (like Wiesner in private) confess uncertainty as to
Soviet capabilities and intentions. We *do* know the Soviets are
building great numbers of ICBMs, capable of highly accurate deliv-
ery. We also know, and publicly admitted as much during the 1963
hearings on the nuclear test-ban treaty, that the Soviets are well
ahead of us in understanding the effects of nuclear explosions.
Combine their increasing offensive capability with their lead in the
technology of defense (our ABM and theirs use the so-called X-ray
effect), and the case for going ahead with at least a limited ABM is
beyond argument.

We must, however, grant Wiesner an important point: to base
the go-ahead decision on the *potential* Chinese threat, rather than on
the *real* Soviet threat, does reflect mighty tortured logic. Of course,
Wiesner doesn't mention the Soviet threat, and McNamara, in his
San Francisco speech announcing the decision [to go ahead with
the Sentinel ABM system], carefully mentioned it only in passing.
The chief reason for going ahead with ABM, according to my

sources, is to have the future option of hard-site defense — that is, defense of our Minuteman missile silos — in case the potential Soviet counterforce (first-strike) capability materializes. It could become a reality by 1970–71 . . .

But we cannot go ahead with hard-site defense and talk U.S.–Soviet détente at the same time. The truth has come out in the open during Senator Jackson's subcommittee hearings, during which experts have compared the Chinese and Soviet threats, but the Johnson administration hasn't yet mustered the courage to embrace the truth.

If you are confronted with Wiesner's presumed expertise on the subject of ABM, you might keep in mind this observation he once made, which effectively demolishes his notions of a technological "stalemate" between ourselves and the Soviets. Said Wiesner: "One of the frightening things to me, and a source of real danger . . . is that some inconceivable development, some new idea, some scientific insight, might give the discoverer a decisive advantage if he chooses to exploit it, and the more fundamental investigations scientists do, the more likely such a discovery is." *

The Soviets are trying their damndest; are we?

———————

When we spoke on the telephone a few days later, Nixon thanked me for the ABM memo and said Buchanan had added the Wiesner quotes to the black-bound briefing book. These were very hard subjects to talk about before the voters, he said, but he intended to discuss them fully later in the campaign.

* According to unimpeachable sources, American scientists learned of the so-called X-ray effect, essential to ABM technology, quite by accident and, ironically enough, from their Soviet counterparts. At a meeting of U.S. and Soviet scientists, one of the latter referred to the X-ray effect, assuming the Americans were aware of it. They weren't, but hurried back to their laboratories and discovered a gap in their knowledge they weren't even aware of — in scientific jargon, a critically important "unknown unknown."

V

1. EARLY IN NOVEMBER, I asked a favor of Nixon. The Georgetown University Center for Strategic and International Studies, where I was writer-in-residence, regularly conducted national security seminars for private groups. In January, the Center would play host once again to the Young Presidents Organization, made up of chief executives who had reached the top of the corporate ladder before their fortieth birthdays. The Center needed a "name" after-dinner speaker, and Nixon, I believed, could benefit from informal exposure before an audience of well-heeled young businessmen of Republican inclination. His Schedule Committee agreed, and John Whitaker, who kept the calendar, passed the word that the Boss would come.

Within a few days, I heard from another volunteer, advance man Dale Grubb, a former Secret Service agent who had guarded Vice President Nixon. Grubb painstakingly reviewed the details of Nixon's planned two-and-a-half-hour stay in Washington. He selected the meeting place just off the ramp at National Airport, and he arranged for the limousine and driver Nixon customarily used; he checked out the banquet room at the downtown hotel where Nixon would speak; he even gave thought to the refreshments (coffee, tea, milk) that should be waiting in the suite Nixon would briefly occupy before speaking. Grubb advanced Nixon as though he were already President. For my part, I could do no less. Nixon's talk would conclude the second day of the three-day seminar, and I made extensive notes on the briefings, speeches, and debates that preceded his appearance.

A capacity crowd of about one hundred businessmen attended the seminar, each paying more than $200 for the privilege of neglecting his business for seventy-two hours in order to worry about the security of the United States. They were earnest and surprisingly well informed, and compared favorably with a like number of academicians, especially in their ability to come quickly to the point. The YPOers — their organization's very name amused the academics — came at a personal sacrifice, and with commendable seriousness, but they were, like the business community generally, uninterested in ideas for the sake of ideas. They came as tourists, venturing briefly onto the edge of the intellectuals' domain. The Georgetown Center, which took no government contracts and did no classified research, was perhaps unique in providing a meeting ground where an audience encountered intellectuals whose persuasions ranged from conservative to left-liberal. Our guests actually heard "both sides," as when the unreconstructed Cold Warrior Robert Strausz-Hupé and the revisionist Ronald Steel squared off on U.S. commitments overseas. The comments they provoked from the audience were intelligent, but afterward I had the discouraging sense that the assembled businessmen would not again think about such issues until next year.

Still, there was one issue many of them thought and cared deeply about — Vietnam. When Walt W. Rostow dropped by for a late afternoon talk and declared the administration's war objective ("We want those fellows to go home where they belong"), he ran into tough, probing skepticism. Rostow, accustomed to facing academic accusers prone to abstract argument, had some difficulty finding concrete terms to convince these businessmen that Vietnam was still a paying proposition. There was no argument, however, when he said candidly: "Since nineteen sixty-six, the war has not been about Vietnam, but about American politics. It's a race between Hanoi's rate of loss of manpower in South Vietnam and Lyn-

don Johnson's rate of loss of support in the United States." I made
sure to write that down.

Nixon, accompanied by Dwight Chapin, his efficient appointments secretary, arrived on the seven o'clock shuttle. He walked
quickly to the car, hands jammed into the pockets of his overcoat,
and settled into the back seat. He had traveled through the dinner
hour without noticing it and he looked tired. "Well, what have
they been hearing?" he asked. Thankful for Grubb's example of
diligence, I drew out my notebook and read aloud. Nixon listened,
his eyes half-closed. Dr. Edward Teller, the luncheon speaker, had
strongly opposed the draft form of the nuclear nonproliferation
treaty ("The last nail in the coffin of NATO"). Nixon broke in:
"Should I come out against NPT? It's like being against mother-
hood. It's going to pass the Senate for sure." He listened closely to
the replay of Rostow's remarks. "Did he say *that?* They must be
worried over there."

With bubbling Howard (Bo) Callaway, former Georgia congressman and Nixon's southeast coordinator up front, the YPO wel-
coming committee at the hotel surged around the candidate. I
hung back but Nixon waved me aboard the elevator. "You haven't
finished," he said. "Let me hear the rest." In his suite, he sipped a
cup of tea and combed his hair, while I followed him around unreeling the final pages of my notes. We finished the briefing just as
Chapin knocked on the door.

As Norman Mailer would observe months later in Miami, Nixon
had learned how to enter a room like a big man with a serene sense
of his own importance — shoulders back, chest out, winning smile
flashing. The audience rose and clapped. After the Center's Director, Admiral Arleigh Burke, gave his old friend an affectionate bear
hug of an introduction, Nixon gave a commanding performance.
He ignored the lectern set up in the middle of the semicircle of arm-
chairs and moved around the edge of his audience like a nightclub
entertainer playing the ringside tables. He appeared to be speaking

off-the-cuff. In fact, page after page of his Bohemian Grove speech of the previous summer was turning before his mind's eye — I knew because I, too, had practically memorized it. When Nixon stood still, his hands kept moving: now clasped behind his back, now sweeping in an arc ("the world"), now drawn close to his body ("America"). He led his rapt listeners on a brisk, well-organized tour of the globe, deftly injecting the names of foreign statesmen and eyewitness assessments of trouble spots from Africa to the Middle East to Asia. He commented on statements the audience had heard earlier in the day, drawing flawlessly on my notes. After twenty minutes, he took questions. Bent slightly forward, he listened with his hands folded in an almost prayerful attitude and mentally spun each question in the air, responding to the side that matched a point he wanted to make. Questions on Vietnam received a strong-sounding but basically cautious response that opposed the administration's policy of gradualism without suggesting an alternative. In foreign policy, Nixon stood on his own authority; in areas of domestic policy, he was well served by material he had gleaned from Buchanan's briefing book. As Nixon exited, beaming and shaking hands, the audience applauded even more spiritedly.

Watching him perform, I was pleased with his effectiveness, yet uncomfortably aware that it was just a performance, another turn on the endless stage at the end of another seventeen-hour day. Few politicians were as candid as Nixon about the small tricks of their trade. He not only squeezed ideas into catch phrases, he also enjoyed talking about it privately. In purely political terms, there was nothing wrong — quite the contrary — with his kind of successful advocacy, with his skillful simplifying and blurring of complexity. He did the office seeker's act superbly well.

But he also did less than he was capable of — or so it seemed to me. Even those who despised him were forced to concede his superior intelligence. Yet he chose not to be directed by his intellect. Instead, he put an intellectual's mind in the service of a salesman's temperament. He did not express ideas, he put them across — and, in the process, turned them into something else. He was often accused of talking down to his audiences. He did more than that. By reducing politics to winning elections, he discouraged those who agreed with him from looking and reaching up.

In this evening's performance, before men who believed as fervently as he did in competitive achievement, the striving side of Nixon had been displayed to advantage. These self-improvers who joined Toastmasters, attended Dale Carnegie courses, and pasted vocabulary-building words on their shaving mirrors could identify readily with the man who was determined to sell himself this time. But Nixon gave his listeners little hint as to *why* he should enter the White House, and *what*, specifically, he would do once he arrived there. Intellectuals would have pressed him hard on his motives and intentions, but these businessmen did not. And Nixon volunteered nothing.

Doubtless this was astute short-run politics. But it was also sterile politics in the long run. Over the two preceding generations, the nation's course had been altered less by elections than by ideas. The ideas of liberalism had triumphed far more completely than the politics of liberalism. The audience Nixon delighted had derived part of its pleasure from the absence of painful thought. It had been sufficient, once again, to damn wicked liberalism's errors, without more than a passing nod in the direction of alternatives. It was too much, of course, to expect these executives to turn into instant intellectuals full of zest for the combat of ideas. But at least Nixon could have encouraged them to recognize the dimension of conflict above and beyond the next election. Nixon privately acknowledged that conflict, yet ignored it publicly. He left his audiences with the illusion that a miraculous short cut might yet be found, sparing them the effort of thinking and enabling them to retrieve everything by winning an election. Behind Nixon, of course.

I rode back to the airport with him, jotting down assignments. He had not known a certain fact about U.S. foreign economic policy and had had to duck it in a reply. Kent Crane, a sympathetic former Foreign Service officer, would supply it. A quick handshake on the ramp, and he was gone. The farewell delegation at the hotel had been large and demonstrative, and several well-wishers looked longingly into the limousine, awaiting an invitation Nixon did not extend. How absurdly important it was who sat where and who saw whom thus seated. Now, as I rode home in lonely splendor, I felt sorry for those who had craved the illusion of a few intimate minutes with "Dick." During the three hours we were together, Nixon and I had communicated like a pair of tape recorders and had not said a directly personal, unbusinesslike word to each other. None had occurred to me, and apparently the same was true of him.

2.   Conversation was almost superfluous in Nixon's method of working with his writers. If someone said something that interested him, he would ask him to write it down. Back would come the memorandum covered with Nixon's scrawled comments and orders. In a way, this was far more reassuring evidence than a nod that he had paid attention. But the distant and formal relationship permitted little casual give-and-take and thinking aloud. An offhand remark could lead to a request for analysis not yet begun, and to urgent follow-up requests while one hastily researched and wrote.

I said to Nixon one day that retiring Secretary of Defense McNamara's concluding review of United States military strength, especially our nuclear arsenal, was an unconsciously self-indicting document. Things had not worked out as he once had been so certain they would. It seemed to me that the deterioration of America's nuclear superiority and its implications ought to be a key issue in the campaign, even though it was surely the most difficult one to discuss with a public that didn't know — and didn't want to know — about such apocalyptic matters. The so-called missile gap that had helped elect Kennedy in 1960 had never existed, but now a very real gap was opening before our eyes.

That was enough to cause Nixon to ask for a paper outlining the background and possible future development of what he called "the nuclear issue."

MEMORANDUM

TO: DC   February 3, 1968

FROM: RJW

In his final military Posture Statement, delivered to the totally distrustful members of the Senate Armed Services Committee, McNamara said, in effect, that his critics are right . . . The United States has lost nuclear superiority, and it is in grave danger of losing deterrence.

Let's review the record. In February 1963 McNamara told a House committee that the Cuban missile crisis had been resolved favorably because "Khrushchev knew without any question whatever that he faced the full military power of the United States, including its nuclear weapons . . . We faced that night the possibility of launching nuclear weapons and Khrushchev knew it, and that is the reason, and the only reason, why he withdrew those weapons." In other words, Khrushchev backed down before a superior *nuclear* force.

Throughout the early 1960s, before and after the missile crisis, McNamara and other administration spokesmen told members of Congress in secret session that the Soviets, for a variety of reasons, would be compelled to settle for *permanent* strategic nuclear inferiority. There would be an indefinite condition of stalemate favoring the United States . . .

As late as April 1965 McNamara was telling *U.S. News & World Report* that the Soviet leaders "have decided that they have lost the quantitative race, and they are not seeking to engage us in that contest . . . There is no indication that the Soviets are seeking to develop a strategic nuclear force as large as ours."

McNamara was dead wrong. The Soviet ICBMs now being deployed — and this point must be driven home to the unsophisticated public — were put into the USSR's defense programs and budgets fully five years ago. This is the minimum lead time necessary to move a new strategic weapon from drawing board to active deployment, and this is what the Johnson administration has given away . . .

In secret testimony in January 1966 McNamara presented, as all military planners must, a theoretical "worst case" that could not be ignored. "Perhaps the worst possible threat the Soviets could mount against our Assured Destruction (second-strike) capability would be a simultaneous deployment of a force of several hundred SS-9s (the SS-9 is a large, three-stage missile, comparable in size to our Titan II, but carrying a much larger warhead, estimated at more than 20 megatons) equipped with highly accurate MIRVs (multiple independently-targetable re-entry vehicles), and a reasonably sophisticated ABM system equipped with exoatmospheric area defense missiles."

As the "worst case" has taken shape, McNamara has argued over the past year that nuclear superiority no longer means anything. In the new era of MIRV, he says quite plausibly, the old numerical advantage in launchers doesn't mean what it once did. But McNamara and the administration cannot have the argument both ways. The present static U.S. deterrent force was planned and built on the assumption that technology had reached a plateau; and that once the Soviets got close, they, too, would call a halt. MIRV is a jarring reminder of the dynamism of technology; our admitted uncertainty about the Soviet ABM system is another. And the Soviet drive for superiority, through proliferation of existing weapons and the development of new ones, is the most forceful reminder of all: they obviously believe in riding technology, not trying to halt it at some preconceived point that fits a cherished "model" of stable deterrence. The United States has lost nuclear superiority because the administration deliberately chose *not* to attempt to preserve it.

Alarming though it sounds, the shadow of a possible nuclear Pearl Harbor looms immediately ahead. Our land-based deterrent force is increasingly vulnerable to the growing Soviet force of MIRVed and more accurate missiles. To preserve the credibility of our deterrent, the strategic nuclear force must be increased and more of it must be based at sea and in space. The need . . . is to explain, as simply as this complex subject allows, the peril in which the nation stands . . . We are entering the most dangerous years in the history of America.

As with the earlier ABM memo, Nixon received this one appreciatively and again said he wanted to discuss the nuclear "blue chip" later in the campaign. This intention, like many others, evaporated in the sunshine of his extraordinary good luck. Except for a single statement applauding the Senate's approval of the Sentinel ABM system, which I wrote and personally walked through the clearance process at Nixon headquarters, nothing was said before the Republican convention. In the election campaign, Nixon made one radio speech on the nuclear balance, was attacked by the Democrats (whose spies had forewarned them of the speech weeks earlier) and the media for reviving Cold War issues, and fell silent. Why should he trouble the voters by speaking of such grim matters when they looked to him for relief from war, disorder, and worry? Thus he entered the White House with "the nuclear issue" unexplained and — more important — with the public uninformed and unprepared for the ABM decision he was at once forced to make.

In the closing days of January 1968 the Communists unleashed the Tet offensive against major cities and American bases in Vietnam. But the most severe impact was felt back home, where we saw nightly on our television screens something that couldn't be happening if we were to believe the Johnson administration. The pictures of death and destruction were worth millions of words of Communist propaganda. One news photograph especially — of South Vietnamese general Loan blowing out the brains of a bound Vietcong suspect — splattered across the front pages and the conscience of the home front. (Weeks later, there would be equally grisly photographs of the victims of methodical Communist massacre in captured Hue, shot and bludgeoned to death and dumped into mass graves.)

Tet marked the turning point in the struggle for American public opinion. If a supposedly beaten foe could fight on for days and even weeks, massively frustrating American firepower, why should anyone listen any longer to the administration's boasts and claims about the war? While I had Nixon's attention, I quickly learned, it was wise to bring up whatever else, related or not, was on my mind. With what I hoped was a plausible transition, I passed from solicited to unsolicited counsel.

MEMORANDUM

TO: DC February 3, 1968

FROM: RJW

If you are willing to entertain my earlier indictment of McNamara and my judgment of the consequences of his folly, I cannot see any compelling reason for restraint in the face of the Vietnam blunder, which is equally his doing.

Once again in the waning days of his tenure, McNamara has felt the sting of suppressed truth stirring in his breast. He now talks of the reversal of several "previously favorable trends" in the war. Let us remember that these trends were deemed "favorable" by McNamara, who hardly qualifies as an objective observer.

Vietnam is a gross failure in conflict management based on precise and logical principles that happen *not* to apply to Asian reality. The only respectable reason for staying on in Vietnam is that the United States is too heavily committed, militarily and morally, to pull out. But this level of commitment was never envisaged in

McNamara's plan for managing the war; far from it. The United States stands imprisoned in a gigantic mistake.

This mistake is currently costing us 200 to 300 lives a week, $30-plus billion a year, almost all our intellectual and emotional energies, the respect and adherence of our European allies, our strategic dominance in nuclear weapons and in conventional forces in such critical areas as the Mediterranean and the Middle East, the stability and growth of our economy on which rests the hope of domestic racial reconciliation and progress — the list can be extended indefinitely. The costs of staying in Vietnam are outrageous — and so are the costs of pulling out.

What is needed, and *all* that is needed, at least for now, is a frank admission of this obvious state of affairs.

Are we bound to hang on and attain "victory"? Within the limits of the Manila declaration formula, there can be no assurance of United States "victory," no matter how long we stay. For the test will come *after* our forces withdraw, as they must following a negotiated "settlement."

You are perfectly correct at this point to rule out any widening of the war and any further American military commitment. You are *not* correct to praise the generosity of Johnson's terms to the North Vietnamese. The supposed generosity of those terms rests on the assumption that North Vietnam is playing the same game as we are — that the North Vietnamese are, in fact, susceptible to "management." They are not. They are fighting their kind of war, in their way, for their objectives. The correct stance, which may be adopted later on, would be to point out the fundamental and partly admitted errors of the administration in its conduct of the war; to point out what the mistake is costing us; to call attention to the perils facing us at home and abroad; to assign the war its proper (and secondary) place among these perils; and to proclaim the intention to "de-escalate" the level of American commitment and effort so as to free our resources to meet more important challenges.

This is not "retreat"; this is sanity. If the Soviets should suddenly confront us with a challenge in Europe or the Middle East, or if the race war we fear should materialize in our cities this summer, we will damned well see Vietnam in its true perspective and perhaps act hastily to trim our commitment there. It would be better to see it for what it is now.

———————

Nixon made no reply to my proposal.

3. A campaign organization acquires a distinctive character from the candidate it serves. The identifying "tone" of the emerging Nixon organization was a quiet hum. Efficient operatives were the rule rather than the exception, and they gave the organization a cool, functional corporate personality, as though Nixon were being assisted by a team hired in a package deal with IBM. Even his declaration of candidacy, customarily a moment in which the candidate displayed real or feigned emotion, wound up displaying the technical virtuosity of his organization. On February 2, 1968, Nixon announced the unsurprising news of his candidacy by sending 150,000 letters to the households of New Hampshire voters — a staggering piece of direct-mail work, made more impressive by being done in secrecy. The press received the word just as the citizens of New Hampshire were opening their letters.

The text said in part: "During the past eight years I have had a chance to reflect on the lessons of public office, to measure the nation's tasks and its problems from a fresh perspective. I have sought to apply those lessons to the needs of the present, and to the entire sweep of this final third of the 20th Century. And I believe I have found some answers." The letter succeeded in making a seeming virtue of Nixon's enforced retirement. But the final sentence — the clincher — had been much labored over. In an early draft, it had read: "And I *think* I have found some answers." That sounded too tentative and wishy-washy, and so we collectively amended it to the more self-assured *believe.* What were these answers, asked reporters? Wait and see, we replied, wait and see.

The first formal campaign speech seemed to suggest, like evangelizing George Romney, that we should seek first the heavenly kingdom. America, Nixon declared, was suffering from "a crisis of the spirit," for which he roundly blamed Lyndon Johnson, who had lost touch with "the soul of the nation." What was needed, Nixon lyricized, was leadership that would give America "the lift of a driving dream." That was Price at the top of his form as a phrasemaker, but Nixon's message was at once too lofty and too muffled to suit me. I had been unable to join the touring party, and so had been assigned the task of monitoring the media coverage of the postannouncement campaign swing and reporting by way of daily memoranda. On the same day that I wrote to Nixon about the impact of Tet, I sent a general note:

MEMORANDUM

TO: DC   February 3, 1968

FROM: RJW

The graceful nonannouncement and the deft handling of the first encounter with the press have put DC off to a splendid start. Johnson is worried. A poor devil who writes speeches for him confides that the President read DC's *Pueblo* statement as it came over the ticker, and that he profanely allowed that it was a "good" (read: politically effective) statement . . .

Yes, America is undergoing "a crisis of the spirit," but Americans are worried and angry about a great many *specific* and *concrete* issues — the war, racial strife, rising taxes and prices, crime and civil disorder, etc. New Hampshire is useful chiefly to strike sparks that will set Wisconsin ablaze. These sparks must be specific, though not necessarily in the form of proposals for action. There should be emphasis on the theme we discussed: America is slipping . . .

Sure enough, when Nixon lashed out at the Johnson administration for "knuckling under to a fourth-rate power" by allowing North Korea to get away with the seizure of the USS *Pueblo,* the crowd that had been nodding at his sermonizing suddenly came alive. Thereafter, remember-the-Pueblo became a standard "cheer-line" — as Nixon called it.

The *New York Times'* account of the first day's campaigning contained an interesting bit of news. Nixon had slipped out of his hotel — and away from the press — for an unscheduled series of meetings with the citizens of Hillsboro. Under the direction of Garment, Treleaven, and Shakespeare, the Hillsboro Town Hall had been turned into a sound studio. The exchanges between Nixon and carefully selected panels of questioners were filmed for use in TV commercials. A Romney man got wind of the taping sessions and alerted reporters, who reacted angrily. Nixon had promised an "open campaign," and now he was sneaking off to unannounced private meetings. Ellsworth and Buchanan, who had been getting along well with the press, sounded a bit testy in their quoted explanations that reporters were barred in order to put the panelists at ease.

In truth, Ellsworth, Buchanan — all of us who dealt with issues — were more attuned to the printed word than to videotape, and we preferred reporters, even sworn adversaries, to technicians in our hire. But this small episode marked the unintentional surfacing of the other side of the Nixon campaign — the side that the media men and their hirelings controlled. What was traditionally the main business of campaigning, the speeches and public appearances that the writing press covered, steadily became less important than the unseen media enterprise. Nixon's performances before the cameras in closed, controlled circumstances, far from the prying eyes of the press, were the ones that mattered. Edited film clips and commercials showing him at his best were beamed to the audience that mattered — the millions of television viewers who ignored the dull political news in the papers. My sympathies were with the working press, whom I thought we had inadvertently snubbed.

MEMORANDUM

TO: DC   February 4, 1968

FROM: RJW

The press relations goof on the TV taping gave the Romney people an opportunity they didn't deserve. Reporters won't try to bull
their way into a private taping, but they should be told well in advance that the session will be closed, and that the candidate won't
slip away without telling them where he's going. The quotes from
Ellsworth and Buchanan were rather truculent and unfortunate
. . . What's needed is somebody to put his feet up on the table with
the reporters around eleven o'clock and swap insults and dope
stories with them over Scotch.

———————

That "somebody" never emerged because Nixon wanted the
press kept as far away and uninformed as possible. Thanks to the
media technicians, he no longer needed the pencil-and-paper intermediaries who had "shafted" him. Now he could go over their
heads directly to the people via the tube.

At least that was the objective. As a practical matter, the traveling press could not be banished, nor could Nixon run away from reporters who awaited him at every stop. So long as they could raise
questions and interpret his answers, the possibility existed of an un-
programmed response. At a press conference in Manchester, Nixon
made an unguarded comment on the Communist offensive in Vietnam, describing it as "a desperate — I would hope last-ditch —
effort." He expressed the conviction that the United States must see
the war through to "a successful conclusion," a formula that
sounded as hollow in his mouth as Johnson's. Just as the press conference was beginning, Buchanan called and told me what Nixon
was about to say. It was too late to do anything but urge that the
question be sidestepped at the next stop in Wisconsin. When the
party landed there, a cautionary note for Nixon's guidance was
waiting:

MEMORANDUM

to: DC   February 5, 1968

from: RJW

I'm told the question of the Vietcong offensive came up and was answered with the Rusk line, to the effect that this was a last, all-out effort by a beaten foe. My sources in the Pentagon and outside privately give a quite different estimate.

What this prolonged, multicity attack demonstrates is: 1) the Communist military infrastructure in the south is intact and functioning efficiently; 2) the cities and the South Vietnamese society, army, and government are heavily penetrated; 3) U.S. troops formerly used in search and destroy operations will have to be pulled back to defend cities thought secure; 4) the Vietcong are courageous, tenacious, and willing to die, and a frightened and demoralized civilian population will draw the contrast with the play-safe attitude of the ARVN. It was the very timidity of the ARVN, by the way, that compelled the U.S. forces to use dubious tactics in the city fighting that were sure to cause heavy civilian casualties — e.g., the use of helicopter gunships flying at rooftop level.

This offensive brings into doubt not only the administration's optimism, but also its basic strategy.

———

For the next few days, I left it at that and kept busy with assigned writing chores, turning out statements on détente, East-West trade, likely budget cuts, guerrilla warfare in Latin America, and a big-navy speech shamelessly calculated to purchase the favor of the citizens of Portsmouth, who lived in the shadow of the announced closing of their town's base. The reports from the road were ecstatic. Nixon was outpolling poor Romney by literally incredible margins. The expensive machinery in Wisconsin was purring.

Yet all was not quite perfectly predictable. Tet continued to send shock waves running through the political landscape. Senator Eugene McCarthy's challenge to the President in New Hampshire had begun to seem less and less quixotic. The Gallup poll showed approval of Johnson's handling of the war falling, with no prospect of a rebound. Although Nixon's victory in the first primary test was certain, the pervasive air of uncertainty concerning the war caused him to begin maneuvering ever so carefully to exploit Johnson's weakness. In his remarks on future United States policy toward embattled allies, he sounded a new note that had present application: "Let's help them fight the war and not fight the war for them." When that line was received enthusiastically, Nixon incorporated it into his standard speech. He also began attacking the Johnson administration for "failing to train the South Vietnamese to take over the major share" of the fighting. Sensing a fresh flexibility in Nixon's position, and encouraged to do so by Ellsworth and others, the press broke out in a rash of stories saying the Republican front runner would soon modify his hawkish stand. He was reported to be preparing a "major statement" on Vietnam.

"What's going on?" I asked Garment on the telephone.

"I don't know, but you'd better come up to New York as soon as we get back."

VI

1. "THE OLD MAN is thinking," Garment informed me on my arrival in New York, "and that's what he wants the rest of us to do." Nothing had been decided on the Vietnam statement, not even whether there would definitely be one. The Nixon staff had moved to new quarters uptown at Fifth Avenue and Forty-third Street, a move made without publicity in deference to Rockefeller's territorial rights. Nixon's name was absent from the building's lobby directory, and only a piece of paper taped to the door guided a visitor to Suite 401. Garment's desk was in a cramped space just off the entry foyer that also served as a passageway. While we talked, people marched through.

In the Nixon organization, the slightest hint of danger created an air of emergency. A telephone call from a worried state chairman would set alarm bells ringing, even though he might want nothing more than to remind New York that he was on the job. There had been a few such calls in recent days prompted by Romney's lunging attacks on "the Johnson-Nixon Vietnam policy." Party professionals wondered how long Nixon would continue to echo Johnson's stand-fast line, and how his apparent me-tooism would affect his ability to criticize the administration in the months ahead.

Thus we were reacting, not to Tet or the policies it had shaken, but to scattered political reactions to the public reaction. We stood at third hand from the event itself, anxious to do something if only a tactically safe inspiration came to us. Our hypersensitivity to danger put us in a self-made bind. Whatever we might do seemed at least as risky as what we were already doing, and so we settled for more of the same.

As Buchanan argued, the asset of victory in New Hampshire was not yet locked up, and nothing should be done to jeopardize its impact. Delay would clarify the post-Tet situation in Vietnam, Price thought, and perhaps reveal the intentions of the White House and the Pentagon. Garment, much as he desired movement on the war issue, disliked attempting to outguess the hurt and cunning Johnson. Our talk came full circle.

Before I left, Garment asked me to join him for a drink at the nearby Biltmore Bar. "Roger Hilsman's coming by to talk to us about Vietnam," he said.

"What does *he* have to tell *us?*"

Our interview with this ex-New Frontiersman, now opposed to the war he had helped plan and manage, was more than an instance of Garment's eclectic brain-picking. Such promiscuous appropriation of ideas revealed, in due course, the near-vacuum where Nixon's own position should have been.

MEMORANDUM

TO: DC   February 23, 1968

cc: Len Garment

FROM: RJW

Len Garment and I spent two hours yesterday afternoon with Roger Hilsman, former Assistant Secretary of State for Far Eastern Affairs, author of *To Move a Nation,* and presently professor of international relations at Columbia University. We were taking up his offer to hear his views on Vietnam. After his fourth Scotch and soda (he set the pace), Hilsman became positively chummy and began offering gratuitous advice on how to handle the Vietnam issue in the campaign . . .

Hilsman, you will recall, was a guerrilla fighter in Burma during

World War II and acted as a prime mover for the emphasis on counterinsurgency during the early Kennedy administration. The war in Vietnam has long since gone past the scenario drawn up by Hilsman and like-minded New Frontiersmen. So we're dealing with a Kennedy Democrat (both JFK and RFK) who feels neither loyalty nor respect for the Johnson administration.

As a result of visiting Vietnam last summer and thinking about what he saw, Hilsman told us, he has shifted from a moderate hawk to a moderate dove position . . . Hilsman said he thought for a while on his return from Vietnam that perhaps the answer was to give "Westy" another half million men, so that he could make "seek and destroy" work and then get back to "clear and hold." But he decided, becoming in the process a self-styled dove, that this steep escalation wouldn't work: everything still would depend on the South Vietnamese, and so far as he can tell, through observation and from his informants, our allies simply aren't up to the job. He has come to the conclusion that U.S. military force cannot reverse the political gains of the Vietcong — not at any level of forces and not *ever* — because we are "white faces" and the Vietnamese people must be rallied by their own kind.

Americans are everywhere in South Vietnam, doing many things that the South Vietnamese should be doing for themselves but won't so long as we are willing to assume their responsibilities. The South Vietnamese want above all to *survive.* Yet, that is precisely what the U.S. cannot in the long run guarantee unless the South Vietnamese reclaim the leading role in the war and in pacification.

What Hilsman's view comes to is this:

1. The U.S. needs a strategy that can be sustained militarily and politically, one that shifts the onus for the war from Washington to Hanoi. It must be a strategy, moreover, that is *not* dependent on any response from Hanoi.

2. That being the case, the U.S. should seek to "cool it," to de-escalate the war. U.S. strategy should shift from seek and destroy to clear and hold. We should halt the strategic bombing of North Vi-

etnam while continuing tactical bombing of northern staging areas and of the infiltration routes, all without any expectation of a quid pro quo from Hanoi. We should make every effort to "de-Americanize" the war, turning back responsibility to the South Vietnamese. The Saigon government should be broadened and made *actively* reformist, with the expectation that this would lead to contacts between new elements in the government and the NLF.

Hilsman contends that such a policy would be realistic, for it steers between the equally disastrous extremes of major escalation and abrupt withdrawal. The success or failure of such an approach would be determined by the South Vietnamese; it would take a year or two for the results to become clear. And by that time, the situation would be sufficiently fuzzed-up and the American involvement sufficiently downgraded, that Washington could go decently to Geneva and negotiate a settlement with Hanoi and the NLF that would be a surrender in fact but not in crucial appearance. Of course, the South Vietnamese *could* surprise us by taking hold and defeating the Vietcong militarily and politically, but Hilsman obviously regards this as a long chance. By the time of the anticipated conference, Hilsman declares, the U.S. would realize that South Vietnam never actually possessed the strategic importance imputed to it; and that, partly because of what the U.S. has done and partly because of what the Asians are doing for themselves, there are no dominoes in Southeast Asia . . .

Toward the end of our conversation, Hilsman pondered how he might advise DC to handle the war issue. It goes this way:

1. Emphasize that he is a "free" man and LBJ is not. Say the war needs to be reassessed fundamentally. Perhaps this would result in the decision to commit greater force, perhaps not — the intelligence data and classified information to make such a decision is available only to the President.

2. Bear down on the theme that the outcome in Vietnam is ultimately up to the South Vietnamese themselves — it's their fight and their country. Echo LBJ's 1964 talk of "Asian boys."

3. Examine Vietnam in the perspective of reality, rather than of outmoded theory. If the domino theory was ever true in Southeast Asia, it isn't true anymore. Thailand can take care of itself. Indonesia is proving it doesn't need "white faces" to save it from Communism and Chinese imperialism.

4. Above all, sound a new version of Ike's 1952 promise concerning Korea, saying this time: "Elect me and I will find an honorable way out."

Hilsman doesn't think DC can beat LBJ, but he does believe that a great many Democrats, who have given up on the President, will respond eagerly to a ray of hope from the Republican side. His presence bore out that eagerness, and his unsolicited offer to present his views . . . shows that our smallest gesture may be magnified by those who want desperately to see a difference between DC and LBJ . . .

—————

Nixon, who remained in seclusion, kept my memo and remained silent. I returned to Washington, disappointed and determined that, next time, I would not go to New York empty-handed. If Nixon didn't have a Vietnam position thought out, I would present him with one.

2. Just as the press was beginning to wonder what had become of Nixon's expected statement on Vietnam, the opposition captured the headlines. Rockefeller, following a fund-raising speech in Detroit on Romney's behalf, faced familiar questions and gave novel-sounding answers. Yes, he allowed, he would accept a genuine draft if it came.

To the Romney camp, this had the smell of betrayal. The Michigan governor was hopelessly behind Nixon in New Hampshire — at least six to one in his own polls — and an unauthorized Rockefeller write-in campaign was making surprising headway. A humiliating prospect loomed: in spite of months of campaigning, Romney might finish dead last, behind an absentee noncandidate. With the election only two weeks away, Romney's aides laid the facts before him and recommended the only alternative to crushing defeat.

The first of the stunning surprises in this year of the unexpected came on February 28. At a press conference in Washington, Romney announced that he was withdrawing from the New Hampshire race. As a face-saving gesture, he made his announcement in the form of a "report" to his fellow Republican governors, meeting in the capital, in the hope that they might rally around another moderate. Ellsworth, who had been attending the meeting and keeping watch over the uncommitted governors, called me as Romney's face faded from the television screen.

I asked if there were a Romney-Rockefeller plot.

"There's no sign of it," said the jubilant Ellsworth. "I think it means that George made up his mind to get out, period. And that means we've won earlier than we thought. Now we can skeletonize the rest of the primaries and go into more nonprimary states. This is the beginning of the campaign against Johnson."

After a day of uneasy waiting, Ellsworth's judgment seemed to be confirmed. The moderate Republican governors, cool to Nixon but all operating independently, stood around and looked at one another while the Nixon agents closed in. They had been busy for months, for their abiding fear was that the governors would sense Nixon's weakness, discover their strength, and join forces around one of their own. Surprisingly, the governors allowed themselves to be persuaded that a do-nothing policy suited their interests. As Sears replayed it, the argument used on the governors went this way: "Look, we all went through the sixty-four bloodbath, and we don't want to go through it again. If the people in your state see you getting too close to one of the candidates, they'll be after you and each other. We're willing to ride on the verdict of the primaries. Why don't you wait and see what happens?"

Ellsworth's claim of victory proved a bit premature. As impressive as it was, the first TKO in American political history was just that — a victory for the technicians. Romney's own pollsters had knocked him out of the campaign. Perhaps it was true, as Buchanan's press-relations directives argued, that Nixon was so strong no one would step into the ring. The fact remained that Romney's early exit had cheated us of the clear-cut triumph necessary to dispose of Nixon's "loser" image once and for all. Moreover, Rockefeller was still alive and unscathed, as Nixon well knew. Talking to reporters, he praised Romney ("I admire men who get into the arena") and challenged Rockefeller, urging him to trust the voters rather than "the kingmakers at Miami."

Typically, Nixon and his strategists exaggerated the danger from Rockefeller, the last man any Republican kingmakers would want to crown. Romney's withdrawal served to make the intraparty situation plainer than ever: the wings of the G.O.P. represented by Rockefeller and Reagan (as Goldwater's heir) were implacably hostile to each other, and Nixon commanded the center. If Rockefeller should become an open candidate, conservatives flirting with Reagan would move toward Nixon and take their revenge on the New York governor, who had walked out on them in 1964. Nor did Rockefeller have anything to gain by entering the arena in such states as Wisconsin and Nebraska, where he was certain to lose. The only primary he might win was Oregon, which he had taken in 1964, but he could not run there without first being beaten in rock-ribbed Nebraska.

Rockefeller's only strategy was to continue waiting on the sidelines, hoping that his poll-rating would climb (especially among Democrats and Independents) and that the front runner would make a mistake. It could not be just an ordinary mistake, but one so damaging as to be virtually unimaginable on the part of a disciplined veteran like Nixon.

With only anticlimax left to report on the Republican side in New Hampshire, the word and picture journalists paid new attention to Senator McCarthy's crusade against the President. If most reporters hesitated to take McCarthy seriously until the Tet offensive, they overcompensated thereafter, turning the primary into a presumed referendum on the administration's war policies.

This grossly oversimplified what was actually happening among New Hampshire's voters, as the exhaustive postelection survey of the University of Michigan Opinion Research Center disclosed. "Among McCarthy's supporters in the primary," the Michigan study found, "those who were unhappy with the Johnson administration for *not* pursuing a harder line against Hanoi outnumbered those advocating a withdrawal from Vietnam by nearly a three to two margin."

In New Hampshire, the President's name did not appear on the ballot. Party leaders were organizing a last-minute write-in campaign and practically blackmailing the regulars into expressions of pro-Johnson "loyalty," using such crude devices as numbered pledge ballots. Around McCarthy, in sharp contrast, had gathered hundreds of young people opposed to the war. They were intelligent, articulate, and liberal to radical in their politics, and they had left the campuses to enlist as volunteers in a "moral" cause. The sympathies of the press were overwhelmingly with the attractive and earnest "McCarthy Kids," and the media formed a mental picture of the senator's constituency based on these unrepresentative followers.

The men behind the typewriters and cameras were just as susceptible as their readers and viewers to "seeing" what their emotions told them was there. It was easy to understand how the word-journalists went astray. Quite apart from their dislike of Johnson and their feeling of kinship with the children of the educated upper-middle-class, the political writers were affected by their working environment, overshadowed as they were by the hulking presence of television. In the competition for public attention, TV won every time. The word-journalists tried increasingly to adapt their medium to the appeals of picture-journalism. When they discovered Sam Brown, the divinity school dropout and chief McCarthy organizer, reporters seized on him as the "image" of the antiwar youth movement sweeping the state. (In just this fashion, instant "leaders" sprang up among white campus radicals and black ghetto militants. Word-journalists, competing with the medium of immediacy, needed embodiments of complicated phenomena to facilitate instant analysis.) The picture-journalists, looking for guidance as to where to point their cameras, read about Sam Brown in the press and hurried off to interview him, thus closing the circuit of unintended misunderstanding and misrepresentation.

Nixon, meanwhile, was all but ignored as he went through the motions of running unopposed. Yet even that lonely position seemed worrisome on second and third thought. He was trying to preserve a semblance of a contest by running against the combined write-in totals of Johnson and Rockefeller, and boredom might eat away at his expected vote. Just a week before the primary, in the midst of a speech filled with his usual generalities on the war, he drew his listeners up sharp by making a bold-sounding promise.

"If in November this war is not over," he declared, "I say the American people will be justified in electing new leadership, and I pledge to you that new leadership will end the war and win the peace in the Pacific."

This promise, implying a plan to fulfill it, splashed across the front pages and brought the reporters and TV crews rushing back to the Republican side of the New Hampshire campaign, eager for details. There weren't any. Nothing lay behind the "pledge" except Nixon's instinct for an extra effort of salesmanship when the customers started drifting away.

Was this promise Nixon's own idea? Was it the result of Hilsman's suggestion? Similar counsel had come out of a meeting of senior Nixon advisers several days earlier in New York's Warwick Hotel. Sears, who regularly attended the Sunday sessions, recalled that the echo-Ike advice originated with Herbert Brownell, the former Attorney General. "Brownell thought Nixon should do what Eisenhower did in nineteen fifty-two — you know, 'I will go to Korea.' It was such dumb advice that I didn't bother to say anything. I thought that a pro like Nixon wouldn't need anybody to tell him to stay out of the tall grass."

I wondered why Nixon had acted without consulting his staff or preparing the next step. It seemed out of character for him to jump into a commitment, particularly one forcing him to spell out his position on the war, which he wished to avoid. But perhaps this impulsive act — taken alone, for unexplained (and perhaps unexplainable) motives — was very much part of Nixon's character. I remembered his snap decision that gray early morning in Los Angeles six years earlier, when he suddenly went downstairs and confronted the reporters and cameras and appeared to commit political suicide. Nixon was not a mechanical man, merely a man who had created unusual self-controls, and these were subject to failure. Like the rest of us, he sometimes saw the glimmer of opportunity in the dark and leaped toward it. When it happened, the thing to wonder about was our surprise at his humanity.

In any event, the "pledge" had been made and Nixon would have to back it up.

MEMORANDUM

TO: DC   March 8, 1968

FROM: RJW

RE: Vietnam

I believe it is absolutely imperative that a staff meeting be held at the earliest possible date to think through our position on the war. The pledge to end the war and win the peace must be given at least a measure of substance if it is to have the desired impact. What, specifically, is our position?

Let me suggest what our position should *not* be. We should not allow ourselves to be co-opted automatically on the side of the administration's impending major escalation of the U.S. military commitment . . .

Are we prepared to support truly massive reinforcement, perhaps even a doubling of the U.S. forces? Last week, the U.S. took at least five times as many casualties as the South Vietnamese. Are we prepared to see this ratio climb to ten to one? In the northern provinces, the much publicized plight of the combat base at Khesanh symbolizes the prevailing U.S. posture of strategic inferiority on the ground. Simultaneous attacks on Khesanh and Hue, which are officially conceded to be within the enemy's capability, could create a desperate emergency, which could see the U.S. suffer local military defeats of literally world-shaking psychological impact. French general André Beaufre is quoted as saying: "The principal Vietcong objective in the Tet offensive was psychological, whereas the principal U.S. objective was military." The purely military response to an emergency in the north would be heavy reinforcement and perhaps an invasion of North Vietnam somewhere above the DMZ, with the objective of cutting the enemy's lines and threatening his rear. But where is the rear in this war? And are we prepared to give assent to military measures such as invasion that could change the whole character of the war *without* achieving a desired result?

In 1954, when the Eisenhower administration weighed the alternatives in Indochina and decided against intervention, an important element in the decision was the attitude of the American people. As I recall the circumstances, the then Vice President sent aloft a trial balloon for U.S. intervention, and when the White House saw the way the wind of public opinion was blowing, the French, rightly or wrongly, were left to their fate. Let us not be either paralyzed or carried along, willy-nilly, by the imagined necessity of appearing "consistent." Johnson, after all, is the man who should worry most about seeming consistent. Since 1964, he has done almost everything he accused Goldwater of preparing to do; and none of it has worked. Policies and options that could be championed in 1954, in 1964, or even a year ago, have been made untenable by the cumulative effects of the administration's tragic misconduct of the war. The mistakes made under a policy of gradual escalation cannot be retrieved by a new and desperate policy of massive escalation. The American people are coming to distrust the identification of escalation with "victory," and with every reason. Further escalation is the surest means of worsening the U.S. position in Vietnam and of increasing the likelihood of eventual humiliating defeat.

In order to gain popular support for new leadership capable of making a tolerable peace in Southeast Asia, we must inspire confidence by speaking candidly — something the administration has not done and cannot do in the months ahead. We must not become accomplices after the fact in a policy founded on a lie, namely, that as some level of *military* commitment, the U.S. will achieve "victory" for its *political* goals. Short of the destruction and occupation of North Vietnam, "victory," so defined, is unattainable. Whether or not it was ever attainable through specifically military means is beside the point; it is not possible now. At the same time, further pursuit of this illusion will further divide a nation already on the brink of civil war, will further dissipate the resources needed to contain this top-priority domestic emergency, and will hasten the worldwide collapse of the economic, political, and military structure of order founded on U.S. strength.

The theme of DC's future remarks on Vietnam should be no further escalation and no wider war, an echo of Johnson (1964) that has the ring of a real choice compared with Johnson (1968). DC should specifically oppose resort to invasion or to nuclear weapons — not on moral grounds, but because they won't work on any rational scale of costs vs. benefits. He should lay increasing stress on the need for new and more vigorous attempts to end the war through diplomacy. While continuing his references to the growing Soviet strategic challenge, which has until recently gone unnoticed in our preoccupation with Vietnam, he should question the administration's obsession with military means in a war that is universally agreed to have only a political solution . . .

Without doing violence to sincere convictions or high principles, I believe a way can and must be found to oppose a war that is fulfilling a long-dreaded American nightmare — a man-for-man, one-to-one struggle on the continent of Asia. We cannot retreat from Vietnam, but neither should we go a step deeper into the quagmire. In attempting to guarantee "no reward for aggression" in Vietnam, the U.S. is risking a grossly disproportionate penalty for principle at home and throughout the world. The American people sense this onrushing penalty, and they will respond, I believe, to a man honest enough to address their doubts and fears in the accents of calm truth.

As I said at the outset, whether or not you agree with any of this, I think the question of our position needs a full airing as soon as possible.

3.   When it finally came, Nixon's anticipated landslide in New Hampshire still strained credulity: he received 79 percent of the vote, more than seven times the total of Rockefeller write-ins. Even so, we had not beaten a flesh-and-blood rival, merely our own predictions, and that took the edge off our celebration at Washington's Willard Hotel. Talk turned to the astonishing result of the balloting on the other side: McCarthy had received 42.2 percent of the vote, compared to Johnson's 49.4 percent, and he had taken twenty of the state's twenty-four convention delegates. For a little-known senator thus to humble an incumbent President was unprecedented, and the room buzzed with speculation. Television analysts saw what the previous weeks' reporting prepared them to see — a resounding vote of no confidence in the administration's war policies. Even if hawks actually outnumbered doves among McCarthy's supporters (as we later learned), the depth of Johnson's unpopularity was shocking.

I joined Ellsworth and Sears in a quiet corner, and we drew up a list of winners and losers. Nixon and McCarthy were winners, obviously. The losers: Johnson, then Rockefeller, who relied heavily on a strong Democrat in the White House to bolster his claims. Then Robert Kennedy, who appeared to have missed his chance. McCarthy, no admirer of the Kennedys, nevertheless would have deferred to the heir apparent, but the regime-in-exile had debated and waited too long. Now McCarthy, the moral victor, was in the race to stay, and Kennedy seemed to be out.

What no one outside Kennedy's circle knew, of course, was that he had already decided to run and was awaiting only the right moment to declare his candidacy. The next day, at the worst psychological moment imaginable, when the McCarthyites had scarcely tasted "victory," Kennedy confided to a reporter that he was "reassessing" his position. That headline raised cries of outrage from McCarthy's young crusaders. Ruthless Bobby was trying to steal Clean Gene's glory. By the time Kennedy formally announced his candidacy a week later, the anti-Johnson movement was irreconcilably split — and the President, for that reason, seemed somewhat more secure.

But nothing was as it seemed in this madly unpredictable year. Except Nixon, who was even more cautious than he appeared. He regretted his "end the war" pledge and did his best to disown it, telling an Associated Press interviewer: "I have no magic formula, no gimmick. If I had a gimmick, I would tell Lyndon Johnson. That would be a moral obligation. But I do have some specific ideas on how to end the war. They are primarily in the diplomatic area." With that, he stepped back toward the sheltering generalities and the safe course. But the public was moving away from him. Ordinary citizens discerned the shape of the future much more clearly and maturely than their supposed leaders. Gallup reported that 69 percent of those polled — Republicans and Democrats, hawks and doves — favored a plan of "Vietnamization," calling for the replacement of 100,000 U.S. combat troops at a time by South Vietnamese and their phased withdrawal from the country.

Not the war but the politics of the war issue absorbed Nixon. On Saint Patrick's day, he telephoned from Key Biscayne, and we talked about the twists and turns of the post-New Hampshire political situation.

Nixon was greatly pleased by Robert Kennedy's plunge into the race and said two or three times: "We can beat that little S.O.B." He believed the worsening Democratic split would give the Republicans a "great, historic opportunity" — potentially another 1932.

If Kennedy were nominated, it would deliver the South to the Republicans, but only behind Nixon — not Rockefeller. Nixon didn't expect Kennedy to oust Johnson. "It's all uphill for him, against the arithmetic. Sorensen was against it and so were others." Among other things, Kennedy had the liability of being a single-issue candidate. "Johnson could take the war away from him in a minute — and then what?" Twice, Nixon mentioned Johnson's "poor health" and remarked: "Bobby may kill him" — apparently by applying terrific pressure. (Evidently he had been talking to someone whose line into the White House he respected.)

Throughout our conversation, it was clear that Nixon was not worried. If Bobby were nominated, he said, it would offer the chance to indict the whole JFK-LBJ tenure ("right back to the Bay of Pigs"). He showed no hesitancy about taking on the brother of the man who had beaten — and awed — him in 1960.

Our immediate (and minor) problem, said Nixon, was to sustain interest in the Republican side while the Democrats tore each other apart. "Rocky's people put out the story they were glad Bobby jumped in. Actually, they're hopping mad — Bobby's upstaged them." Nixon expected Rockefeller to announce the following week. In any event, he expected to face Rockefeller in Oregon. If and when Rockefeller announced, Nixon also expected "the liberal press" to open up on him, but he regarded this as an index of his strength. It might not happen, he said, if all the play went to the Kennedy-McCarthy fight.

With the Democrats working the antiwar ground, Nixon wondered how Rockefeller could stake out a distinctive position on Vietnam. "He's supposed to have *six* different position papers on his desk — talk about *flexibility!*"

In spite of his tone, Nixon was intent on being at least as flexible. He wanted to know how we might "pre-empt" positions and thereby narrow Rockefeller's room for maneuver. He had read and approved my memo on the administration's possible escalation of the war. When I suggested that we could use this paper as the basis

of our position, he countered with the suggestion that we discuss it
further. Evidently we would have the staff conference, but he didn't
share my sense of urgency about stating a position.

"I'm waiting to see the whites of their eyes," he said.

4.   The ability to wait and see what an opponent will do, and
then judge the result objectively, is a priceless asset in a politician.
It is what the gift of "timing" consists of. Nixon did not naturally
possess it, but he had trained himself in the ways of patience and
curbed his combative impulse. His wait-and-see attitude had
served him well in dealing with Romney. Yet the success of this un-
demanding strategy lent an air of unreality to the campaign. It became plausible to imagine the impossible — that Nixon could continue indefinitely to pursue the presidency at an unhurried walk.

His first objective, of course, was the favor of a Republican party
badly needing ideological tranquillity after the rending Goldwater
experience. With only 29 percent of the nation's voters identifying
themselves as Republicans, the G.O.P. obviously needed internal
unity if it was to have a chance of winning. The Republicans
bound for the Miami convention hoped to choose a candidate who
could win, but the first order of business was to call a truce in the
fratricidal warfare. In this light, Nixon's blandness became positively attractive.

Nixon men kept up a front of unshakable confidence in the inevitability of his nomination. To the skeptical challenge that they encountered — "Yeah, Nixon's a mile wide and an inch deep" —
they answered: "And solid as a rock." Skeptics remained uncon-
vinced. "We don't believe it ourselves," Sears laughed. He had an
unorthodox theory that the center of the Republican party, from
which Nixon hoped to lead, was in fact the weakest point. "There
really aren't any delegates there. Every delegate is either a conservative or a liberal — that's the way Republicans are made. They're
moralists and ideologues. What we have to do this time is seduce
them into being practical, like Democrats."

To mention the Democrats was to reveal the missing dimension of the Nixon strategy. Assuming he won the nomination, what then? How did he propose to expand the Republican base into a plurality? At some point, Nixon would have to break into a run. He acknowledged as much in his morale-boosting talk of the "great, historic opportunity" awaiting the Republicans in 1968 — the chance to beat the divided, bloodied Democrats and seize the shifting middle ground of American politics. Such talk implied a dramatic change in strategy and objective, one which would give substance to Nixon's image and slogans. But when? "After the convention" — this was the phrase commonly heard around headquarters as we put off decisions, and no one used it more often than Nixon himself.

We assumed that the man in the White House would remain immobilized by his problems, a fixed target open to attack at our convenience. We were mistaken. The President was about to move in a way that opened a path to Republican victory yet narrowed our great opportunity.

VII

1. ONLY LYNDON JOHNSON knew his presidency was drawing to an end. Paradoxically, his secret recognition of weakness gave him enormous strength. When he chose to make known his stunning decision, the man who seemed to have lost control over the country would, at a stroke, gain immeasurable influence over both parties and the choice they offered to the electorate.

One day before he left the White House, Johnson spoke with a visitor in a way that shed revealing light on the collapse of his presidency.* "Our most tragic error," he declared, "may have been our inability to establish a rapport and a confidence with the communications media." For a President forced to step down in the face of near-disaster abroad and near-anarchy at home, this was a remarkable assessment of his misfortunes. By thus identifying the source of his tragedy, Johnson confirmed the decisive effect of the so-called credibility gap — the chasm, as the media saw it, between the administration's statements and the truth. He attributed unprecedented power to the media — almost veto power over the exercise of presidential leadership. Another embattled President in another time, say, Harry Truman, would have blamed his woes on flesh-and-blood enemies and tangible obstacles. Johnson blamed the intermediaries between himself and the people and saw himself frustrated by his "image" in their words and on the three-screen television consoles scattered throughout the White House. One evening,

* A transcript of the conversation was made available to the author by a former assistant to the President.

while walking with *Life* columnist Hugh Sidey, he wondered aloud: "Why should Ho Chi Minh believe me when the newspapers and the broadcasters in my own country won't believe me?"

Was this self-pity, tinged with a persecution complex? Johnson's host of flesh-and-blood enemies might insist it was. In fact, his assessment contained much truth.

2. Presidents had complained against the bias of journalists since the earliest days of the Republic. So long as wide diversity of view and sharp competition characterized the printed medium, the reader, including the reader in the White House, had a variety of biases to choose from. The marketplace acted as a self-correcting mechanism for the worst partisan excesses. In the important New York and Washington markets, for example, liberal, conservative, and middle-of-the-road newspapers not only chronicled the day's events but also kept watch over each other's treatment of the news.

Yet forces at work in the economic marketplace inexorably reduced the number of newspapers and magazines, which at once narrowed the range of views offered and weakened journalism's inner defenses against bias. By 1968, the field of standard morning newspapers serving New York and Washington had shrunk to a pair of monopolies. Although the *New York Times* and the Washington *Post* were professionally excellent, they were papers with a distinctly liberal point of view, which presented the rest of the spectrum of analysis and opinion poorly or not at all.

In addition, by the late 1960s America suffered from media "tilt." So completely did the New York–Washington communications corridor dominate the rest of the country that the "provinces" seemed to begin on the western edge of Georgetown. Once-resounding regional voices such as the Chicago *Tribune* (which clung to its pathetic boast — "the world's greatest newspaper") waxed fat as commercial enterprises, yet exerted waning influence on "national" opinion. The prosperous and well-edited Los Angeles *Times* airlifted copies to Washington for distribution to government officials, but it could not buck the east to west flow of "national" news and opinion. The privilege of speaking to and for the country rested, like so much privilege and power down through the nation's history, with the cosmopolitan East.

A great many "national" opinion molders were transplanted provincials, a fact often cited as a rebuttal against the charge of "eastern" bias. But most of these migrants adhered to the traditional pattern and became, in spite of their origins, determinedly chic, sophisticated, and progressive, in the New York manner. Their arrogance was typically unconscious, being built into their jobs. As a fledgling *Time* writer from the provinces of Queens, New York, I experienced the process in the late 1950s. When assigned to write "The Nation" lead, the magazine's thinly disguised editorial, I used to stare across the Manhattan skyline toward Hoboken in the small hours of the morning and wonder what the people *out there* really were thinking. It was my task to express their "mood" in a hundred lines, boiled down from the files of correspondents and stringers who shared my desire to please our primary audience, the senior editors.

New York journalism was a chamber of mirrors and echoes, and the "mood" we called America's was ultimately our own mood, distilled mainly from talking to each other. Within blocks of my cubicle at Time Inc. were acquaintances similarly engaged in pleasing their bosses and peers, at the *Times,* at *Newsweek,* at NBC and CBS. Outsiders, particularly conservatives, suspected a liberal conspiracy to brainwash the population. The newsweeklies ran identical cover stories, and the networks treated the nightly news in similar fashion. It was futile to explain that such concurring news judgments arose innocently, as the result of the people involved having a similar point of view. The interrogator would pounce — Why were they all liberals? Why didn't the magazines and networks hire conservatives? The answer, invariably unsatisfying, was that conservatives usually found better and more rewarding professions in which to invest the college degree now required of aspiring journalists.*

* From *Monday,* a publication of the Republican National Committee, December 13, 1971: "The Media Industry Newsletter has surveyed 2,309 New York City executives in and out of the media and has found that overall they are 57 percent Democratic, 40 percent GOP, 2

The strong link between higher education and higher journalism was one of the most powerful forces shaping the news media. *The Front Page* stereotype of the journalist as hard-drinking and uncouth dissolved before the tweedy, pipe-smoking new professional who looked and talked like the Ph.D. he sometimes was. The inclination of the college-trained journalist to burrow deep into a specialty and become an acknowledged expert in his field was all to the good, insofar as it improved communication among the educated and informed. But the journalist who resembled an academic intellectual, and who continued to give authority to academic fashions in social and political ideas, stood on the opposite side of a cultural gap from the public he was presumed to serve. If he was not actually "alienated," as so many academics affected to be, he was surely detached from the common life and conventional opinions of ordinary people.

The new journalist was a crusader quite different from the old typewriter-populist who championed the common man against the "interests." The academy had trained him to be a critic of society and especially of the uneducated common man whose defects were the apparent source of so many evils. The journalist's assumed role of social critic and reformer conflicted with his traditional function of "objective" observer, but this was explained as technological progress: he had given that job to the ubiquitous television camera. Talking with a college-student interviewer, the *New York Times'* resident philosopher, James Reston, reflected on the changing role of the press. "Television has taken away the great descriptive story. How can you sit down at a typewriter and try to describe the killing of John Kennedy when the reader has seen the tears on Jackie's cheeks? I happen to think this has been a good thing because it has forced the press to get more at the causes of events and not just the effects of the events or the recording of the events . . . So we have a

---

percent for Wallace, 1 percent undetermined. In the book publishing field, 74 percent of the respondents said they are Democrats, only 25 percent GOP. Democrats also dominated broadcasting, 56 to 43; newspapers and magazines, 50-45 (4 percent for Wallace); but the GOP won in advertising, 50-45 percent . . ."

much more exciting role . . . for a new generation of more analyti-
cal and better-educated reporters. You've got scope now for
thought and analysis of causes and consequences that I never had
when I was your age."

Now Reston modestly neglected to point out that the men who
packaged and presented the network television news digests relied
very heavily on the "national" press for ideas on where to aim their
cameras. This bias in identifying "news" was compounded by the
bias arising from the nature of television itself. With its cumber-
some equipment and intrusive presence, television became part of
any event it covered and to some extent changed and contrived it.
Selective analysis in the printed media and selective coverage in the
electronic media combined to *standardize* the news profession's intramural opinion of what was news and what it meant. Once that
notion had been communicated to the largest audiences in human
history, it became the media's "truth," locked in place by the profession's inability to criticize itself and admit error.

Politicians, whose power and tenure depended on being attuned
to popular sentiment, were at once fascinated by and afraid of the
national media. When David Brinkley impaled a victim with a wry
smirk, the politician shared Brinkley's delusion that millions of
NBC viewers agreed with the wounding words. In truth, Brinkley
and other leading opinion-molders performed for each other and for
the politicians who took them so terribly seriously. The millions of
viewers in the non-Eastern provinces did not surrender their own
opinions (and biases) by watching Brinkley, Cronkite, and other
television superstars. They simply availed themselves of the convenience packaging that wrapped up the day's events in lively,
thirty-second "takes" instead of columns of gray newsprint. The
truly brainwashed were the inhabitants of the media-enclosed environment of New York and Washington, for they reacted (and *over-
reacted*) to words and pictures that ordinary nonpolitical citizens
scarcely noticed.

What neither the politicians nor the opinion-molders were able
to see — the former because of fear, the latter because of pride —

was the sovereign contrariness of the people. Imagery, in the end, did not outweigh substance. The people watched and listened — and came to their own conclusions. By the middle of 1968, they had formed a distrust both of news-makers and the news media.

Lyndon Johnson and his media enemies were not, as they supposed, competing for the pliable, monolithic mind of America — each citizen would make up his mind independently, as always. The antagonists actually were waging a grudge battle, a conflict originating with John Kennedy's reign, the splendid fakery of the New Frontier and the prominent part the new breed of journalists had played in it.

Kennedy, a one-time Hearst by-liner, a Pulitzer Prize winner, and a press buff who enjoyed the inside gossip of journalism, dealt with the media as a fellow professional. He knew precisely how to capitalize on the admiration and acceptance he enjoyed. More than any President in modern history, he was obsessively interested in every word written about him. If he missed something, his staff and network of indefatigable readers and clippers would not. For most members of the Washington press corps, the transition from Eisenhower to Kennedy was exhilarating. "Ike never read what I wrote," recalled the White House correspondent of a news magazine. "Kennedy read it before I did and called me up." And then came Lyndon Johnson, who also read everything but reacted quite differently, as a professional of another kind.

"Some of our troubles," Johnson said in his 1968 conversation with a visitor, "must be attributed to simple geography. There is simply a good deal of prejudice in the East toward anyone who comes from my region. We said that in the first weeks of the administration, when they were all talking about how we had taken over and saved the country and so forth. I said: 'It will be a very short time until people in your profession will be pointing out the evils of Texans, the sins of personality, style, and so on.' It happened as we thought and feared. But in the early days I failed to visualize the intensity of it or the duration of it, and the completeness of it."

A staff assistant put the failure of Johnson's presidency in a somewhat different perspective, yet laid the same stress on style and personality. "When I read some of the things the college kids write about Johnson, they make it very clear why they hate him. Johnson took something that was great and important in their eyes, and he made it small. It's as though he defecated in the Oval Office. What they're angry about, and not only the young, is the *vulgarization* of the presidency. Johnson couldn't help showing off his operation scar — that's the kind of man he is. If he had been different, if he could have changed, you might not have seen all that legislation pushed through Congress. But people see and remember only the scar — the *Vietnam* scar."

The people whom the President and his assistant had in mind were the same people described by Midge Decter in a probing essay, "Kennedyism." She defined the new "ism" as "the assertion of the right of those properly endowed — by education, upbringing, leisured high purpose, and, yes, by birth, if need be — to rule. The New Politics, even for the 'kids' who find other names for it, is the assertion of the right to be ruled by attractive men, morally attractive, aesthetically attractive, in a morally and aesthetically attractive society." *

After the first phase of gratitude to Johnson, the Kennedyites, who felt that their learning, taste, and moral sensitivity set them apart from the mass of ordinary Americans, came to feel ever more estranged from the man occupying the presidency. In their view, the office was as much cultural as political, one which ought to exemplify the "best" in American life — as they judged and exemplified it. When Johnson reeled off the honor roll of Great Society legislation, trying to justify the record of the most productively liberal administration in the nation's history, the Kennedyites tuned him out. Theirs was not old-fashioned, porkchop liberalism, to be crudely quantified. Theirs, they asserted, was a qualitative liberalism. Though liberals and radicals opposed Johnson politically, their vehemence stemmed from a basically snobbish rejection. They fancied themselves aristocrats, and a boorish, twanging Texan

* *Commentary*, January 1970.

was simply *unworthy* of being the kind of symbolic leader they demanded as *their* President.

3. In 1968, the fault line dividing America split the country into unequal and dissimilar parts. On one side were the conventional parties and their constituents, brought together by familiar interest politics. On the other was the Kennedy party, brought together by and around the media, and dedicated on the surface to "moral" and disinterested politics. On one side stood the majority of Americans, passive viewers who would eventually be voters. On the other, caught up in a fever of activity, was a small elitist minority acting on behalf of its favored plebeian following. The elitists asserted that being "right" — by their own standards, to be sure — counted for more than being in the majority. With Robert Kennedy's entry into the campaign, the dispossessed elite could hope to rally the resentful of all races and classes. For the shirt-sleeved, scrambling Bobby was acting out a cosmic grievance, a rebellion against fate, the system, and — most of all — the usurper sitting in his martyred brother's place.

By occupying it, John Kennedy had transformed the presidency. In a sense, he brought it up to date, presiding as emperor of a newly imperial America. The handsome, youthful-seeming leader standing coatless in chill Capitol Plaza, flanked by his beautiful wife and the gray, assembled elders of the nation — surely, this was the hero America craved. "In the long history of the world, only a few generations have been granted the role of defending freedom in its hour of maximum danger," cried Kennedy. "I do not shrink from this responsibility — I welcome it." Only a few days earlier, in his farewell address, Eisenhower had taken calm measure of the nation's peril and warned — strange words for an old soldier — against the danger of an overweening "military-industrial complex." Now Eisenhower sat wrapped in his muffler and lap robe, the perfect image of age and irrelevance, while Kennedy depicted himself as the West's brave captain and projected an image of virile purpose.

The opening moments of the Thousand Days inaugurated the

coming triumph of appearances. The first President of the electronic age of American — and, therefore, world — politics conveyed his message through his image. His enthralled audiences at home and overseas received it as children "read" the pictures in a storybook. Eagerly, viewers embraced the evidence of their eyes. Kennedy treated his office as though it were a throne and presented himself as the exemplary American. By embodying those attitudes and qualities that most Americans held in esteem, by living as Americans — and envious foreigners — dreamed of living, he bore witness to the apparent success of an idealized America, less the world's leading power than a radiant fairy-tale realm.

Delighted Europeans especially saw Kennedy as an urbane and literate aristocrat, whose coming marked America's long-awaited maturity as a culture and a civilization. It had been galling for the Old World to defer to Truman, with his loud sport shirts, and only the memory of his wartime exploits excused Eisenhower's golf. But Kennedy was civilized and his wife spoke French. Kennedy was acutely conscious of his novel cultural role and deliberately enlarged the presidency to include it. As Richard H. Rovere wrote, "He thought that a President might help a fundamentally good society to become a good, even a brilliant civilization. And it pleased him to think of himself as a promoter, and impresario. He was a shrewd enough observer to know that there are always a number of Americans who look in the mirror and see reflected there the President of the United States — or who will make certain alterations that will enable them to see that reflection." *

In Kennedy-enchanted America, "style" was everything. Not style in the familiar sense, as mode, manner, or aspect of something, but style as a supreme value in itself, style for its own splendid sake. The line between image and substance disappeared. A thing well said was a thing accomplished. What answer did the people receive when they asked what they could do for their country? None — the desired effect had been achieved by asking the striking question.

* Richard H. Rovere, "Letter from Washington," *The New Yorker,* November 30, 1963.

What were the 16,000 U.S. troops sent to South Vietnam and Laos doing there? Their physical presence there was secondary; their primary purpose was symbolic: to represent "strength" to the Russians. Scenes shifted swiftly in the drama of power centered on Kennedy, and theatrical gestures and declarations were assumed to be effective in the real world. If they weren't, the failure went unnoticed for the moment, as the next scene was played.

At home, the dazzling pageant had a narcotic effect. The glamorous President and First Lady were objects of a public fascination previously unknown in America, one that exceeded in depth and intensity anything seen in countries accustomed to monarchy. Marya Mannes returned from the Kennedy inaugural balls confessing "undemocratic emotions," for she had watched while "packed thousands merely stood and stared at the President and his wife like mesmerized cattle." The media, as fascinated as their audience, sustained the magic spell in a torrent of words and pictures. Americans told Kennedy stories, wore Kennedy hair styles and Kennedy clothes, took up Kennedy sports and diversions, read Kennedy books, listened to Kennedy records. Just as avidly, they told Kennedy jokes and traded Kennedy gossip, enjoying the satisfaction of mixing awe and irreverence. It almost seemed as though an entire people forgot themselves in their preoccupation with the Kennedys.

The academic and media liberals, with few exceptions, were as entranced as ordinary folk. A fashionable enthusiasm sprang up for "cool," tough-minded, pragmatic liberalism such as Kennedy's — "liberalism without tears," in the phrase of his biographer, James MacGregor Burns. Kennedy, Burns wrote, is "a different type of liberal from any we have known. He is in love not with lost causes, not with passionate evocations, not with insuperable difficulties; he is in love with political effectiveness." *

In fact, Kennedy was not any kind of liberal, as he had made clear on more than one occasion earlier in his career. Though Harvard-bred and rich, he was the grandson of Honey Fitz, and, true to

* *The New Republic,* October 31, 1960.

his antecedents, he matured into a highly polished pol. What MacGregor and others advanced with an air of discovery was actually traditional machine politics repackaged and redefined around Kennedy's personality. Where ordinary people altered their hair styles in imitation of the Kennedys, the liberal intellectuals updated their ideology, and for the same vain, self-flattering motives. Praise of Kennedy's skeptical temperament and questing intellect reflected gloriously on the men who supposed they shared his qualities — and who imagined his rise to power lifted them as well. But the spirit of the old liberalism, passionate and tear-filled, survived in the extravagant expectations aroused for Kennedy's success. He would break the grip of the past and make a sweeping fresh start. He and his vigorous men of ideas would mold a plastic reality according to their abstract desires. History would smile on the bold, majestic enterprise. As though announcing a certainty, Burns said Kennedy had "prepared the way for the most consistently and comprehensively liberal Administration in the history of the country."

The Kennedy liberals thus made a recklessly heavy emotional and intellectual investment in the illusory liberalism recast in his image, and they established in advance the criterion of effectiveness — specific, concrete accomplishment — to determine whether or not their investment had paid off. Not surprisingly, when the reckoning came unexpectedly, they balked and directed attention away from Kennedy's unproductive liberalism and toward his shining image and tragic myth.

A hundred million Americans watched John Kennedy's televised funeral, like his inaugural an event of perfect contrivance. Before their tears dried, however, people found they could not express what Kennedy had meant, now that his distinctive face and voice were gone. Nor could the grieving commentators tell them, except to say that Kennedy had been a "great" President and must be remembered. In their confusion over a fit memorial, people hastily renamed many places after him, few of which related to his career. All that was commemorated, in spite of the soaring eulogies, was the emotion of the mourners.

Lyndon Johnson reminded us who we were — and some conceived their dislike of him in that moment. As much as we fanta-
sized, imitated, and gossiped, the Kennedys, who moved through
life behind massed wealth, were not at all like the rest of us. Alas,
we lived in circumscribed worlds, rose with difficulty if at all, and
frequently encountered obstacles that could not be bowled over but
had to be crept around. Johnson had come up by this route. His
flaws, unlike those of the legend-wrapped Kennedys, were easily
recognizable, for we could see them in our own mirrors as well as on
the television screen.

A thoroughly American trait Johnson brought to the presidency
was his need to be well liked. He yearned for the security of popular affection, for the kind of love the people had showered on Kennedy and Franklin D. Roosevelt, who were similar in being completely different from the people they ruled. "The most stimulating
thing in my kind of work," said Johnson in a typical plea to a group
in the White House Rose Garden, "is the feeling that the people
care about me." He sounded the same plaintive note in many such
self-revealing moments. Amid his complex and sometimes contradictory motives, this was a constant in Johnson's character — the
urgent search for popularity.

When it came within his grasp in 1964, self-doubt gave way to
euphoric self-confidence. "I would say," Johnson exulted to visitors
aboard his campaign jet, "that I am the most popular presidential
candidate since FDR." He wanted to roll up the biggest plurality
ever, and did, winning by nearly 17 million votes. But reaching for
every last vote (and token of affection) carried him beyond the limits of honesty and responsibility. He ignored future contingencies
he might face as Commander in Chief and played the demagogue
on Vietnam, making loose statements about "Asian boys" and
"American boys" and their respective roles that sounded like promises then and broken promises later.

After the election, Johnson set the goal of *his* administration:
"Our purpose must be to bind up our wounds, to heal our history,
and to make this nation whole." Within a year, he seemed to have

succeeded. In the media, he loomed larger than life, the take-charge Texan who picked up beagles and people alike by their ears and made them like it. The consensus underlying the Great Society seemed to stretch as far as the eye could see, and LBJ towered as Leader of All the People — a Super-President. He swept the unfortunate, the forgotten, and the excluded into his embrace and brought them at least to the fringes of the affluent society. Whatever he promised, he seemed able to deliver. He vowed to wipe out poverty. He pushed civil rights legislation through Congress with the fervor of a revivalist booming, "We Shall Overcome." More than once in those days he was heard to remark that he had the chance to serve nine years in the presidency, longer than any other man but FDR.

Even at the peak of his power and persuasiveness, however, Johnson could not please everyone. The Kennedy liberals hung back, even though the generation-old unfinished agenda of New and Fair Deal welfarism was being enacted at breakneck speed. "The President never really had the support of the Democratic left," George Christian, Johnson's press secretary, recalled as we talked one day in 1967. "The liberals wanted him for the things they wanted, and then they didn't want him. They always looked down on him." Johnson, hypersensitive to real and imagined slights, lashed out bitterly in private at the Kennedy liberals. "I don't believe that I'll ever get credit for anything I do in foreign affairs, no matter how successful it is, because I didn't go to Harvard."

While sunk in the purgatory of the vice presidency, Johnson had been the butt of cruel jokes around the White House. "Whatever happened to Lyndon?" the New Frontiersmen inquired, laughing. He had been remote from the stage-managing decisions in Indochina. As President, he tried to keep the war out of his mind and the public's. Then, early in 1965, the suppressed truth burst out in the open, and Johnson faced the consequences Kennedy had bequeathed him.

Scarcely a month before Kennedy's death, Ngo Dinh Diem, the

mandarinlike autocrat who ruled South Vietnam, had died vio-
lently. An authentic nationalist with effective control over most of
his wartorn country, Diem had invited U.S. military advisory assistance. He also had the unquestioned authority to withdraw the invitation, which seemed important at the time only as a *threat.* Because
little thought was given to what the U.S. was getting into, even less
was given to the means of eventually getting out. Officials in Washington knew of the coup against Diem and had reason to suspect he
would not survive its success, but they declined to interfere. (Roger
Hilsman, the latter-day Nixon adviser, went so far as to suggest, in
a memo to Secretary of State Rusk dated August 30, 1963, that, if
necessary, U.S. troops might be used "to assist the coup group to
achieve victory.") Diem, who refused to conduct the war and ad-
minister his country as U.S. officials desired, had become totally ex-
asperating. He seemed an expendable ally.

With Diem removed, however, the revolving door began to spin
in Saigon. As one fictitious "government" after another rose and
fell, the only source of stability was revealed — the American presence. Diem, it turned out, had been the difference between stability
and instability — and therefore between an Asian war and an
American war. The U.S. was committed beyond recall. In the August 1964 Tonkin Gulf Resolution, authorizing the President to
take "all necessary steps" against aggression in Southeast Asia,
Congress proved as reluctant as Johnson to declare that the U.S.
was indeed fighting a war.

When Johnson did what the now open-ended American commitment in Vietnam seemed to require, the Kennedy liberals who were
loyal to the empty throne unfurled the banner of "dissent" and
went into opposition. Was it the war that drove them away? With
a fine show of moral indignation, they asserted that, if Kennedy
had lived, the war somehow would not have involved large-scale
American military intervention. Such disregard of historical fact
and evidence, such brazen falsification, carried the day. The myth
served to conceal, among other things, the liberal surrender to Ken-

nedy and the liberal complicity in his "awful mistake." It had seemed necessary to falsify history, argued a disillusioned Kennedyite, for "it made it possible to blame Johnson alone, or primarily, for the stupidity of the war. It was intolerable to believe that John Kennedy, who represented the best in us, could have prepared the way for the most sordid episode in our history. It was, in short, too difficult to blame ourselves." *

Johnson was ill-equipped to comprehend, much less deal with, the Eastern-based political-cultural insurgency. Kennedy had the knack of patronizing the liberal intellectuals, giving them a great deal of time yet not nearly as much influence as they imagined. Johnson, who could not remember reading a half-dozen books all the way through since leaving Southwest Texas State Teachers College, was less sophisticated and more vulnerable. He took men of formal learning seriously. No urbane Harvard man would have dreamed of uttering the earnest testimonial Johnson delivered before a Princeton audience: "Each time my Cabinet meets, I can call the roll of former professors . . . The three hundred and seventy-one major appointments that I have made as President . . . collectively hold seven hundred and fifty-eight advanced degrees." Such gestures at appeasement only stirred deeper scorn among the self-protecting intelligentsia.†

The uprising of the political-cultural elite turned a part of the American Establishment into an *anti*-Establishment — and made the liberal intellectuals happier than they had been in years. During and after the Kennedy era, they had served as pedestal-builders, using words to legitimatize a mythical hero. Now they were

---

* Gerald Clarke, "JFK — Bitter Memories of a Cold Day," *The New Republic*, January 16, 1971.

† Consider the sharply shifting attitude of Professor Hans J. Morgenthau, a leading antiwar spokesman, toward Kennedy's intellectuals and Johnson's. After Kennedy's death, Morgenthau wrote: "It is the historic merit of Kennedy to have made the intellectual respectable as a manager of national affairs . . . It was indeed an extraordinary and awe-inspiring spectacle to see the Department of Defense, over which a succession of businessmen had presided in hapless ineffectiveness, transformed by a group of young intellectuals" (*The New Leader*, December 9, 1963). In 1967, Morgenthau wrote of the same people in the Pentagon: ". . . the great national decisions of life or death are rendered by technological elites, and both the Congress and the people at large retain little more than the illusion of making the decisions which the theory of democracy supposes them to make" (*The New Republic*, October 28, 1967).

free to take up the more congenial work of building a gallows for a villain. Their effectiveness, as they *de*legitimatized Johnson and the war, depended absolutely on the deference of the media, which did not disappoint them. Literally any assembly of intellectuals could not only command publicity for its views on American and Asian politics, which was fair enough, their views, which were often uninformed, also were certain to be taken very seriously by media personnel who condemned such ignorant outpourings from *non*intellectuals. Under intellectual sponsorship, the anti-Johnson insurgency soon spread from the campuses to the streets and escalated from violent rhetoric to aggressive actions in front of the cameras.

Swiftly, the Johnson consensus crumbled as though it had never existed. The goaded majority stirred in anger, anger at the war's cost in blood and dollars — and at violent war protests. Anger at the upsurge of the "youth culture." Anger at the riotous blacks — and fear of a suspected "get Whitey" motive behind soaring black crime. Above all, anger at a fallen Super-President. Was *this* the promised Great Society? At a Cabinet meeting early in 1968, as plans for expanded antipoverty spending were being discussed, Johnson, according to one who was present, spoke a haunting epitaph to his dreams: "Galbraith says liberalism died with President Kennedy. I sometimes think we are lonely voices speaking in the wind."

Johnson struck a stoic pose and fell into the habit of comparing his ordeal with Abraham Lincoln's during the Civil War. The White House staff kept the President supplied with two sets of cards — blue cards bearing a quotation from Lincoln, describing his loneliness as war leader, and pink cards summarizing the latest weekly Vietnam casualty figures — and Johnson pressed the cards into visitors' hands. The reporters who heard the President's pleas for understanding were unmoved except to write that he was pleading. He failed to evoke public sympathy. The ordinary people who had seemed to care about Johnson now seemed to have ceased caring. Placards and buttons reading, "Lee Harvey Oswald — Where Are You Now That We Need You?" brought no rebukes, but drew half-smiles from those who had wept for Kennedy. The professional President-watchers in the press, studying Johnson at bay, found him weary, defensive, and deflated. He no longer made grand promises but issued grave warnings that went unheeded. "We don't have to act like animals to get our revolutions and reforms translated into action," he lectured. "That comes through the ballot."

The ballot boxes in New Hampshire contained an unmistakably clear message: the anti-Johnson insurgency might succeed. All at once, with Kennedy's terrible swift sword raised against him, Johnson's Civil War frame of reference became less fanciful. The President realized that he had *personally* become the chief issue in the tormented society, the symbol that gave the insurgency cohesion. Moreover, beyond the angry minority, he faced a frustrated and discontented majority. Johnson realized that he could not reasonably hope to unite the majority if he ran for re-election. To win by the biggest margin in history and then squeak in as a minority President — or perhaps not to win at all, but suffer humiliation at Kennedy's hands or Nixon's. These were possibilities Johnson's pride could not bear.

A decision that had been forming within him now hardened into resolve.

4.   It is essential to Johnson's enemies that "a struggle for the President's mind" occurred in the weeks before his March 31, 1968, speech. When Johnson gave his televised recollections in February. 1970 a reviewer, citing the authority of one Townsend Hoopes, went so far as to brand the President's version of his actions and motives "revisionist." * The scenario of a many-sided struggle not only inflates bystanders like Hoopes, it also validates the fashionable view of Johnson, the villain. If the President dug in his heels until the very end, and caved in only under the weight of his revealed error and guilt, then his voluntary retirement is without redeeming grace. It can be portrayed less as an act of self-sacrifice than as an

* Townsend Hoopes, *The Limits of Intervention* (New York: McKay, 1969).

overdue penance. Johnson must remain stubbornly "wrong" because his detractors are determinedly "right" and, demand to be publicly vindicated. Their ultimate vindication would come with U.S. humiliation and defeat in Indochina, permitting them to say of an American and Asian tragedy: "We told you so."

From the sources available, both published and previously unrecorded, a picture of "struggle" indeed appears, but it is an interior struggle, a clash between the opposing sides of Johnson's personality. The picture is unclear because the process of presidential decision-making — *any* President making *any* major decision — cannot be reconstructed in detail. No single participant, however intimately involved, no group of advisers who might miraculously agree on the effect of their counsel, is in a position to say how the process occurred, for such observers see and hear only a part of it.

Even the President, on whom all the uncharted streams of information and influence converged, may wonder afterward which were truly decisive. Or he may choose to ignore certain influences. For example, Abe Fortas, then an Associate Justice of the Supreme Court, was in the White House day and night during the latter stages of the decision-making period. It was Johnson's custom to have picture-and-text booklets published recording important moments of his administration. Months after Johnson's withdrawal speech, a handsome booklet was duly produced commemorating the event. The President flipped through a copy fresh from the printer and suddenly stopped. There, in a group picture taken in the Cabinet Room, was an embarrassing face — Fortas, who had resigned under pressure from the Court after being denied confirmation as Chief Justice. Johnson ordered the booklets kept in storage and, when he left the White House, they were removed to Austin. The Johnson Library was off to a flying start, with several thousand copies of the same volume.

When the President speaks with his unique authority, he naturally works backward from the outcome of the decision process, seeking less to enlighten his contemporaries than to justify himself before the historians of the next generation. For Johnson, whose reversal of policy meant a wrenching away from personal commitment and prized position, justification is all-important.*

"The President made up his own mind, in his own way," recalled Harry McPherson, an aide who worked as closely with Johnson as anyone throughout February and March 1968, in an interview. Johnson's "way" was erratic, inconsistent, and intensely emotional. At one point, he emphatically declared that he had no intention of curtailing the bombing of North Vietnam when, according to his own account, he had already accepted the idea in principle and asked for recommendations on how to implement it. "Contradiction is a life-technique of Johnson's," said McPherson, "the way he meets the world. Whoever you are and whatever you're suggesting, he'll argue the opposite, he'll challenge you." This approach arose from something more than deep-seated contrariness. The secretive Johnson found concealment behind the uncertainty he created and gained additional time to calculate his moves.

In the weeks after the Tet offensive, Johnson had scant time and maneuvering room. The Asian enemy had simulated a bold initiative and his domestic enemies were in full cry. Shaken by the coordinated attacks on more than thirty Vietnamese population centers, worried by the danger of a second-wave assault, and alert to the possibility of Communist pressure at points of American vulnerability from Berlin to Korea, the President ordered a review of U.S. military strength measured against the full range of contingencies, up to and including catastrophe. Late in February, General Earle G. Wheeler, Chairman of the Joint Chiefs of Staff, flew to Vietnam for an on-the-spot conference with General William Westmoreland. Both by top-secret cable from Saigon and in person on his return, Wheeler recommended reinforcements.

The magnitude of the military build-up proposed was stunning — nearly 206,000 additional men, or a 40 percent increase above

---

* The initial, "overview" volume of Johnson's memoirs — *The Vantage Point, Perspectives of the Presidency 1963–1969* (New York: Holt, Rinehart and Winston, 1971) — was published after this manuscript, based on interviews and other sources, had been completed, and it has been used mainly for corroboration.

and beyond the 525,000 troops already authorized. Such a steep escalation of the war would have staggering political, economic, and social ramifications. With the strategic reserve largely depleted, the build-up would require mobilizing reservists and increasing draft calls. It would mean adding billions of dollars to a budget already deep in deficit, perhaps tipping the shaky dollar off the razor's edge and plunging the world's financial markets into chaos. It would mean revolt on Capitol Hill by outraged doves and fed-up hawks alike. It would mean anger among politicians feeling pressure from reservists forced to leave jobs and families and combined anger and fright among governors asked to give up National Guard units they would need if racial unrest flared into another long, hot summer. It would mean condemnation from the media, displaying newly truculent righteousness in the wake of Tet, and antiwar demonstrations of unprecedented size and intensity.

The President faced the obvious question — Is it worth it? And, in his fashion, he sought assistance in answering it. At the Cabinet meeting on February 28, former Cabinet officials recall, General Wheeler gave a somber briefing on Tet ("It may be the start of what they call their 'new war' ") and Secretary of State Dean Rusk assessed the grim diplomatic implications, pointing out that Hanoi had been laying its Tet offensive plans even as it put out peace feelers. Johnson wound up the discussion in his familiar rambling fashion. He was worried about the impression the administration made with the public and cautioned against statements like Westmoreland's claim the previous fall that he saw "light at the end of the tunnel." An aide to Johnson remembers watching the President's eyes as he spoke ("That's how he got his message across"). He noted that Vice President Humphrey, the chief spokesman for the administration's optimistic line, came under Johnson's particularly sharp gaze.

The President took note of the various peace proposals "from the Javitses and the Gavins, from Fulbright and the Kennedy boys and the rest." After calling the roster of doves, Johnson delivered a request. He said he wanted the State Department and the Pentagon to examine every proposal "and let me know how we can escalate peace." As he spoke, a former Cabinet member recalls, Johnson's voice took on a plaintive tone. "We have our shirttails out all around the world . . . We have people out traveling, hunting for peace." There was no mistaking the President's intentions and desires, for he repeated them. "So what are all these options? Let's look at all these new, fresh, imaginative proposals and explore them so we know what the options are, how we can escalate peace."

That same day a presidential directive went to the Secretaries of State and Defense. "I wish alternatives examined," Johnson said in the memorandum and gave a list of questions to be answered. These included: "What military and other objectives in Vietnam are additional U.S. forces designed to advance? What specific danger is their dispatch designed to avoid? . . . What probable Communist reactions do you anticipate in connection with each of the alternatives you examine? What negotiating posture do we strike in general? . . . What major Congressional problems can be anticipated? . . . What problems can we anticipate in U.S. public opinion?" Johnson closed with an admonition: "You should assure the highest possible degree of security up to the moment when the President's decision on these matters is announced."

When Johnson quoted from his memorandum on television in 1970, historian John Roche, a former aide to the President and a maverick liberal with the impeccable credentials of an ex-chairman of the ADA, waded into the controversy. Drawing on his own files, he quoted further in his newspaper column from Johnson's February 28 memorandum: "What specific goals would the increment of forces *if recommended* aim to achieve?" (Italics added.) Roche also reported that Johnson in the same document sought recommendations for "modifications" of the bombing policy. It is perfectly clear, he concluded, "that the initiative for exploring alternative strategies in Vietnam came from Johnson." *

Roche is on firm ground here, and so is the President, who gave

---

* Roche treated Johnson's decision in three columns for release March 26, 28, and 31, 1970. See also his devastating attack on the "instant" historians, "The Jigsaw Puzzle of History," *The New York Times Magazine*, January 24, 1971.

unmistakably clear instructions to his Cabinet. Indeed, Johnson's critics are left standing in midair when they assert that the President who asked the questions above was an obsessive warmaker, whose mind had to be captured by "hidden doves" within the administration.

The role of impassive Dean Rusk remains hazy, which is in large measure a tribute to his loyal reticence. Next to Johnson, Rusk, who served on the New Frontier but never joined it, is the favorite target of spiteful liberal attacks on his alleged rigidity. In fact, Rusk, though skeptical that the plan would work, had favored a partial bombing halt to induce negotiations as early as November 1967. In his only public reminiscence of March 1968, he said: "I myself recommended on March third, and on March fifth, that we prepare for a bombing halt in Vietnam. At no time was I ever in favor of an additional two hundred thousand troops in Vietnam." Loyal to his loyalist, Johnson remembers Rusk saying around March 5: "I think the time has come to stop the bombing above the twentieth parallel." To which Johnson recalls that he replied: "Get on your horses and get back to me as quick as you can with your recommendations."

Clark M. Clifford replaced McNamara at the Pentagon on March 1, 1968, and thereafter played a pivotal — in Hoopes's eyes, an heroic — role in the events of that month. Unquestionably the most esteemed Washington lawyer of his time, as well as the highest priced, Clifford moved as a skilled, subtle emissary between alien worlds. The go-between and power broker, by definition, belongs to no camp. Clifford entered the Pentagon a conventional hawk, but changed his mind as the result of examining the subsurface realities of the Vietnam war.

It is clear that something like a struggle for Clark Clifford's mind occurred, for the hidden doves within the Pentagon practically besieged the new Defense Secretary with oral and written arguments for a shift in U.S. strategy. As late as mid-March, however, those who heard Clifford speak in the Cabinet recall that he laid out pol-

icy alternatives without offering any recommendation and that he
seemed to suggest that the President had weeks and perhaps months
to make his decision. What was forming in Clifford's mind evidently was not so much immediate counsel as a strategy for the long
pull.

He wrote afterward: "I became convinced that the military
course we were pursuing was not only endless, but hopeless. A further substantial increase in American forces could only increase the
devastation and the Americanization of the war, and thus leave us
even further from our goal of a peace that would permit the people
of South Vietnam to fashion their own political and economic institutions. Henceforth, I was also convinced, our primary goal should
be to level off our involvement, and to work toward gradual disengagement." *

Clifford, whose once intimate relationship with Johnson ended
with the publication of his "personal history," may have privately
pressed his new-found convictions on the President. Certainly he
succeeded in launching the process that came to be called "Vietnamization." But he carefully refrained from making a claim for
the influence of his views. Interestingly, near the end of his account, Hoopes quotes a wise observer, who does not so much sum up
as dispute the book's thesis. The observer is Clifford, who says:
"Presidents have difficult decisions to make and go about making
them in mysterious ways. I know only that this decision, when
finally made, was the right one." †

The decision to be made was finally drawn sharp and clear because the President faced a speech deadline. Special Counsel
McPherson, a quiet-spoken young Texan and gifted writer, regularly drafted the President's speeches. In preparing for the State of
the Union Address in late January, he had proposed a comprehensive discussion of the war, but it had been deferred repeatedly.
Through February and into March, against the background of Tet,

---

* Clark M. Clifford, "A Viet Nam Reappraisal: The Personal History of One Man's View
and How It Evolved," *Foreign Affairs*, July 1969.
† Hoopes, p.224.

McPherson wrote and circulated drafts for comment. His own doubts about the war, first formed during a visit to Vietnam the previous May, had steadily deepened. In our conversation, he recalled sending memoranda to the President urging, "as candidly as I dared," steps toward de-escalation. Specifically, he recommended a halt to the bombing, arguing that "the average middle-class American" didn't understand its necessity, was losing heart for the seemingly endless conflict, and was coming to feel that the war was a matter of blindly obstinate pride on the part of the President.

Until late in March, the drafts McPherson wrote and rewrote — Lady Bird Johnson, with an eye to history, collected every draft, a total of twenty-two — remained faithful to the policy assumptions undermined by Tet and the changing domestic attitude toward the war. Then, on March 27, in a meeting in Rusk's office at the State Department, Clifford held forth at length. His fingertips pressed together and his sonorous voice rolling on, he argued point by point the case for the U.S.'s doing better in Southeast Asia by doing less. "He said that we were furnishing the South Vietnamese with the world's biggest police force," McPherson recalls, "and as long as we did, they would do nothing."

The meeting lasted several hours, and became, according to Hoopes, an unexpected, full-scale review of U.S. policy and strategy in Vietnam, dominated by Clifford's forceful eloquence. Clifford doubtless performed superbly, but perhaps Rusk, whose admirers have not been heard from, also may have been turning in a performance of his own. It is not hard to imagine him pretending for Clifford's sake to be brought around to conclusions he had already reached and privately communicated to the President three weeks earlier.

In any event, by the time the group went to lunch, Rusk seemed prepared to try McPherson's idea for a two-phase bombing halt: the President would announce an unconditional end to the bombing above the twentieth parallel and would offer to extend it throughout North Vietnam if Hanoi would show matching restraint at the demilitarized zone and would stage no further attacks on Saigon and other population centers. Rusk approved giving the President a clear choice between *two* texts — a "war" speech proposing more of the same policies and a "peace" speech offering a partial cessation of the bombing, in the hope that it would produce tacit cooperation, steps toward de-escalation, and negotiations.

Working through the night, McPherson completed a draft of the "peace" speech early on the morning of March 28. That was the draft Johnson chose and labored over for the next four days —especially the peroration.

VIII

1. UNAWARE OF WHAT was happening inside Johnson's White House, Nixon decided late in March that he should make a radio speech — indeed, the first of a series of speeches — explaining his position on Vietnam. The speech was scheduled for the evening of March 31, and he came within a matter of hours of delivering it. Never again did the Nixon campaign come so close to telling the American people how a Republican President would deal with the issue tormenting the country.

The timing of Nixon's decision had little to do with the state of the war itself or his pledge to "end" it, which he had been trying to play down. Rather, the decision was made chiefly because the latest surprise in this year of the unexpected created an inviting political opportunity.

On March 21, before a crowded press conference in New York City, Governor Nelson Rockefeller declared — incredibly — that he would *not* campaign "directly or indirectly for the Presidency." He would not enter any of the remaining primaries, nor would he do anything "by word or by deed" to encourage a draft movement on his behalf. Rather than mount a "divisive challenge," Rockefeller said he would be a "responsible Republican" and bow to the apparent will of the majority of G.O.P. leaders who favored Nixon.

Primed by the media to expect an announcement of active candidacy, Rockefeller backers were stunned, disappointed, and, in some cases, deeply hurt. Maryland's freshman governor Spiro T. Agnew, leader of the draft-Rockefeller effort among the governors, had invited reporters into his Annapolis office to watch the televised news conference. Agnew's face reddened. He was placed in the most humiliating position a politician can occupy — a supposed Rockefeller insider, he had not gotten the word. The next day, Ellsworth paid a sympathy call, heard Agnew's tale of misplaced trust and resentment, and arranged for the pride-stricken governor to visit Nixon in New York. From that moment, the draft-Rockefeller campaign was dead.

Rockefeller described his course as "realistic," and so it was, according to the conventional political wisdom. His original strategy had called for Romney to wear Nixon down in four contested primaries, after which the Michigan governor would step or be elbowed aside. Rockefeller then would enter the Oregon primary, score a spectacular victory, and ride into the convention aboard his cresting popularity in the polls. He would claim to be the only Republican who could win in 1968, and the delegates would put hopes of victory above revenge and nominate him. Romney's collapse had wrecked the timetable and strategy for stopping Nixon. So effective was the Nixon propaganda — avoid another '64 — that George Hinman and Emmet Hughes, Rockefeller's top strategists, echoed the Nixon theme in their advice to the governor: do nothing.

But 1968, as McCarthy's emergence proved, was the year to defy the odds. Within six weeks, Rockefeller would reconsider and re-enter the contest. By then, however, it was too late for him to be anything except a good loser.

The heart of Rockefeller's miscalculation was psychological rather than political. While he dreaded facing again the kind of Republicans who had hooted him down in San Francisco in 1964, he failed to understand Nixon's more personal and potentially crippling dread. Nixon was not quite sure he could beat Rockefeller, who inspired much the same awe in him as the Kennedys. These wealthy, famous, and well-connected Easterners always *expected* to win; Nixon didn't. They did not feel compelled to "prove" anything. Nixon, for whom New York was "the fast track," all too ob-

viously did. Moreover, the vociferous anti-Rockefeller conservatives shared Nixon's insecurity and were suspicious of his (and their
own) ability to measure up to the challenge of the wicked, liberal,
and damnably superior East. Living in his very remote world,
Rockefeller was insensitive to the undercurrent of doubt among
rank-and-file Republicans, the feeling, which they confided to one
another, that "we shouldn't be doing this after the way Dick blew it
in nineteen sixty."

An imaginative political gambler, sensing his psychological edge,
might have crowded the favorite, forcing him to justify his candidacy in positive, concrete terms. But Rockefeller failed to apply
such pressure. Although he guessed the emptiness of Nixon's Vietnam "pledge," he did not realize how much even his mild needling
irritated and worried the "new" Nixon. Our fear of Rockefeller
was symbolized by a neatly tabbed, one-hundred-and-five-page research report documenting his career as a party-wrecker. Our
strategy against him depended entirely on directing right-wing distrust away from Nixon. Under relentless goading from Rockefeller,
Nixon might have slipped back into his familiar, self-defeating
ways. The reappearance of the old Nixon would have brought conservative uncertainties rushing to the surface. But all such might-
have-beens vanished when Rockefeller decided to play the percent-
ages.

Rockefeller's withdrawal astonished Nixon — "The Boss couldn't
believe it," Buchanan reported — and he reacted with public praise
of his rival's exemplary devotion to party unity. But more than a
shadow of suspicion lingered that Rockefeller had not really withdrawn. It was true enough, as Nixon told reporters, that the only
remaining obstacle to his nomination would be "my own mistakes."
But he realized that Rockefeller, by seeming to sacrifice personal
ambition for the party's sake, had positioned himself more strongly
than ever to take advantage of any serious mistake.

Memoranda flew back and forth within the organization, advising "DC" on his course. I saw, from the copies I read, that
Nixon was learning little he did not already know. The common

inspiration behind the advice seemed to be to anticipate what
Nixon would do — and then to suggest that he do it. Safire, for
example, counseled Nixon to avoid arm-twisting as he locked up a
first-ballot nomination. To counter "the boredom problem" and
keep his name and views before the people, Nixon, Safire suggested,
should make "several" speeches on Vietnam — "not lumping 'the
position' into only one speech, but taking parts of it and expanding
on them in depth." If this intriguing suggestion indicated the current drift of Nixon's thinking, I could expect to hear from New
York. Within a couple of days, Garment called: "RN wants to talk
about a speech on Vietnam."

Before leaving Washington, I sifted through clippings and press
releases, reviewing what Nixon had been saying about Vietnam in
New Hampshire and Wisconsin. His position up to this point was a
grab bag of phrases, from which audiences could draw whatever
general conclusions they pleased. He invariably faulted the Johnson administration for "frittering away" the overwhelming U.S.
military superiority through a policy of "gradualism." He also crit-
icized the failure to strengthen the South Vietnamese army "so that
they can take over the fighting and we can leave." In recent weeks,
he had emphasized diplomacy: "We should now be waging a diplomatic offensive with the Soviet Union and others who might influence the North Vietnamese to come to the conference table."
But the hope of flexibility raised by mention of diplomacy was
dashed whenever the candidate answered a specific question.
Nixon opposed a bombing pause ("I'm for keeping the pressure on
militarily"), a coalition government in Saigon ("the first install-
ment on a complete Communist takeover"), and, most of all, unilateral U.S. disengagement from Southeast Asia ("We can end the war
by withdrawing, but we would lose the peace").

When Nixon spoke of the future direction of American diplomacy, his words had a double echo. He sounded uncomfortably
like Johnson, but even more disquieting was the echo of the 1950s,
Korea, and the supposed efficacy of diplomacy-by-ultimatum. A
new administration, Nixon said in a New Hampshire radio inter-

view early in March, "should make very clear to the enemy that we are not going to tolerate this war going on and on, that we are going to mobilize our economic and diplomatic and political power . . . If the enemy . . . does not go along with a program of live-and-let-live, then we have to have the option to move with more military power."

Was Nixon still toying with General Norstad's talk-or-else scheme for frightening Hanoi into negotiations? His talk of applying more military power flew in the face of speculation that the administration's post-Tet reappraisal would result in downgrading the U.S. military effort. Suppose Johnson chose de-escalation and another "peace" offensive? We would be left defending our opponent's indefensible and abandoned policy.

For several months, I had been meeting informally with combat officers returned from Vietnam, trying to get away from the parochial Washington perspective on the war. As I reread my notes on these private debriefings, the futility of the U.S. military strategy leaped from every page in the words of military men. *A Marine general:* "We teach our young officers to find, fix, and finish the enemy — to *kill* him. But we're not sure who he is." From across the generation gap separating World War II and limited-war officers, *a Marine captain:* "Destroy the enemy? Protect the people? That's bullshit. Somehow, the South Vietnamese people and the South Vietnamese government have to be brought together at the village level. And we can't do it for them." *An Army colonel,* as he complained against quantified claims of U.S. "victory" in Vietnam: "It takes one and a half U.S. infantrymen in-country per year to kill one enemy soldier. And it takes five noncombat personnel to support one infantryman. Let's say there are some two hundred thousand enemy soldiers to be killed. You add it up and tell me who's ahead in this goddamned war."

No such voices were to be heard among the very senior retired military advertised as Nixon's "national security advisers," or among the war hawks of the Republican Coordinating Committee, or among the party leadership. I listened in disbelief one morning as House Minority Leader Gerald Ford earnestly told a breakfast gathering that the answer to Tet was to *Americanize* the war effort. On the evidence presented so far, Nixon and the Republicans had no idea how to end the war. Nixon wanted to speak now only because he saw the chance to pre-empt ground from Rockefeller. But it seemed to me, as I flew to New York and remembered what the men in uniform had said, that he faced a moral obligation rather than a tactical opening.

2.   In those March days, the men pursuing the presidency did so in ways faithful to their contrasting styles and personalities. Kennedy dashed across the country, a comet of fierce emotion trailing near-hysteria. "The contest in nineteen sixty-eight," he cried, "is not for the rule of America but for its heart." McCarthy sniffed the Wisconsin breeze, studied the polls taken by his youthful crusaders, and before a campus audience announced matter-of-factly: "I don't wish to sound overconfident, but I think the test is pretty much between me and Nixon now." And then there was Nixon.

I found him alone in the farthest back room of the New York headquarters suite. Slumped in a chair, with both feet propped up against a battered desk, he was methodically telephoning uncommitted Republican politicians. As I walked in, he was talking with a deflated Rockefeller booster, Pennsylvania's governor Ray Shafer. ". . . Yes, I know . . . and I understand your position completely . . . but I hope you'll be with us later . . . Fine." While he talked — how many times had he repeated this banal, essential conversation? — he twirled a pencil and stared out the soot-darkened window. But his voice did not betray the boredom evident in his expression. The governor in Harrisburg heard only friendly Dick Nixon, a sympathetic pro reassuring him that he could play his own game without penalty. After a parting round of pleasantries, Nixon put down the receiver, crossed Shafer off a mental list, and turned to me.

He had decided to begin talking "substantively" about Vietnam, generally along the lines I had been urging. But he had not yet settled in his mind on precisely what he should say. His thoughts, usually so clearly organized when he discussed a speech, on this occasion cautiously circled the subject. It was apparent, as I scribbled notes, that Nixon wanted a speech drafted for size, so to speak, and he would decide afterward whether the text fitted his requirements.

He began — half thinking aloud, half dictating possible language — by criticizing the administration's "military emphasis," which cost so much in terms of lives, dollars, and pain without producing satisfactory results. "The military emphasis in Vietnam erodes our credibility everywhere else in the world. We look like a paper tiger . . . We must not discuss Vietnam apart from the rest of the world . . . Unless the administration acts dramatically, the war will be in such shape as to force us to fish or cut bait. Do we want to take big risks? We can't send another three hundred thousand men. We can't invade North Vietnam. The only thing left is Haiphong, and that involves risks with the Soviets . . .

"So we must get away from the military emphasis, and we must put Vietnam in the world context . . . We have to look at the war and Vietnam and the rest of the world in a fresh way. A new administration could do that. A new administration wouldn't be stuck with Johnson's policies. It could find ways to get off dead center . . .

"My utter conviction about this stupid war is that we must restrain China," Nixon continued, his hands locked behind his head. "We must encourage China's historic caution and inwardness. China and the hard-line philosophy will be the big winner in Vietnam if we're defeated. The other nations around China will be open to her. But Vietnam could inflict a great loss on China. Therefore it is vitally in the interests of the Soviets to see us stay there or at least *not* be defeated. We don't want to stay, and the Soviets should see their interest in that respect, too.

"Now, there could be a new era in our relations with the Soviets, a new round of summit meetings and other negotiations. We have to make that plain to them. We have to say, 'Look, if you go on supporting North Vietnam, we will have to act dramatically.' We won't add — '*If* we have the power,' of course. On the other hand, we have to say, 'If you are willing to give ground and help us out of this morass, it could mean lots of good things. Otherwise, we're going toward confrontation. If the war goes on, if China feels strong enough to challenge us in a few years, there could be a confrontation that neither the U.S. nor the Soviets could control. So let's both get out.' "

Nixon paused and considered the effect of those words. Obviously, he did not want to say anything so bald. In view of his past statements, he could not even hint at the possibility of U.S. withdrawal. "What we want to get across is that Johnson can't end the war, and that Kennedy and McCarthy would end the war but lose the peace. A new administration can end the war and win the peace. But don't put that in the form of a promise. Just say something like, 'As I have stated . . .' We can't put everything in this first speech. Indicate somewhere that this is the first of a *series* of talks on Vietnam."

Nixon went back to the telephone, and I went to find a typewriter. I disagreed with some of the things he had said — for instance, the illusion of restraining Communist China would lure the U.S. deeper into futile ground engagement in Asia — but I was pleased that, finally, he would say something, and generally along the lines I had advised. If he emphasized the Soviet Union's involvement in Vietnam, he would cross an extremely important divide, one likely to shape the course of his campaign and his administration. For he would squarely confront the myth that the Cold War was "over."

What had in fact ended was the post–World War II era of unquestioned U.S. strategic superiority. Our strength had enabled us to project American influence far beyond national interests, while simultaneously curbing the expansion of a militarily inferior Soviet Union. Now the Soviets had gained the strength to deter and frustrate the U.S. at the periphery, as in Southeast Asia, and soon they were likely to gain the power necessary to face us down in more critical areas. If we were not to see our overextended global perimeter

rolled back on a broad front, we had to begin at once a selective disengagement and redeployment, starting with an orderly withdrawal from Vietnam. The growing external threat of the Soviet
Union, combined with the growing internal weakness of our weary,
impatient population, compelled us to redefine our truly vital national interests and security requirements.

Yet the transition from a false world view to a truthful one could
not be made in a single leap; the American people were psychologically unprepared. It was necessary to make still another appeal to
Moscow's self-interest in a prompt settlement of the war and to express the hope of progress toward genuine détente. There was the
chance that it would succeed. But even if the Soviets could not reasonably be expected to accommodate Nixon where they had disappointed Johnson, it was essential to identify Moscow as the primary
source of our frustration in Southeast Asia. If stern tests with the
Soviet Union should develop in the 1970s and beyond, we had to
begin preparing now for the possible onset of such a *second* Cold War
— a contest of equals. This meant banishing the popular miscon-
ception that Vietnam alone barred the way to peace. Some U.S.–
Soviet differences were negotiable, but the incentive to negotiate
would be seriously reduced if the Soviets saw a weak, divided adversary, confused as to its real interests and priorities.

Nixon, the senior anti-Communist on the American political
scene, was well equipped to execute the dual maneuver of simultaneous tactical withdrawal and strategic redeployment. It would be
in character for him to say hard things about the Soviets, even as he
invited them to parley. But the mythmakers of détente in the
media would be prevented from automatically dismissing him as an
outdated Cold Warrior, for he would meanwhile take a markedly
softer line on Vietnam, their blinding preoccupation. By making
plain his determination to wind down the war, he would disarm
critics under the sway of the Vietnam-centered world view and
would prepare the framework for debate on the future U.S. course
in the world at large.

I borrowed a portable typewriter and settled down to work in

Charles McWhorter's vacant cubicle. (When delegate-hunter
McWhorter came in later that evening, he accepted my tenancy
with a nod and dragged the telephone, his indispensable tool, to a
chair; in this fashion, we went about our respective crafts until past
midnight.) The next morning, Tuesday, March 26, I sent a draft of
some two thousand words around for comment.

Price, Buchanan, and Garment were somewhat less than enthusiastic. Price was reluctant to challenge the Cold-War-is-over assumption quite so frontally and equally reluctant to judge Vietnam
a tragic misadventure. Parts of the draft were attuned to Garment's
dovish sentiments, but he had qualms about putting the war in a
stark context of U.S.–Soviet global rivalry. Buchanan, the hard-
liner, thought the context was fine — what concerned him was the
risk of making *any* speech. Yet Nixon wanted a draft, here it was,
and none of them offered a satisfactory alternative. Finally, I incorporated some of Price's suggestions into a second draft and gave it
to Rose Mary Woods.

Nixon decided at once that it "fit." That afternoon, the press was
informed that the candidate would make a nationwide radio talk
— "a major address" — on Vietnam the following Sunday evening.
I was surprised and pleased by Nixon's swift decision, for the draft
contained implicit and explicit commitments. Implicitly, it committed Nixon to keeping the Soviet Union in the foreground of his
future statements on U.S. foreign and defense policies. Explicitly,
as he had instructed, it committed him to say a great deal more
about Vietnam. From Price's prose stockpile, I had borrowed a
self-challenging assertion — "We need a new approach and a new
policy, but first we must speak with new candor and clarity" — by
which Nixon's views would henceforth be measured. Fully as much
as his "pledge," that statement bound him to tell the American people what he proposed to do and why, under pain of acute embarrassment if he tried to back away.

Now that the decision had been made to go ahead, Price and I
shared the task of polishing the draft. The next morning, Wednes-

day, a new version, expanded but thematically unchanged, went to the Nixon apartment, and that afternoon we were summoned uptown for an editorial conference.

Nixon met us at the door and led the way to the small study off the living room. Tricia was reading there, and he displaced her with a paternal word of apology. Settling into an armchair, with his feet on an ottoman and the manuscript balanced on his knees, Nixon said he had marked a few passages he wanted reworked, but first, he invited us to argue the text as a whole. Buchanan, the writer least involved in the drafting, assumed the role of devil's advocate and guardian of Nixon's consistency. How would the press interpret the new line? How could Nixon say *this* when only a few months ago he had said *that?* Price and I debated other questions. He thought it unwise to criticize U.S. battlefield tactics without suggesting alternatives. I insisted that in this talk especially such issues were secondary — even if we won the battles, the war could still be lost in the absence of coherent and attainable political objectives. In this argument, he seemed the "conservative" and I the "liberal." But as we debated the Soviet Union's influence, we switched sides.

All the while, Nixon listened closely, as though we were lawyers and he an appellate judge. At points of dispute, he stood outside the text, waiting to be persuaded to enter it. I soon discovered that he did not wish to be persuaded of the validity of our ideas. Rather, he sought guidance in the procedure that was the sum of his "centrism" — the pragmatic splitting of differences along a line drawn through the middle of the electorate. The line could go left or right, depending on the persuasiveness of claims made for the popularity of competing views. Nixon's aim was to find the least assailable middle ground. The grand theme interested him less than the small adjustment, which might provide an avenue of escape. The only major change made in the text was the inclusion of a section written by Price urging curtailment of "search and destroy" operations against the enemy and a shift to a "protect and expand" strategy

centered on the South Vietnamese population. The rest of the
changes were minor equivocations, often introduced by Nixon's admonition: "Let's copper that."

We met daily for the remainder of the week, and Nixon, who
clearly enjoyed honing the cutting edge of words, allowed the sessions to run for two hours or more — longer, I thought, than was
necessary for the actual work. Then it occurred to me that Nixon
was getting himself "up" for this talk and that we served as an audience and cheering section. He would read lines aloud, praising the
"good rhetoric." When he asked for a barbed reference to Robert
Kennedy, we worked to come up with a crack that would satisfy
him. After we did, the three of us didn't like it anymore. We then
found ourselves in the unusual position of wanting Nixon to sound
stuffier than he wanted to sound. At last he agreed to drop the line,
complaining: "Oh, hell, why does Bobby get to be so mean, and
why do I have to be so nice?"

When we arrived to work with Nixon on the afternoon of Friday,
March 29, he had just received important news. On Monday and
Tuesday, the Senior Advisory Group on Vietnam, made up of elder
statesmen, former diplomats, and retired military officers, including
several prominent Republicans, had met at the White House. The
group had received long and unusually candid briefings on the war
from representatives of the State Department, CIA, and the Joint
Chiefs of Staff. At a luncheon meeting with the President, the
doubts troubling these distinguished men had come out in the open.
Among those present was General Omar Bradley, co-chairman
with former Senator Paul Douglas of the bipartisan Citizens Committee for Peace with Freedom in Vietnam, formed at the inspiration of the White House the previous October. As a result of this
outspoken meeting of the Senior Advisory Group, the consensus
underlying the Citizens Committee collapsed.

The Bradley-Douglas Committee, Nixon told us, had reversed its
former stand. It no longer believed that the war could be brought
to a successful end by military means. Even if 200,000 more U.S.
troops were committed, there were far more and better equipped

North Vietnamese troops in South Vietnam than our intelligence had estimated, and the prospect was for a long, inconclusive war. Tet had destroyed the pacification effort. The Citizens Committee, Nixon said, was advising the President to seek peace by offering a bombing pause, restoration of the 1954 and 1962 Geneva agreements, and new elections throughout Vietnam. Fresh rumors from Saigon told of an intensifying power struggle between Thieu and Ky, perhaps resulting in still another coup. Johnson, Nixon had been informed, would move within two months — and would probably "go for peace." "He's afraid of Bobby," said Nixon, adding that he thought Johnson would try to outflank his opponents by promising to "bring the boys home."

Nixon spoke more rapidly than usual, but this was his only sign of excitement. The developments he reported, though fateful for U.S. policy, seemed to have a calming effect on him, as though freeing him from an unwanted burden of choice and decision. Now he could think exclusively in political terms, preparing counters to Johnson's expected moves. As he spoke, I made notes, anticipating a request for further revision of the text. But as he announced the conclusion he had reached and the course he intended to follow, my pen stopped.

"I've come to the conclusion that there's no way to win the war. But we can't say that, of course. In fact, we have to seem to say the opposite, just to keep some degree of bargaining leverage."

I recalled from Nixon's *Six Crises* his account of the "most difficult decision" of the 1960 campaign. John Kennedy had called for U.S. intervention against the Castro regime, and Nixon, aware of Eisenhower's plan to invade Cuba (which would culminate in the Bay of Pigs fiasco), decided he had no choice but to "protect" the covert operation by attacking Kennedy's proposal as dangerously irresponsible. This time, however, the circumstances were entirely different. Nixon had before him the cautionary disaster of Lyndon Johnson, who had been elected as the apparent advocate of one policy in Vietnam only to execute another as President. If Nixon hoped to bridge the credibility gap and cross it to the presidency, he would have to play straight with the American people. As the polls revealed, the people were coming to regard the war as a losing proposition and were unlikely to support a prolonged war for the sake of bargaining leverage rationalized by talk of "victory." Moreover, as Nixon well knew, the Communists came to the conference table only to ratify the outcome on the field of battle. Hanoi felt it had traded away the fruits of total victory over the French and would not be so hasty in seeking accord again.

I doubted that Nixon would be able to sustain such a misleading approach through the campaign — indeed, the talk he was preparing to give said nothing about U.S. "victory" in Vietnam, but instead beamed a message to Moscow emphasizing "realism" and encouraging a far-ranging deal between the superpowers. Hence I took Nixon's conclusion as sincere and remained skeptical of his declared tactics as we reviewed the fourth and final draft.

Some key passages:

. . . The answer to failure is not simply more of the same. The continuing debate over military escalation versus military de-escalation misses a fundamental point: that this is more than a military war. Its progress depends on the way it is waged on all fronts — military, economic, political, diplomatic, psychological — and even in military terms, the direction of our effort can be as important as the level of our effort.

. . . In the present situation, the first need is not to do *more* of what we have been doing militarily, but to shift priorities and change directions . . .

Just as a narrow, traditional military framework does not fit the reality of Vietnam, neither does our equally narrow view of Vietnam as an isolated trial, a war in a vacuum . . .

The war in Vietnam has long been explained as an effort to contain the expansive force of Communist China. And so it is — it remains the principal testing ground for Mao's "wars of national liberation," and is being watched as such in Asia, Africa, and Latin America. But in terms of aid and political support, Peking is no longer the senior partner that it once was in North Vietnam's aggression. It has now become a very junior partner to Moscow . . .

Hanoi is not Moscow's puppet, but it must remain a respectful client in order to keep Soviet aid flowing and to balance the influence of nearby Peking. If the Soviets were disposed to see the war ended and a compromise settlement negotiated, they have the means to move Ho Chi Minh to the conference table. The Soviets are not so disposed and, in terms of their immediate self-interest, it is hard to see why they should be.

The Soviets hold a position of extraordinary advantage in Vietnam. They hold what could be decisive influence over the duration of the war, and yet they escape the normal hazards — and, more important, the responsibilities — of involvement. Also, they enjoy immense strategic advantages. While the United States is tied down in Vietnam, the Soviets are loose in the world . . .

The drive for broad understanding with the Soviets — for détente — has now faltered and come virtually to a halt. We can and must recover this lost momentum — resolving not only the war in Vietnam but also many other of the questions which divide the two super-powers . . .

We need a new policy that will awaken the Soviet Union to the perils of the course it has taken in Vietnam. This should be done, not through belligerent threats, but through candid, tough-minded, face-to-face diplomacy cast in the language of realism that the Soviets understand. The Soviets are unable to comprehend an adversary who confuses the military and political aspects of warfare. Worse, they cannot respect him or take him seriously. And when this erosion of strength undermines the credibility of American will and strength . . . the danger to the world grows enormously . . .

When the leaders of the superpowers again meet at the summit, as I believe they must and shall, the situation and the atmosphere should be entirely different [from the hastily arranged and fruitless

Glassboro conference]. We should be certain of our strength and clear about our purpose . . .

What seems insoluble in a narrow context often becomes soluble in a larger one. The larger the table, the more that can be placed on it, and the more traders there are, the greater the range of possible combinations. Precisely because both Soviet and American interests in Vietnam extend beyond Vietnam itself, the two superpowers can discuss the problem in a broader perspective. Bargaining counters that would be irrelevant in the narrow context of Vietnam itself, or even of Southeast Asia, become usable when the discussions are global in nature . . .

All who see the struggle in Vietnam clearly, and who recognize its cruel and almost infinite complexity, recognize that there are no swift and simple "solutions," no push-button answers, no gimmicks, no neat or concise "plans" to assure the success of our objectives . . .

This evening, I have indicated some aspects of the new approach I believe should be taken toward . . . ending the war in Vietnam and winning the peace in the world. These mark, I believe, the beginning of realism about the war and about its larger context. There is far more to be done — and in the weeks and months ahead I will be explaining in greater detail my views on other aspects of the effort needed. But the first needs are those I have spoken of tonight . . .*

3.   We met for a last review of Nixon's speech in midmorning on Saturday, March 30. At two o'clock that afternoon, he would go to the studio and tape the broadcast. Printing and mass-mailing personnel were standing by. Supporters in Washington had been alerted and were waiting to be telephoned quotes from the final text. A press release was ready, and girls were waiting at headquarters to duplicate the final version of the speech for distri-

* The full text of the final draft of Nixon's speech appears in the Appendix.

bution. The well-oiled machinery needed only the go-ahead signal.

A couple of minor revisions were necessary, and Price excused himself to use the typewriter in the small den down the hall. (There, the candidate preserved his glowing tan with the sun lamp he denied owning.) Buchanan and I sat with Nixon in the study, eating sandwiches and sipping beer. The Boss was in good humor, based in part on his belief that he had reliable intelligence on Johnson's likely moves and timing. Confidently, he questioned Buchanan about the probable impact of the speech. What would be the lead in the Monday papers? In wire-service fashion, Buchanan rattled off a crisp fifty words and even put a head on the story: NIXON ASKS U.S.–SOVIET SUMMIT TO END VIETNAM WAR, SEEK PEACE.

Much later I learned that Mel Laird, on the basis of his highly original reading of the *Pueblo* incident, had advised Nixon to follow the same course. Laird saw the Soviet-sponsored North Korean seizure of our spy vessel as a typically blunt Soviet signal indicating willingness to engage in sweeping negotiations with the U.S. As early as mid-February, Laird told Nixon he might be able to work out some kind of Asian "package deal." Nixon, for his part, needed little encouragement to engage in summitry. He conceived the presidency almost entirely as a foreign-policy-making office. He also had a lively appreciation of the potential domestic political rewards of personal diplomacy. Whenever Johnson's Glassboro meeting with Kosygin came up, Nixon noted with amazement that nothing had happened there, yet Johnson's poll-rating jumped sharply.

The telephone on the desk rang, and Buchanan picked it up. He listened for a few moments, then put down the receiver and faced Nixon with a puzzled expression. "That was Frank Shakespeare. Johnson's called the networks and asked for television time for a speech tomorrow night."

Nixon put his head down for a long moment. Then he flipped the pages of manuscript in the air in a gesture of resignation. "Dammit. We've got to cancel. That's all we can do."

Buchanan returned to the telephone while I went down the hall to break the news to Price. Mindful of his misgivings, I told him: "Ray, the governor's just called — you've got a reprieve."

Nixon sat slumped in his armchair, frowning. He pointed a finger toward Buchanan and demanded: "All right, Pat. What's Johnson going to say?" He would announce a bombing pause, Pat guessed. Nixon pointed at Price, who answered: "He'll wrap himself in the flag and answer Bobby." Now it was my turn. There wasn't any reason for Johnson to speak on Sunday, I said, except that it came two days before the Wisconsin primary, where Johnson had every reason to expect very bad news. If he wanted to make a move without seeming to react to defeat, I concluded, he had to make it now. Nixon received our guesses in glum silence. Johnson had taken the initiative much sooner than expected. Before leaving Nixon, we talked about rescheduling the radio address later in the following week, but quickly agreed that nothing could be decided until after the President's speech.

On Sunday evening, March 31, Lyndon Johnson did as we anticipated, announcing a dramatic turn in war policy toward de-escalation and a limited halt to the bombing of North Vietnam as a means of getting talks started with Hanoi. Then he did the unthinkable. With a glance toward his wife, he began the secret peroration of his speech, summing up a career of more than thirty years and the beliefs behind the conclusion he now announced. ". . . With America's sons in the fields far away, with America's future under challenge right here at home, with our hopes and the world's hopes for peace in the balance every day, I do not believe that I should devote an hour or a day of my time to any personal, partisan causes or to any duties other than the awesome duties of this office — the presidency of your country.

"Accordingly, I shall not seek, and I will not accept, the nomination of my party for another term as your President."

A few minutes later, Price, who had had a hurried conversation with Nixon, relayed his impressions of the speech and Nixon's reaction. "At first, it seemed to be a bid for a draft, but it was too Sherman-like. Johnson's looking at the history books — he wants to play the peacemaker. Can he do it? We don't know what moves have been made off the board" — the last was unmistakably Nixon. "Hanoi may never be in a better bargaining position than now."

Ellsworth called a few minutes later. "We're *much* stronger. And Rockefeller's weaker. By all the traditional rules, if any Republican can win, the party won't give it to the man who took a walk. *But* now we've lost that nice, easy target of Lyndon. Now we have to be *positive*, have *ideas*, offer *programs* — and that could be Rockefeller's strength, such as it is. His idea-factory will be going full blast. Nixon's great strength is that he's the only guy on the scene with any high-level international experience."

The next day, Nixon's statement to the press exuded confidence. He tossed off a jaunty quip: "This is the year of the dropouts. First Romney, then Rockefeller, now Johnson." But he was privately shaken and uncertain. As one of the New York staff told me later: "For a day or so, RN couldn't understand it. He had expected to face a bloodied, beatable opponent, either Johnson or Kennedy — preferably Bobby, because he wanted to beat a Kennedy. Johnson's withdrawal left him a bit scared. Now he couldn't be sure whether it would be Kennedy or Humphrey."

Faced with this new situation, Nixon fell back on his do-nothing strategy. The important difference was that he now admitted it, although he took pains to make his silence appear to be synonymous with statesmanlike responsibility. He announced that he would observe a personal "moratorium" on Vietnam and would say nothing about the war or the peace-seeking initiative until he could judge the effects of the bombing halt and North Vietnam's response. "In the light of these diplomatic moves, and in order to avoid anything that might, even inadvertently, cause difficulty for our negotiators," Nixon told the press, "I shall not make the comprehensive statement on Vietnam which I had planned for this week."

The talk we had prepared, of course, had been something less than "comprehensive," and we would have been hard-pressed to go beyond it in detail, particularly if Nixon had insisted on saying the opposite of his basic conclusion about the war. But the media did not know this, and his silence invited wishful speculation and much more favorable publicity than if he had given the talk as planned. His moratorium also allowed him to retire from the renewed battle between the lame duck President and his Democratic critics. Although Nixon's statement warned Johnson against "the temptations of a camouflaged surrender," his maneuver tacitly conveyed a friendlier message to the White House — "You can trust me not to make any trouble for you." Thus was laid the groundwork for a nonaggression pact between incumbent and challenger that would become increasingly apparent in the months ahead.

All in all, Nixon's withdrawal into silence was a brilliantly executed political stroke — and a cynical default on the moral obligation of a would-be President to make his views known to the people. But politics imposed no sanctions on maneuvers that worked, and Nixon's worked superbly. On the following Tuesday, the man whose views on Vietnam were unknown, and not likely to be made known, received a resounding 79.4 percent of the Republican vote in the Wisconsin primary.

IX

1. BY REMOVING HIMSELF from the competition for popular favor, Johnson, for the moment, recovered it. His critics were lavish in their praise. Senator McCarthy, full of triumph and magnanimity, said the President deserved "the approval and honor and respect of every citizen of the United States." The stock market, hearing the magic word "peace," leaped as it had during the heady days of the Great Society. As a wave of good feeling and optimism rolled over the country, only the antiwar radicals seemed unhappy. Plans to disrupt the Democratic National Convention, one leader grumbled, were "shot to hell."

But the spell cast on the eve of April Fools' Day proved short-lived. Toward dusk on April 4, the false calm was shattered by a bulletin from Memphis. The Reverend Dr. Martin Luther King, Jr., who was leading demonstrations in support of the city's striking sanitation workers, had been shot by a sniper as he stood on a motel balcony. Within an hour came word that he was dead, and the report that the police were seeking a white man as his assassin.

That evening, scattered window-breaking, looting, and arson occurred in the slums of the District of Columbia, the first large U.S. city with a black majority. During the next two days, the disorder in Washington grew into full-scale riot and spread to some one hundred and twenty cities. Before the violence abated, thirty-nine persons had died, all but five of them Negroes, and more than 3500 persons had been injured. Some 20,000 persons were arrested. Property damage was hazily estimated in the scores of millions of dollars.

Anyone who saw the April riots as an explosion of grief misread the mood and motives of the blacks who took over the streets. These were not followers of King and his code of nonviolence — that movement had expired before its leader. Since the first riots in the Northern slums in the mid-1960s, a new breed of self-styled black "revolutionary" had sprung up and elbowed King aside in the competition for media attention. At once terrified and fascinated by the big-talking, gun-toting newcomers, King's white supporters had drifted away, taking their guilty consciences and checkbooks. King had tried to organize a following in Chicago's huge ghetto, but the city-bred blacks regarded him as just another Southern preacher — "de Lawd," they mockingly called him — and they continued to trade votes for groceries with the ward heelers. Next King plunged to the forefront of anti-Vietnam protest, but alliance with Dr. Spock and the genteelly radical upper middle class carried him further away from the tenements and the welfare mothers. When he died, he was under the shadow of irrelevance, in search of a movement to which he might attach himself.

In Washington, where the looting extended into the downtown shopping district, almost within sight of the heavily guarded White House, a black teen-aged girl spoke to a newspaper reporter. King, she said, had "compromised his life away . . . If I'm nonviolent, I'll die. If I'm violent, I'll still die, but I'll take a honky with me." There was small chance of her dying or killing anyone, for the police, outnumbered and under orders to show restraint, fell back. In some instances, they directed traffic in the riot areas, and looters hauling away their booty in automobiles obeyed the signals. What was evident among the throngs of happy people, smashing, stealing, and burning in a carnival atmosphere, was not a hunger for revenge, but a hunger for *things*.

Compared with the capital — by far the hardest-hit city with more than a thousand fires burning — New York experienced only minor disorder. The eye of the hurricane was the Nixon headquarters. The staff argued worriedly without reaching any conclusions. The uncertainties raised by Johnson's withdrawal had not yet been sorted out, and now the racial crisis had come to a violent boil.

"There's no consensus," Price told me on the telephone. "We talked all around it. You know the positions — everything from law and order to compassion." Nixon had made a statement deploring Dr. King's death, but he showed no inclination to go beyond it. "At this point," said Price, "he doesn't feel the need to reach for attention, and I agree."

Television was showing spectacular scenes from Washington — pillars of smoke rising above the cherry blossoms, machine guns mounted on the steps of the Capitol — but it seemed to me that the worst damage was invisible. This was the widespread collapse of confidence in authority. Panic-stricken white suburbanites, after fleeing downtown Washington offices, succumbed to another, equally primitive instinct: to stand and fight. From locked drawers and closet shelves came the long-accumulated arsenal of fear. The District of Columbia, according to conservative official estimates, contained "a bare minimum" of 75,000 handguns alone. No one knew how many tens of thousands of lethal weapons were owned by the citizens of the surrounding Virginia and Maryland suburbs. While the target of the rampaging blacks was property, the anxious whites, hearing the wild harangues of Stokely Carmichael and other extremists, were prepared to take aim at black "troublemakers." The mob spirit was infectious. The looters swiftly produced their opposite numbers outside the law, the white vigilantes.*

Garment dutifully briefed me on the altered campaign strategy. "Our revised target is the Democratic philosophy. None of the Democratic candidates has anything *new* to say, none of them offers a real choice, and none of them can unite the country — that's the theme." But he sounded no more convinced than I was that it dealt with the situation created by the riots. Those were Nixon voters arming to the teeth in the suburbs; what did he propose to say to them?

* In September 1968 suburban Montgomery County's Council rejected a strict gun-control ordinance after three days of hearings before overflow crowds disrupted by the racial jeers and catcalls of hundreds of white gun enthusiasts. The controversy continued in the Letters column of the Washington *Post,* with most of the supporters of the ordinance lamenting the demise of democracy under mob pressure. An opponent of gun control unintentionally stated the real danger when he described the mob's victory as "democracy in full motion."

"I don't know. He may decide to make a speech soon. You know, something on the theme of violence and reconciliation, preserving the decent middle, whites helping blacks and blacks helping whites to keep the country going. He might make that kind of speech, maybe at some small Negro college like Hampton in Virginia."

I lost patience. "Len, there are troops stationed on my corner. The capital of the United States is being occupied in order to protect it against its own population. The whole goddamned world is watching and wondering whether this country will come apart at the seams — and you're telling me that Nixon may get around to making a speech. He's got to do better than that."

Garment responded with a question: should Nixon attend Dr. King's funeral in Atlanta? I was amazed to learn that the question was being seriously debated and that several senior advisers were opposed — not only conservatives such as Senator John Tower of Texas, but liberals too, including Ellsworth and Bob Finch. They were afraid, Garment said, that if Nixon went, some of the Southern delegates would bolt. "Even Eisenhower advised him against it. I think Nixon wants to go, but he knows that the Southerners will call him a traitor if he does. He's in a hammer lock."

Whatever King had been personally, he had become a symbol of something greater, a dream of accommodation between races and classes. His vaunted "soul-force" had much less to do with the realization of that dream than the force of changing life-circumstances that brought Negroes and whites closer together in jobs, schools, and neighborhoods, compelling them, as individuals, to adjust to each other's presence with civility and restraint and mutual respect. If Nixon genuinely believed in the theme of unity, he had to behave in exemplary fashion and pay his respects to the murdered man's widow and children. "Tell him I think he has to go," I said. "Otherwise he can forget about the 'decent middle.' If he stays home, there won't be any moral difference between him and Wallace."

Garment answered with a mixture of sadness and disgust. "Things have come to some pass when a Republican candidate for

President has to take counsel with his advisers about whether he should attend the funeral of a Nobel Prize winner."

In the end, Nixon attended the funeral and called on Mrs. King. Quite properly, he drew the line at joining the procession that trudged behind the mule-drawn wagon bearing the coffin — that was the other side's media politics. Yet Nixon, after having done the right and necessary thing, continued to be worried by the imagined perils. Several times thereafter, he rebuked those of us who had urged him to go to Atlanta, calling it "a serious mistake that almost cost us the South."

When Garment called again, he relayed an assignment from Nixon: review the first draft of the previous December's NAM speech and rework unused material into a fresh statement. That speech, I pointed out, had been a warning against a possible war-in-the-making. What was needed now was a fresh judgment in warlike circumstances and in advance of what might be a nightmarish summer. What had been Nixon's reaction to King's death and the riots? Were there any thoughts to guide me as I worked on a statement?

"He's given us almost no clue as to what he believes," said Garment, sounding dejected. "He hasn't done his homework on the racial problem or the cities. I guess he doesn't know what to say."

The Nixon organization's operational environment was like that of a studio control booth: hushed, sealed off from distractions, all buttons and dials set for carefully timed, skillfully executed moves. The racial crisis was not part of the scheduled program. The man in the booth did not live emotionally in this time, in this country set aflame, yet he was determined to preside over it.

As our conversation ended, Garment said: "Either Nixon will move into the urban crisis now, or his candidacy will remain technically alive but sink beneath the waves." Whether or not that remark was for my benefit, to spur me to my task, I believed it, and set to work.

But it was no use. If Nixon had roared with anger, or been moved to weep; if he had telephoned the White House and volunteered his services — but he had said and done nothing and had given no sign that he felt anything.

I could no longer find phrases to express Nixon because I could not find him. He had eluded me; he was not *there*, a felt presence behind the words in my typewriter. I stared for a long time at the blank paper reflecting the sum of what I knew of his convictions. Finally I called New York and asked to speak with him. I learned that Nixon had gone to Florida and then on to the Bahamas, where his friend Robert Abplanalp, the multimillionaire inventor of the aerosol can valve, had a villa. He would not return until the middle of the month.

By retreating into impenetrable silence and seclusion, Nixon doubtless was being politically shrewd. But why should ordinary citizens who could not escape trust and support him? Whatever I wrote would give the misleading impression that he understood and cared; that he should occupy the presidency when the racial volcano next erupted. I was no longer certain that he should.

MEMORANDUM

TO: DC   April 10, 1968

FROM: RJW

RE: Order and Justice

As requested, I have reviewed my draft of the NAM speech with an eye to restating one of its themes in the light of recent racial upheaval. I've had no success. I have also spent three days trying to write a new draft from scratch, guided by Len Garment's injunction to combine compassion with firmness. It sounds fine, but it doesn't work very well. After at least two dozen false starts, I have abandoned the effort and will pass on my thoughts via this memo instead.

It seems to me that we face an issue that cannot be convincingly straddled or fuzzed up with fancy rhetoric. We have heard all the familiar stuff about the underlying causes of Negro riots, and we have heard ditto about the jobs, housing, education, etc., etc., that are presumed to do something to prevent riots. All this strikes the ear politely, moderately, and very dully, for the reality revealed by the latest outbursts is quite different. Most of the rioters in Washington looted and burned because they damned well felt like it and discovered they could get away with it. Most of them had jobs (many with the government), a striking number held college degrees or were attending college full-time, and very few had anything but contempt for King's nonviolence jazz. What the rioters had in common was a hatred of "honkies" and a determination to scare Whitey and grab his goods and property.

It is hard to work up much compassion for this element of the Negro population, and particularly for the wild and increasingly aggressive teen-agers who are the spearhead of violence . . . The real victims of the rioting are the middle-class Negroes, but they suffer their losses in silence. As they see whites retreat before Negro hoodlums, moderate and responsible Negroes must wonder whether they have chosen the smartest role and values, and the ultimate winning side. But just try to frame an argument that speaks of "good" and "bad" blacks, and you see at once how it will offend everyone . . .

The presently forgotten man in all that's happening is the lower-middle-class white citizen. He doesn't like Negroes, and he is close enough to them in status, employment, and place of residence to be reminded daily that most of them don't like him. This white man feels threatened from below and browbeaten from above. He is scared enough to run like a rabbit at the first sign of trouble — witness last Friday's stampede out of Washington — and he is worried enough about the resolve of his government to protect him that he owns and intends to use a gun to protect his home and family.

This white citizen is withdrawing his trust from the system that disappoints him in dealing with Negro violence . . . (Not to be overlooked is the underlying white desire for a bloody confronta-

tion, which grows out of boredom, tension, frustration, and an attitude of let's-get-it-over-with.) The white man we have defended
against the charge of being a racist is showing that he does, in fact,
fear and hate blacks.

I am convinced that a policy decision, or at least some guidance
on where the emphasis should fall, must precede any full-dress
speech on the present and future of race relations . . .

If there is a black revolution brewing below, it is because of paralysis above. Paralysis in the government, in the press, in the
churches, wherever men of good will and heavy guilt feelings are
able to exert their influence to suppress an ugly and unacceptable
truth, namely, that the driving force of Negro aggression is not economic deprivation as much as it is class and racial hatred. To
break this paralysis above, it will be necessary to overthrow a number of social myths . . .

Through Buchanan came word that the Boss had decided not to
say anything for a while.

2. On Nixon's return from Florida, the speech-writers assembled in New York. The organization had moved again, this time to
the soon-to-be-demolished former headquarters of the American
Bible Society at the corner of Park Avenue and Fifty-seventh Street,
and we met in an office decorated with an incongruous religious
mural. Nixon was tanned and presumably well rested, but he
showed a testy impatience. Plainly, he was keyed up in anticipation of the encounter that brought us together — his appearance a
few days later before the annual meeting of the American Society of
Newspaper Editors in Washington. Not only would this give him
an opportunity to impress a sympathetic and influential audience of
editorial writers, it would also produce the next thing to a personal
confrontation between Nixon and Rockefeller, who would address
the editors a day earlier.

Rockefeller clearly was a candidate again. The governor had just announced the appointment of Emmet John Hughes as his personal chief of staff. Hughes was a one-time Eisenhower speechwriter and a long-time foe of Nixon's. After describing his old antagonist ("Hughes is a dirty player and always has been. He'll pull every trick"), Nixon opened the meeting by putting himself in Hughes's shoes. "If I were Rocky's adviser," he said, "I would tell him to make a strong pitch for fiscal responsibility and strengthening the dollar. That would be an unexpected move. Instead, I think he's going to go for a major statement on the cities and call for all-out spending programs. In the same breath, he'll probably promise to balance the budget." This estimate of Rockefeller's intentions, which proved accurate, was less a tribute to Nixon's guesswork than his agents' intelligence-gathering from Rockefeller informers who wished to be remembered after their candidate's defeat.

Nixon raised the possibility that he could try to outbid Rockefeller, but rejected it, revealing in the process a general attitude and approach. "I don't believe you can allow any single occurrence to force you to take a position before you have to take it. There will be other battles — this is only the first one. Rockefeller and I won't be scheduled this way again. When I took it six weeks ago, he wasn't coming. This isn't a time to rush in. We might have to live with any proposal we make."

As the discussion moved into proposals that Nixon could reasonably make, Martin Anderson reviewed University of Chicago Professor Milton Friedman's negative-income-tax scheme and its variants, which were familiar to Nixon and the newspaper editors. The candidate could talk about these without getting caught in a hard-and-fast commitment. "The family allowance thing intrigues me, and we may have to come to some kind of income guarantee later," said Nixon. "But I'm not ready to cross that bridge."

It was not his sense of timing alone that stayed Nixon. He seemed fundamentally uninterested in the programs that his young staff members discussed so earnestly. Nixon's weariness with big, new ideas showed in his edged words. *"Everybody's* against slums and unemployment and rats. That's why it's a waste of time spelling out a position as though somebody disagreed with it. Only the press is worried about programs. So take that crap from the coordinating committee and put it out — it doesn't mean a damned thing. But it will appease the press people who say you only speak in generalities."

Nixon warmed to the subject and his weariness with the conventions of democratic politics became explicit: "You know, it hasn't changed in twenty years. You still have to put out a folder saying what you're for and against, where you stand on the issues. Women particularly like it. They don't have the slightest idea what it means, but the voter's been taught to expect it." A deep strain of pessimism ran through his remarks. "You're not going to change people on welfare, whether they're white or black, for a century. As for preventing violence, I don't think *anything* is going to work. The more people get, the more they'll want. All we have is hope — and maybe Lindsay walking the streets" — a surprising reference to the New York mayor's effective tour of black neighborhoods following King's death.

For his appearance, Nixon had chosen a "Meet the Press"–like setting. He would make a brief opening statement and then field questions from a panel of editors. This format, of course, was similar to the one being used successfully for producing television ads, which showed Nixon in Q & A sessions with selected groups of citizens. It conveyed the impression of informal give-and-take, yet actually was structured and controlled by preplanning. Nixon directed us to draft material for his opening statement, including key sentences and any quips we could think of — "But *don't* write it all down. I want to keep it informal." We were each also to supply him with ten sharp questions and brief, fact-filled answers that he could study before his interrogation. Nixon planned to spend an entire weekend holed up in a Washington hotel preparing for his appearance.

He also laid down guidelines for the future. He wanted no further attempts to arrive at a policy consensus before a speech was written. "When too many people get into it, the speech is too bland and no goddamned good." Instead, each of us, working in his assigned area of responsibility, was to draft what he pleased and then submit it to "an editorial board" charged with ironing out problems of consensus and consistency. Nixon, typically, did not announce who would sit on the board. Evidently we would compete for seats. (Safire, I noticed, had already assumed the secretary's function and was keeping the minutes of the meeting.)

While the staff talked about the cities and programs for relieving the problems of the black population, Nixon seemed genuinely interested only in the failing health of the inflated economy. Respected advisers were telling him, he said, that a financial crisis was imminent and that the dollar might be devalued before midsummer. Alarm was warranted, to be sure, but it soon became apparent that his emphasis on the precarious state of the economy had another, politically useful side. Later in the month, Nixon began attacking promises of billions of dollars to rebuild the cities as "dishonest and a cruel delusion" and insisting he would not join in the game "whether it costs the election or not" — which, of course, it would not. *His* supporters didn't want to spend money on the riotous cities. The temporary weakness of the dollar gave him a decent excuse for pushing costly responses to urban problems into the indefinite future. Once or twice, he almost gave his game away, as when he said: "I am not prepared to say that we should give the Negro a certain program in order to buy his allegiance." He did not identify any other politician who *was* prepared to say anything like that.

Nixon wanted a "major statement" drafted on the economy, one which would look beyond Vietnam to noninflationary expansion, new spending priorities favoring the cities, and a revised tax structure permitting sharing of federal revenues with states and localities. "I know the economic thing is dull," he said, selling the job, "but it's vital, and it's going to be a big issue in the campaign."

When no one else spoke up, I asked for the assignment. Eventually, in collaboration with Nixon's friend and mentor, Arthur Burns, I produced a 10,000-word white paper, "A New Direction for America's Economy."

Talk about the dollar naturally led back to Rockefeller. Someone asked whether Romney, the champion of the financially beleaguered cities, would endorse Rockefeller. His doubts about the sincerity of the support he had received in the primaries were well known. Nixon noted that Romney owed some $350,000 in campaign debts to Rockefeller. "The money matters," he said drily.

Money indeed mattered decisively in the making of a President, as I saw illustrated in small and large ways. For a small example, Nixon told us that he wanted a full-dress statement on education, declaring that he proposed to spend "a lot of money on it." The staff, however, did not include anyone with credentials to write the paper. Pick the man you want, Nixon said, and pay him whatever you have to pay to get a good statement. "Don't worry — the money's there." A large example of the success of Maurice Stans's fundraising effort, which gathered some $30 million, occurred during our meeting. Although I had heard Nixon instruct Rose Mary Woods not to disturb him with calls, the telephone rang. Nixon picked up the receiver and at once approved his knowing secretary's discretionary breach of orders. When the caller came on the line, the candidate fairly purred his gratitude and appreciation. "In all my years in politics, nothing like this has ever happened," he said, beaming.

"That was Clem Stone," Nixon explained after the two-minute conversation. "He's given us a half-million dollars." The self-made Chicago insurance multimillionaire — his fortune was estimated at some $400 million — was by far the biggest single contributor to the campaign.

Clement Stone's staggering generosity put Nixon in a better humor, and he relaxed for several minutes tossing around a question of propaganda. "Should we put it out that we want Bobby as our opponent? Hell, we can beat him. Or should we say Hubert?" Bobby jokes were exchanged around the table and Nixon jotted down a couple to supplement the output of gag writer Paul Keyes, former producer of "Laugh-In." Finally the weighty question was resolved: we would tout Robert Kennedy to the press as Nixon's preferred opponent.

It was no contest in Washington. Rockefeller gave a dull, serious speech proposing $150 billion in joint government-private spending for the cities over the next decade and was interrupted only twice by polite applause. Nixon received more than a dozen enthusiastic bursts of hand-clapping. Standing on a nightclublike runway, his smile flashing and hands clasped behind his back, he treated the editors to a tour de force of crisp, quotable answers laced with humor. Columnist Charles MacDowell, a colleague from Richmond newspapering days, leaned over to me midway through the dazzling show: "Dammit, Dick, tell him that the anti-Nixon working press was mighty impressed." A couple of days later, the ideologically hostile Washington *Post* set aside Herblock's Nixon for the moment and complimented the real one in an editorial, "A Gifted Professional."

After Nixon exited, I saw the traveling staff aboard the bus for the trip to the airport. Ellsworth, Price, and Buchanan were elated. They were convinced that Nixon, by rising to the occasion, had finished Rockefeller and locked up the nomination. Well-briefed, his homework done, Nixon faced no surprises and made no mistakes. As I drove through streets that had been patrolled by troops only two weeks earlier, I thought of the editors now composing rave notices. Supposedly hard-boiled skeptics, they were reacting precisely according to the plan of the man in the control booth.

3.   A week after capturing the editors, Nixon received another boost in the media with a nationwide radio speech advancing the attractive, hopeful concept of uplifting slum-dwellers through "black capitalism." Price had written the text while campaigning,

always a miserable chore, and his difficulties were increased by a gaggle of hard-line critics who felt he erred on the side of sympathy for rioters. After much arguing and rewriting, Nixon made the speech proposing that private enterprise be encouraged to assist blacks toward "a share of the wealth and a piece of the action." It was a high point of the campaign.

The only objection to black capitalism was a practical one: small capitalists, white and black alike, were being squeezed into extinction beneath colorblind economic forces. It was hard enough for a small businessman to compete with a chain store in the best of circumstances, but when he was black and his shop was in a rundown, low-income neighborhood, he faced a challenge only the most exceptional man could overcome. Blacks had to be given the same opportunity as whites to be ordinary and yet successful enough to make their way independently. What's more, the desire to bring capitalism to the ghetto overlooked the reality that the ghetto was largely a creation of capitalism, in the form of urban real-estate economics. Black capitalism was valuable for the Republican concern it signaled and for establishing the relationship between Republican ideology and the individual Negro's aspirations. But any ghetto-centered approach seemed to me to lead to a dead end, and I proposed instead a commitment to the "open society."

MEMORANDUM

TO: DC   April 27, 1968

FROM: RJW

RE: The *real* issues in the cities

Irving Kristol invited me to lunch the other day, and we spent more than three hours discussing how DC might add to his growing reputation for awareness and realism in dealing with the problems of the cities . . . Kristol is a liberal Democrat who concerns himself rigorously with finding real and workable answers to properly defined social questions. He told me that his candidate is Humphrey, but his money is on DC — literally; he is a betting man — and so he wants to do what he can to bolster his investment.* (His ideas and mine are freely intermingled in the account of our conversation below.)

The Republicans in general and DC in particular are quite free to move in the city area, for until recently they had no special position on urban problems. In contrast, the Democrats are encumbered with the institutionalized and bureaucratized "solutions" of two decades, and with an urban constituency that is falling apart as the result of racial antagonisms. The Democrats cannot continue to woo the Negro without offending the lower-income white. The Republicans — especially DC — can afford to deal with people in and around cities as individuals, on the basis of broad national values, rather than attempt to manipulate competing values to appeal to conflicting interest groups.

Kristol dismisses the Riot Commission Report as a "mindless document." Were it not for the fact that this is a political year, he believes that men like Nathan Glazer and Pat Moynihan would be attacking the report openly. He endorses DC's rebuttal of the indictment of "white racism," which he describes as "a grave dug by men who are loaded down with guilt feelings."

Kristol believes that DC should base his entire approach on the assumption that the Negro American wants to be just that: Negro *and* American. He wants to be like everybody else. The whole thrust and intent of DC's approach can be summed up: Let the Negro be himself. Let him be proud of his blackness at long last; let him even become intensely nationalistic in his race pride . . . Let there be no artificial and imposed restraints on the Negro's march toward self-awareness and confident identity . . .

All the talk of "rebuilding" the ghetto, of giving the Negro "decent" housing (government-owned or subsidized), isn't what the Negro wants to hear. Like every other American underdog, he

---

* Kristol, co-editor of *The Public Interest* and Henry R. Luce Professor of Urban Studies at New York University, is that rarity: a gifted intellectual who is also a very practical man.

wants to move up and out — he wants to get out of the damned slums. It makes little sense to propose rebuilding nineteenth-century tenements when the Negro wants to participate fully in the twentieth-century economy. Kristol believes (and I agree) that DC must proclaim the *openness* of American society to the Negro who wants to enter it.

Above all, this means an unequivocal commitment to open housing in the suburbs, where the mainstream of American life now flows. (This doesn't necessarily mean racial integration throughout suburbia; most Negroes can't afford to move out and most who can aren't looking to force themselves on whites; but *all* must believe that the way is open and that they can make it if they can afford it.) In order to get the outward flow moving, and in order to build faith and purpose among those who, for now, must stay behind, various forms of government assistance are necessary and desirable. These should *not* be self-defeating handouts, but carefully conceived means of facilitating a natural social progression . . .

The point is to open up, to the greatest number of Negroes possible, as rapidly as possible, access to the satisfactions of American middle-class status. If we are not to be two nations, then we must extend the majority style of life as widely as possible within one nation. Of course, this status and style of life carry not only satisfactions but also responsibilities, and it is the latter that white America wants Negro America to accept.

Kristol, recalling the assumption on which this whole approach is based, says the *only* way to gain Negro acceptance of white middle-class values and responsibilities is through a fully credible open-door policy, so that the Negro who succeeds and the Negro who (for the present) fails do so as *individuals*. The system that rewards merit and punishes lack of merit, on an individual basis, cannot be convincingly discredited as "racist." With the traditional emphasis on individualism in Republican doctrine to build on, there's nothing subversive about even radical-sounding programs designed to help the aspiring Negro make it . . .

No federal programs, however ambitious, can do as much for

Negro progress as can the sound and balanced advance of the economy. The Negro moves fastest when the economy as a whole is
moving briskly. The problem for the city-dwelling Negro is to find
the entry job, the one that gets him into the economy. If he's
young, tough, and regarded as a potential rioter, he may have no
difficulty getting a temporary "job" doing absolutely nothing under
one or another of the federal "cool-it" programs, which are at once
cynical and self-defeating. The Negro hates those who pay him for
remaining reasonably peaceful, and he probably hates himself for
taking the nonjob — he is just as worthless as the whites think he is
— but "a hustle is a hustle" and so he gets paid for nonwork that
leaves him nowhere.

An enormous amount of work goes undone or gets only half-done
in our society, principally in the booming area of government and
private services. Our postal service may be the lousiest in the world
among advanced nations. Our hospitals are closing for lack of un-
skilled and semiskilled workers. Our teachers could do more teach-
ing if they had someone to turn their clerical burdens over to. We
have people who want to work and who should work — who, in the
deepest sense, *need* work in order to gain individual self-esteem and
an incentive for striving toward personal fulfillment.

Why not consider an arrangement by which the government
would bring the workers together with the work, on a temporary
basis and with a view to turning over such projects to regular government agencies or to private corporations within a definite period
of time? Of course, this would mean setting up the government as
"the employer of last resort." But everything depends on the spirit
in which this formula is acted upon. If a person performs real work
for real wages, the arrangement is economically valid, and it doesn't
matter very much who hires him.

As I see it, the government could act as intermediary between the
jobless and the work to be done without gearing up a massive, de-
pression-style, leaf-raking boondoggle. Those who think only in
terms of make-work don't know much about the jobless or the economy. Because their ignorance has given an interesting formula a

bad name, we should not reject it out of hand. Those of us who respect the innovative abilities of private enterprise can surely see
ways in which government–business joint ventures could be worked
out with minimum violence to the work ethic and maximum benefit
to the jobless and society as a whole.

The Negro needs what work can give him — and society needs
the work the Negro can do. Is it really so difficult to work out the
terms of this urgently necessary bargain? I don't think it is.

A final thought. Just about everybody has tried to get into the
street-walking act in the ghetto, and most of the latecomers have
failed to upstage Lindsay and Kennedy. In time of crisis, we all feel
DC should do something — but where and how? I suggest that a
neglected social frontier exists. It is where the doors must be opened
and the people prepared for the next great phase of the American
experiment. It is suburbia.

Should Washington blow up again, which seems a fair possibility
with the Poor People's Campaign beginning this week, I suggest
that DC consider making two or three informal appearances in
places in the suburbs like Bethesda and Arlington, to tell it like it is
and like it must be among those who have a stake in the future . . .
If DC were to speak out for the open society against a background
of panic and barricades, I believe it would have an enormous impact on white and black Americans alike.

In due course, my memo came back bearing a large check mark
— meaning Nixon had read it — and much underscoring in his distinctive scrawl, including an intriguing circle around the phrase
"open society." Perhaps it appealed to his appetite for slogans, but
he did not mention it in our subsequent conversations, and I saw no
point in pressing it. The way the campaign now turned, slogans of
a different sort were in demand.

4.   As though determined to provoke the white majority, black
militants and their white sympathizers persisted in pointless demon-

strations. Only weeks after the inner city of Washington had burned, the first of several thousand squatters began taking over a fifteen-acre grassy site east of the Lincoln Memorial, renamed Resurrection City — a sad misnomer. With this squalid and self-defeating charade, what remained of the organized movement for black equality passed into oblivion, propelled by the same force of publicity that had originally helped it gain momentum.

The scene on that first morning resembled the arrival of a chaotic, electronic circus. Amateur carpenters hammered away putting up prefabricated plywood huts. Trucks carrying radio and television equipment lined the field. Technicians hurried about snaking cables through the confusion. Microphones and tape recorders were everywhere. The only performers on hand were a few dozen Negro children, wide-eyed and weary from long bus rides. They sang and clapped their hands for the benefit of the cameramen, but the encampment's "marshals" — tough, swaggering youths — forbade interviews. I watched as the correspondent of the *New York Times*, wearing a hand-lettered badge in his lapel, reacted with shocked disbelief to being turned away.

For a couple of hours, the children sang, reporters interviewed each other, and work on the huts proceeded between arguments over where the streets of the City were to be laid out — no one seemed to know. We were awaiting the ringmaster, the Reverend Ralph D. Abernathy, King's long-time collaborator who was now struggling to succeed him. He had been delayed en route from the motel where he intended to live, a decision that would be the source of much unhappiness among his followers. Finally Abernathy came, attired in new blue denim jeans and jacket, the official costume of the Poor People's Campaign. He was to drive the first stake, and the jostling crowd of newsmen encircled it. Earlier, I had witnessed the preparations. Two young blacks dug a hole, refilled it, and set the stake gingerly in the loose dirt. Now, as the cameras rolled, Abernathy stepped forward, raised a hammer, and brought it down with a lusty stroke. He intended to chant *Freedom* with each stroke, but at the first whack, the stake all but disappeared into the soft earth. The stagehands had done their work too diligently. Abernathy put aside the hammer and held a news conference.

Conceived by its architects as a symbol of the disgraceful plight of the nation's poor, Resurrection City, in the next six weeks, became simply a disgrace. Torrential rains turned the ill-drained field into a quagmire. Marauding youths terrorized the inhabitants, beating, robbing, and raping under the eyes of the useless "marshals." Tourists visiting the nearby shrines were accosted and relieved of their wallets and cameras. All the while, the demonstrators marched and picketed and had their pictures taken, but no practical measures for the relief of their evident misery were laid before Congress. The campaign had everything media politics required — a scenario, actors, and slogans — but it had no political program. It was an exercise in make-believe that produced real suffering and violence, including a near-riot in the Negro slums, but nothing concrete for the dwindling number of squatters. In truth, George Wallace received more benefit from Resurrection City than the demonstrators, for it projected against the backdrop of the capital every racial stereotype obstructing the Negro's advance.

At the beginning of the sixties, as a *Time* editor reporting on the Negro lunch-counter sit-ins in the South, I had interviewed a Negro minister in the basement study of his bullet-pocked, wiretapped, police-watched church in Montgomery, Alabama. "We must get ready to die," a youthful Ralph Abernathy had told me. "We must get ready to die, singly or in great numbers." What had begun nobly now ended badly. The pathetic rear guard in the damp ruins of Resurrection City, after being told by their leaders that they might face injury or death ("Tomorrow some will be beaten; tomorrow some will be killed"), were driven away, unharmed, under a police barrage of tear gas. The press later reported that Abernathy had secretly arranged for his followers to be arrested — the only escape route he could find from this muddy and meaningless stage.

X

1. IN MAY Nixon swept the last three primaries he had entered — Indiana, Nebraska, and Oregon — and clinched the nomination. The Oregon campaign, long identified as the make-or-break contest, consumed more than half a million dollars, an immense sum for a small state. Much of the money poured into a media blitz and an election eve telethon. As usual, Ellsworth attempted to play down Nixon's strength, telling skeptical reporters 40 percent of the vote would be sensational. Well in advance, secret contingency plans were laid against the slim possibility of an upset: Nixon would go from Oregon to Arizona for a visit with Barry Goldwater and then would swing along the Southern flank shoring up any wavering delegates.

When the ballots were counted, Nixon had received more than 73 percent of the vote, and he took off for Goldwater country a confident winner. After meeting the Southerners in Atlanta, campaign manager John Mitchell crowed: "The ball game for all intents and purposes is over."

So it was — without Nixon ever having gone to bat against a standup opponent. With the victory bandwagon rolling in high gear, he was now halfway to an amazing comeback. And he was making it appear strangely easy and inevitable. The supposed loser and his staff of newcomers led by Mitchell had taken seven primaries in a row and wrapped up the Republican prize, as the press and professional politicians invariably noted, without making a mistake. It was the most impressive organization feat in national politics, all agreed, since John Kennedy's 1960 takeover of the Democratic party.

Yet there was less to Nixon's success than met the professionally appreciative eye. He had succeeded in a vacuum, as it were, free of the pressures of time and frontal challenge that a candidate normally encountered. (Even amateurs knew how to use these extraordinary advantages. As early as December, before Nixon had even announced, we were devoting daylong meetings to mapping the distant Oregon battlefield and thereafter continually refined our plans, all in preparation for phantom opponents.) A candidate forced to take the primary route as Nixon had usually saw himself and his organization tested for several months in full view of the press, the party professionals, and the voters. Nixon had evaded this process — and he had no intention of testing himself. To an extraordinary degree, he and the men around him were still unknown quantities.

In the two and a half months remaining before the convention, Nixon continued to talk encouragingly to us about changing pace, sharpening the issues, and moving aggressively into "the final," as he called the fall election. But it was only talk. Long before the triumphal march to Miami, the campaign was "set."

It was in this period that Mitchell, whose status had been in doubt, finally emerged as the man in charge. Outsiders chalked it up to Nixon's determination to apply the lessons of his 1960 defeat, in this case by delegating power and responsibility. Such a view oversimplified Mitchell's rise and his actual function. Behind the organization's façade of cool superefficiency lay a much shakier reality.

Contrary to his reputation Nixon doled out authority rather freely, but only in small and ambiguous doses, often to more than one person at a time. He liked to please useful people — that was the salesman — and he also liked to see them run scared and perhaps become more useful. Standing apart from the rivalries he arranged and pretending unawareness, he watched as the stronger defeated the weaker. The loser knew his fate when Nixon shunned him, but the winner could never be confident of his victory. For if someone appeared who seemed smarter and stronger, Nixon might set up another conflict, which would begin without notice to the winner of the previous round.

Ellsworth's fate illustrated the technique in action. He carried out Nixon's orders well in such tasks as purging the Washington office, but he remained unsure of his standing with the candidate and therefore unsure of his position vis-à-vis Mitchell. Although Mitchell seemed to have a tight connection with the Boss, he, too, was unsure of himself. At the beginning of 1968, he had been just another of the Nixon partners lending a hand on the campaign, using contacts he had built up as a highly regarded state and municipal bond lawyer. These served him well in organizing Wisconsin. But he stood outside the larger network being built as Ellsworth, Sears, and others crisscrossed the country. As that network gained cohesion, control of the campaign would slip away from the original insiders in the law firm. Seeing the danger, Garment, Buchanan, and others closed ranks around Mitchell, urging him on Nixon as the man to run the show.

Meanwhile, Mitchell mounted a formidable bluff in dealing with Ellsworth, subjecting him to incessant second-guessing. At any point Ellsworth might have resisted the bullying and moved to undermine Mitchell, who had made some damaging errors. Instead, he submitted, and Mitchell, by exercising authority, acquired it. The competition came to an end in late April when Mitchell ordered Ellsworth and Sears to leave Washington and work out of the New York headquarters, directly under his control. They balked, but the order stuck — the signal that Nixon endorsed it and recognized a winner.

An observer within the law firm, retracing Mitchell's rise, confessed afterward that he had expected him to make a common mistake: to assume too much too early and behave as though he had Nixon's irrevocable favor. "I thought Mitchell would try to give Nixon advice and he would get fed up and say to Rose, 'I don't want to see him.' But Mitchell didn't give advice. He and Nixon would just sit and *gossip*, and he'd cut up Ellsworth. He was adroit."

Mitchell, respectful of Nixon's position as supreme strategist, offered something far more valuable than advice. Wreathed in pipe smoke and an aura of imperturbable certainty, he gave reassurance. When he nodded his balding head, strength flowed to Nixon's side of the table. In the precarious calling of politics, Mitchell was an anomaly: a man of secure accomplishment, who showed the talent for getting and keeping what he wanted. While Nixon had been striving and losing, Mitchell had been making it big on the fast track. He was at ease with Nelson Rockefeller and others who made Nixon uneasy. To have a $200,000-a-year man as counselor and executive officer was comforting to Nixon.

Yet his comfort came at the sacrifice of a certain protection. With Mitchell's emergence, Nixon's technique for keeping assistants in dread of their mistakes fell into disuse. Now the staff lived in dread of Mitchell, which made a great deal of difference. With no challenger in sight, Mitchell had no one on whom to blame errors — therefore, he could acknowledge none. At the same time, he was astute enough to recognize the dangers of his inexperience. While he maintained a pose of unshakable certainty, he opted for caution. Any suggestion involving risk faced him with a personal as well as a political threat, and Mitchell crushed it. Under the guise of strength, he reinforced Nixon's timidity.

Under his captaincy, the ship was pulled taut and steered on what seemed the safest course — steady as she goes, more of the same, an undeviating straight line. The hazards of a risk-free course would become apparent only as Election Day loomed.

2.   When taken by surprise, as by the quick succession of Johnson's withdrawal, King's death, and the nationwide riots, the Nixon organization simply stopped and waited. The nudge of good fortune never failed to get the campaign moving again. Contrary to Garment's premonition, Nixon's candidacy, though immobile, did

not sink. Instead he was swept forward by the wave of popular out-
cry for "law and order."

The problems that threw the staff into confusion and sent the
candidate fleeing southward appeared to resolve themselves. In
place of the retiring President stood a more inviting target: the law-
breaker. There was no need to draw the symbol too precisely, for a
great many disturbing figures crowded together in the inflamed
public imagination — the mugger lurking in the shadows, the antiwar demonstrator burning the flag, the campus revolutionary, the
drug pusher, and — most vividly — the black rioter and arsonist.
Crime, especially *Negro* crime, was all that people seemed to talk
about, vehemently and profanely. Every poll showed overwhelming public agreement with Mayor Richard Daley's order to the
Chicago police: Shoot arsonists to kill, looters to maim. The best-
selling bumper sticker in America was the old John Birch Society
motto: SUPPORT YOUR LOCAL POLICE.

Unlike the issue of Vietnam, which stirred tricky crosscurrents,
the issue of civil disorder drained a vast watershed of fear, anxiety,
and racial prejudice. Streams of unrelated emotion converged in a
broad torrent of opinion favoring repression. George Wallace was
riding the wave, but not guiding it. He did not rally his following;
the neglected and resentful cast him up as their spokesman. The
Wallace constituency appeared in surprising places — even within
the federal government. The *Federal Times*, polling postal and other
employees in forty states and the District of Columbia concerning
their presidential preferences, found Wallace the winner in every
section of the country and at every job level. Union locals hooted
down their leaders and adopted fiery resolutions in support of the
new champion of the white working man. Ominously, Wallace
buttons began turning up on police uniforms — and met with approving smiles.

Within a month of King's death, Nixon's lift in the polls wore off.
By mid-May, although Gallup showed Nixon continuing to lead
Hubert Humphrey, 39 percent to 36 percent, the gap was nar-

rowing. Meanwhile, Wallace jumped from 9 percent to 14 percent, drawing much of his fresh support away from Nixon. In some Southern and Border States, the race was entirely between Nixon and Wallace.

Plainly, if Nixon's stance toward Wallace remained passive, his base of support would suffer erosion. Wallace's campaign slogan — *Stand Up for America* — was inspired and activist; ours — *Nixon's the One* — merely contrived. His assertion that there was no difference between the major parties was uncomfortably accurate and forced us to contend defensively that there was enough meaningful difference to make a Wallace vote a "wasted" vote. That argument might have carried weight if Wallace were the leader of a political movement organized around a program and intent on achieving concrete objectives. But his was a cultural protest movement, and his followers saw themselves as defenders of a way of life. They wanted to see upheld not only the values of their upbringing, but also the values supporting a way of life their children might enjoy. Campus radicals were abusing what Wallace's audiences regarded as the privilege of higher education. They and the blacks and the uncaring rich liberals were spoiling the America that these protesting lower-middle-class citizens had not yet fully entered. "America first," a New York policeman attending a Wallace rally told a reporter, "that's all I can think of — Wallace will put America first."

Wallace, in his harangues against liberals and radicals and "pointy-head professors," knew his constituency and frequently catalogued the "plain people" — policemen, firemen, filling station operators, barbers and beauticians, small shopkeepers, all the wage earners sprung from working-class origins and lately arrived in the lower, shaky reaches of the American middle class. The cocky ex-truck driver, his hair slicked down like a drugstore cowboy, chin thrust forward defiantly, spoke from a confident class-cultural identity that guaranteed electric rapport between speaker and audience. While Nixon's television commercials and the half-hour campaign film (*Nixon Now*) synthesized immediacy, Wallace was a vivid presence on the stump and on the evening television news.

So, too, was Robert Kennedy. After King's death, he spoke spontaneous words of consolation to a crowd of blacks, in which he shared their experience of loss through his own. The film clip of this moving scene disclosed how little abstractions affected people's lives. Whatever ideology Kennedy's New Left writers might inject into his speeches, he came before angry blacks and whites alike as the embodiment of a uniting legend that all understood, an heroic romance of family loyalty, victory, and early death. In a curious way having nothing to do with politics, the Kennedy and Wallace candidacies were linked by the emotions they released. These wiry and pugnacious men, though enemies at the level of abstraction, made the same visceral appeal and stirred the same people. Ordinary men and women who saw mostly the bottom side of life could identify with these underdogs challenging the remote masters and the unfair system.

With Johnson's withdrawal, Nixon, packaged and protected, seemed the system's inheritor, as well as the President's silent accomplice on Vietnam. In this year of rebellion from every quarter against status quo liberalism, Nixon should not become by default its defender. Taking advantage of his special sensitivity to the Kennedys, I underscored the factor of personality in addressing the issue of law and order.

MEMORANDUM

TO: DC
FROM: RJW

May 18, 1968

. . . Right now, the conventional wisdom of political analysts holds that Bobby Kennedy is hurt by his black following and seeming radicalism. Maybe so, but just suppose he were to say, "I'm the *only* man who can deal with these people. I know where to draw the line. Choose me and I'll take charge."

Now is the time, I believe, to speak candidly about the tide of fear running in this country . . . In the *simplest* and most straightforward language, the message should be gotten through that the Johnson administration is responsible for the disintegration of law and order and public trust. A new administration would do everything necessary to protect and defend this society . . . The country does not need vigilantes; it needs leaders who will lead and who will merit the trust that is the real foundation of order.

I think we have made the point successfully in a couple of speeches, but somehow it got lost in the rhetoric. There is nothing intellectual about the fear of violence. It is basic and primitive, and it needs plain speech to be soothed. Bobby speaks plainly, you can hear *steel* in his sentences. Even people who say they hate him, if they are scared enough, will turn toward the sound of steel. Let's remind people that we are not so entranced with private enterprise in the ghetto and long-term solutions that we are unaware of short-term dangers.

Early yesterday morning here in Washington, a bus driver for DC Transit was shot to death, and the police have taken into custody four young Negroes. He was one of five drivers held up last night. There have already been more bus robberies since the beginning of this year than in all of 1967 . . .

The police who captured the bus driver's suspected killers near the scene of the crime picked up the murder weapon. They also found another gun on the bus, unfired, which was identified as belonging to the murdered man. He had carried it for protection, but never got a chance to use it. What kind of America are we living in when bus drivers feel, with good reason, that they must go armed?

Up to now, we have spoken of our cities as "jungles" as though using a figure of speech. Things were bad, but not *that* bad. Well, the word "jungle" now precisely and literally describes the situation. And *the* issue in this campaign is the encroaching jungle versus what remains of a shaken free society.

———————

Nixon viewed the plight of ordinary people with alarm — but from a safe distance. Ghostwriters could not bridge the gulf. Only

Nixon ultimately could convince the voters, in whatever way and words he chose, that he really cared.

Kennedy was defeated in the Oregon primary, the first reverse in the family's career, and this strengthened Nixon's conviction that Humphrey would be the Democratic nominee. "If it's Bobby it will be a contest between men, and if it's Hubert, a contest between policies," he told the *New York Times'* Robert Semple in an interview. "Bobby and I have been sounding pretty much alike already, and we can't hold his feet to the fires of the past. But Hubert — Hubert can be portrayed as the helpless captive of the policies of the past."

While Nixon proceeded at a winner's pace from Oregon through the South on his way to another rest in Florida, Kennedy dashed the length and breadth of California, needing a victory in that state's climactic primary to keep his candidacy alive. He won it, and then, as he left a hotel ballroom filled with cheering supporters, he lost his life as his brother had, senselessly, to a deranged young man with a grudge and a gun.

Once more the tragic legend engulfed America. I saw in my children how the Kennedys had entered our lives as figures making personally felt history. On the morning of the day the Kennedy funeral train was to arrive in Washington, when the children learned we would watch the cortege, they went, unbidden, to put on their best clothes and presented themselves carrying flowers from the garden. Through much of the afternoon and into early evening, we waited, with a pair of close friends, on the sidewalk on Constitution Avenue. The children were strangely quiet. At last, as matches and candles flickered in the dusk like fireflies, the procession glided past toward Arlington. On the steps of the Lincoln Memorial a choir sang. We arrived home before the conclusion of the graveside rites, and the mournful day came to a familiar end. We watched another Kennedy funeral on television.

My attitude toward Kennedy had changed in the final months of his life. I didn't often agree with him, yet I had come to respect him. Once committed, he held nothing back.

3.   The Wallace phenomenon demanded a response, and the
Nixon organization debated it. Or, rather, as Wallace might have
said, we engaged in a pseudo-debate. The conclusion was obvious
from the beginning — we must attempt to draw support away from
Wallace. Nevertheless, in the absence of an acceptable, risk-free
strategy, the obvious was ignored, and we wasted several weeks in
elaborate but pointless analyses. The essence of the pseudo-debate
was to avoid the real questions; failing that, to raise them only in
the context of a kind of antiseptic, value-free political science that
pretended to explore all options, including some that didn't exist.

Early in June, Buchanan wrote a memorandum on the approaching need for "hard decisions with regard to where RN is
going to get his *Democrats* to form his majority." He could seek them
among the most visible bloc of Democratic voters, the Negroes.
"No one would disagree with this," wrote Buchanan, sounding un-
recognizably agreeable. Unfortunately, the Negroes also were the
most monolithic Democratic bloc, by roughly a nine to one margin.
Through a massive effort, Nixon might win over perhaps 30 percent
of the Negroes, which meant an additional million votes. With a
fine show of objectivity, Buchanan turned the coin over. Wallace's
poll ratings projected to November amounted to some 12,000,000
votes. By cutting away only 8 percent of that total, Nixon could get
an additional million votes. "Which is easier for RN to accomplish?" Buchanan asked, leaving the question unanswered.

The pretense that the choice was real, and that Nixon could attract Negro support by adjusting his appeals, stemmed from an ex-
cusable desire not to appear "racist" or, as another staff member
wrote, "eager to exploit or create a backlash." Such an intention
recalled the fatal error of Goldwaterism, which tried to exploit an
incipient backlash — the triggering phrase was "crime in the
streets" — and failed. The intimidating memory of that failure
made Nixon men slow to admit that this time the backlash was real.

In another memo, Buchanan zeroed in on the state where Nixon almost certainly would win or lose the election, California. At worst, Nixon would get about 30,000 black votes there; at best, a judgment Price agreed with, some 100,000. There were seven million voters in California, Buchanan noted, and the increment to be gained by all-out campaigning among Negroes amounted to "an addition of one damn percent of the electorate." Again, he reversed the coin. Pointing out that the Wallace following in the state might cost a million votes, he closed with another question: "How many of these can a good tough campaign get?"

Director of domestic research Alan Greenspan, a brilliant economist and president of his own consulting firm, was an expert in playing political war games on the computer. He shuttled between his downtown office near Wall Street and Nixon headquarters bearing stacks of print-outs indicating the reaction of the electoral model to rightward and leftward maneuvering. The computer consistently awarded the game to the rightward moves. This displeased the conservative Greenspan not at all, but he maintained scholarly detachment as he sifted the evidence and stated his findings. "It's my judgment that we can win five percentage points back from Wallace, at a cost of one, or at the most two points moving from RN to Humphrey," he wrote late in June. Nevertheless, a strong campaign against Humphrey producing such a shift might not be enough to win the election: "The major potential of our additional votes at this stage is from Wallace, not from Humphrey." Echoing an earlier plea that would come to sound prophetic as the summer advanced, Greenspan concluded: ". . . we need a strong gut issue to swing a large bloc of Wallace votes to us. I wouldn't want to guarantee that such an issue would win us the election, but I am concerned that if a major effort is not made against Wallace, we may not make it past November."

In the comments he scribbled along the margins of the staff memos before returning them, Nixon enthusiastically endorsed our views and gave crisp instructions. When a memo-writer suggested the need for "a little more passion on the Boss's part, a determination to keep hitting on these gut issues in phrases which stick in the mind of the average voter," especially the disaffected Independent and Democrat, Nixon responded with numbered points: "1. RN thinks this is very perceptive. 2. Discuss with Whalen, Haldeman and Safire as to: 1. Sharp phrases. 2. Media program in South."

We did as directed, with less than satisfactory results. No phrase as telling as Wallace's contemptuous dismissal of the major parties — "There's not a dime's worth of difference between them" — seemed to fit in Nixon's mouth. Too, there was a problem of shifting images abruptly. The "new" Nixon depicted in the media campaign so far was mature, responsible, and statesmanlike — a quiet problem-solver. The still newer Nixon now requested from the creative department was an emotional, hard-hitting crowd pleaser.

The heart of the problem, however, was not phrasing or imagery. As usual, the problem was Nixon. The plea for "a little more passion on the Boss's part" summed it up. None of us could say with confidence what, if anything, Nixon felt passionately about. As a result, our attempts to sharpen his appeals tended to reveal more of our beliefs than his. In the suppressed atmosphere of headquarters, this could be imprudent. Strong conviction seemed as out of place there as strong drink had been when the American Bible Society occupied the premises. Occasionally, Nixon surprised us. When I shepherded a defense policy paper through the clearance process and gained its release as written, my more conservative colleagues were astonished. They had not realized that Nixon believed *that* — nor had I. We were rather like bootleggers serving a client of unpredictable taste and thirst; all we could do was leave samples on his doorstep.

Toward the end of June, the subject of intramural debate changed, by no means accidentally, from the Wallace problem to Nixon's selection of a running mate. Without admitting it, the younger staff members were coming to the conclusion that Nixon alone would be unable or unwilling to cope with Wallace, and that the second man would have to carry much of the fight. Newspaper speculation on the vice-presidential prospects of Senator Charles Percy of Illinois (which were nil) provided the opportunity to propose as the best available man California's governor Ronald Reagan.

Sears led off with a superb analysis of Reagan's strengths and weaknesses, supplemented by a detailed, state-by-state breakdown of a Nixon-Reagan ticket's likely electoral success against Hubert Humphrey and two quite different running mates: Edward Kennedy or John Connally. In contrast to 1960, which had been a "center-left" year, the paper judged 1968 a "center-right" year. It identified the South as by far the most volatile region of the country, showing extreme sensitivity to the vice-presidential choices of the major parties and as very probably being the decisive battleground. After making short work of the Percy straw man, the analysis advanced the case for Reagan as "the only officeholder in the country who can outtalk and outcampaign George Wallace."

Sears highlighted *two* blocs of Democratic voters among whom significant gains could be made: not only the Wallace supporters but also the overlapping "ethnic groups in the large cities (Irish, Italian, Polish, etc.)" — that is, urban-suburban *Catholics.* "No matter who we put on the ticket in second place," Sears wrote, "RN will have to make the appeal to this latter group." In his judgment, no prospective running mate added anything "politically sound" to the ticket — the choice of Reagan could not, for example, guarantee a Republican victory in California. But Reagan could at once tie down and stir up the conservatives who were the G.O.P. shock troops, and he could breach Wallace's Southern citadel like no other Republican. His all-important function, Sears concluded, "should be to relieve the burdens on RN's time so that RN can spend the vast majority of the campaign in eight or nine critical states."

Buchanan, in still another memo, declared that "the Nixon campaign is confronted with the old German problem — the two-front war . . . We are going to have to stave off the assaults of Wallace from the right, to keep him from making any further inroads, and we are going to have to defeat the challenge of Humphrey in the center of American politics. It is almost impossible for one can-

didate to do both of these things well at the same time." Reagan
would free Nixon of "the burden of fighting George Wallace, a burden we would otherwise have to assume totally, a burden which
would necessarily cost us something in the center." In the primaries, with Nixon the favorite and leader, a "conservative" campaign
addressed to Republicans had been the sound and successful strategy. In the fall, however, with two fronts active, it would be entirely different. "We are going to have to be bold to win this one, I
think," Buchanan concluded, "and I can currently think of nothing
bolder than to put the hero of *Bedtime for Bonzo* on the G.O.P. ticket."

Richard Allen, newly arrived from the Hoover Institution on
War, Revolution and Peace to direct research on foreign policy
issues, joined in with a pro-Reagan memo declaring a change in
personal attitude. He had been convinced, he wrote, "that a ticket
headed by RN would need leftish ballast to make a credible attempt to capture the lion's share of the independents." But no
longer: "the Establishment *forbids* a Nixon presidency. Thus, all
who consume and swear by the Establishment views are votes lost
forever, votes we cannot capture . . ." Allen based his argument
on "what the Wallace vote is *actually* doing to us," compared with
wishful thinking that it would just go away, and on Reagan's
proved effectiveness as a campaigner. "With him, there is no crude
appeal — his 'old-time religion' is founded on the very elements
which are missing today: law, order, patriotism, thrift — and in
language which the common man can understand."

I framed my argument for Reagan in terms of the future. "If we
do not kid ourselves about the situation a Nixon administration
would face, I think we can see more clearly what will be required of
the man who stands beside Nixon as Vice President." When the
two stood in the proper relationship to each other, the Vice President served as the front-line advocate, the President as the more
aloof moderate. "The Vice President, far from being a well-liked
bystander, must take the heat and lightning in order to spare and
conserve the presige of the man in the White House." By putting a
liberal on the ticket, "we tacitly accept the notion that RN is a con-

servative" — something I was no longer sure of — "and it defeats the whole intention of running him as a centrist who, if anything, leans to the liberal side on important domestic issues."

Not only would such a concession to the center-left deny Nixon tactical freedom and flexibility. It also would misread the movement of the country to the right of the former liberal center. "In the special, closed environment of New York City in particular and the media-oriented subnation in general, everyone is fascinated by the McCarthy phenomenon. But the people who read and react to print, the people who argue and write, are an extremely unrepresentative minority. The truly fascinating phenomenon is the breakout of Wallace from a sectional to a national base . . . Outside the South, Wallace is attracting low- and middle-income voters formerly tied to the Democratic party through their pocketbooks and ethnic-cultural backgrounds . . . Why should we not appeal to them? Why, if the momentum of events and the mood of the people are running toward conservatism, should we deny ourselves access to this potential majority? If the Democrats had a governor of the most populous state in the nation, who had sex, glamour, and expert proficiency on the tube, who projected the image of the 'citizen' politician to an electorate fed up with 'professionals,' would they rule him out for a place on the ticket because of ideological qualms? They would not."

Those, of course, were imprudent words to address to a rather colorless professional. The more attractive we made Reagan appear, the less he appealed to Nixon, who would suffer from the inevitable, side-by-side comparison. The main defect in my argument, however, was the assumption that Nixon's horizon extended beyond the election.

One morning early in July, Nixon and I talked alone in the small den in his apartment. Word had come back to us that he was concerned over the stream of memos and had asked Rose Mary Woods: "Are they all talking about the vice-presidential thing down there?" In a thoughtful paper, Martin Anderson had made a pair of important points: "So far our major communications effort seems to have

been aimed at dispelling myths about RN's personality and character . . . It seems that we should now turn our efforts toward communicating (his) ideas through the media to the great mass of people who do not yet have a comprehensive view of where RN
stands." I asked for the opportunity to summarize the feelings of
most of the writers and researchers. In our conversation, Nixon said
he agreed with Anderson's judgments completely. (When he replied to the memo several days later, as usual referring to himself in
the third person, he wrote: "It is time to move away from fighting
the old battle of image to the new battle of where RN stands —
only this way do we cut the Wallace vote.")

The two overriding issues, Vietnam and law and order, I said,
suggested alternative strategies pivoting on the selection of a running mate. Nixon could move "left" on Vietnam by saying hard
things now that would have to be said later anyway and by choosing for the ticket someone like Oregon's senator Mark Hatfield, an
early, consistent, and responsible critic of the war. After the Oregon primary, Hatfield, a moderate with excellent credentials as a
party loyalist, had offered to endorse Nixon on the basis of his Vietnam "position" — which, in ghosting the Hatfield endorsement, I
carefully avoided stating. By giving dramatic evidence of a new administration's commitment to end the war, Nixon could turn from
Vietnam and spend most of his time in the fall campaign appealing
to the voters from the center rightward on domestic issues.

But this was a relatively unpromising strategy. The one we much
preferred turned on the choice of Reagan and a domestic emphasis,
for the reasons outlined in our memos. This strategy, I said, by no
means excluded — in fact, it might facilitate — taking a "left" position on the war.

Nixon listened closely and then asked me to draft a comprehensive statement on Vietnam for submission to the convention platform committee. He gave no instructions on what it should contain.
Yet neither did he give me — or, more important, himself — a free
hand. The only clue to his thinking that I carried away was a

parting admonition. "Remember," he said, "I want to keep Hubert lashed to the mast."

A few days later, Sears and I lingered over dinner in a dim, quiet restaurant on Madison Avenue before returning to work. Until recently, he had seemed the very model of a modern young professional who enjoyed playing the game well for its own sake. During our collaboration in the memo-writing effort, he had revealed a side on which he asked the worth of winning the game. When I mentioned Nixon's apparent enthusiasm for spelling out his position on the issues, yet his strange reluctance to do so, Sears smiled. When I spoke of the need for planning not only the campaign, but the program and personnel of the Nixon government, he laughed aloud, a quick, mirthless laugh.

"Nobody's looking that far ahead," he said, draining his glass. "November is when all this stops."

4. On the morning of Sunday, July 14, several members of the Nixon staff assembled at New York's Marine Air Terminal and boarded a chartered Convair. After flying east over Long Island for forty minutes, we landed at the Hamptons airport, where cars met us and took us the rest of the way to Montauk, Gurney's Inn, and a strategy meeting with the candidate.

The "Jolly Roger," the hilltop bungalow of Nick Monte, owner of the Inn, sat at the end of a winding dirt road. A pair of Secret Service men carrying walkie-talkies and wearing sunglasses, their badge of recognition, met the cars. Other agents could be seen patrolling the scrub pine woods around the house, part of the protection force ordered by the President for all candidates following Kennedy's murder. We filed into a glass-enclosed porch with a fine view far out across the sparkling Atlantic. In a few moments, Nixon entered, slipped into an armchair, and propped his foot against a coffee table. Seated around him on long couches were nine staff men — Ellsworth, Sears, Garment, Shakespeare, Anderson, Buchanan, Price, Greenspan, and myself — and two volunteers from the citizens' committee: Nixon's younger brother Ed and Charles Rhyne, Nixon's classmate at Duke Law School and the former president of the American Bar Association. (Rhyne, I noted, was the only man present who had worked in the 1960 campaign.) In the background, straddling a chair behind Nixon, sat a swarthy, smiling man who was not introduced and said not a word the entire afternoon. He was Charles "Bebe" Rebozo, Nixon's friend and constant companion, who was staying with him in the bungalow this weekend.

Nixon opened the meeting by firmly laying down a ground rule: he wished to hear no discussion of possible running mates. Then he analyzed the situation as he saw it. Since the King funeral, the Wallace vote among *Republicans* had gone from 2 percent to 8 percent. In 1960, Nixon had received 96 percent of the Republican vote, and he would need to do equally well this time. Two out of three of the Wallace votes, he believed, were protest votes, which might be drawn away. He dismissed the idea that there were "great numbers of people sitting around, trying to decide how they'll vote." The vast majority of the voters polarized around their parties. He set Humphrey's "bedrock" strength at 40 percent, his own at 35 percent. "This game will be won or lost," he said, "by the sixteen percent Wallace vote and the six to eight percent vote of the true independents."

We should have no illusions, Nixon declared, about where the votes were. Ten percent of the Wallace vote was in the big-city states — "that's the swing vote." The election probably would be decided in California, he said, and the shift of the Wallace support late in the campaign would tip the state. He was convinced that the Wallace vote would shrink as the election drew near, "perhaps to twelve to fourteen percent even if we do nothing" — a forecast that proved exactly on the mark.

To bid for those votes, Nixon said he could not merely "echo" Wallace — he would have to be "more sophisticated." In the primaries, the campaign had emphasized personality. "Do we go for issues now?" One effect would be prompt attacks from "the Eastern

Establishment press." Should he take the risk of seeming "simplistic" in the eyes of the liberal media in order to reach the Wallace sympathizers? (Nixon seemed to be backing away from — or had he forgotten? — his approval of Anderson's points.)

Nixon went around the semicircle and each of us spoke for a few minutes, repeating again what we had told him and each other in memos and conversations. After that, we argued, as we had before, the question of how to attract the Wallace voter. Unlike the intellectual who wanted to know what Nixon thought, the lower-middle-class suburbanite wanted to know how Nixon *felt* about what the voter saw as *moral* issues. I was troubled by Nixon's choice of the word "simplistic," as though he imagined that he could talk down to ordinary people and be believed. If he didn't meet them at eye level and tell them the truth simply and directly, they would see through him.

As the meeting broke up, the choice between "issues" and "personality" had been aired rather than made. (Evidently Nixon's decision was *not* to decide, to coast a while longer.) Someone referred to the approaching end of the long trail from New Hampshire to Miami. "I knew it was all over after Wisconsin — you couldn't be denied the nomination after that," said Nixon. After a pause, he added with a smile: "But I didn't tell any of *you*."

Late that afternoon, the Convair landed at New York and refueled for the flight to Washington. Those of us going on with Nixon stretched our legs on the ramp and made small talk while we waited. From behind the low wire fence, a middle-aged couple waved at the celebrity. Nixon slowly walked over, shook hands, and then took up a position at a distance from the rest of the group — alone, unapproachable, and content. I remembered his words at the end of the Montauk meeting: ". . . *I didn't tell any of you.*" Anyone who imagined he knew the thoughts of this strange, solitary man deceived himself. A colleague later compounded the mystery, saying, "Don't believe a word of what he said about Wisconsin being the clincher. That was just Nixon boosting his ego at our expense."

5.   On Thursday, July 25, Haldeman called from California and informed me that Nixon would arrive in Washington the following day for a meeting with the President. "This trip must be kept *absolutely* secret," he said. I found his concern somewhat surprising. Didn't Haldeman know that Johnson, as part of his nonpolitical posture, was scheduling briefings on the war and the Paris talks with each of the candidates? Or was something going on that I didn't know about? In any event, I assured Haldeman that the statement on Vietnam would be ready, and he told me to meet the group at the Madison Hotel.

For three weeks I had been interviewing experts on Asia, civilian strategists, recently resigned Pentagon analysts, and Republican politicians. From this miscellany of sources a consensus emerged: it was time for the U.S. to begin extricating itself from Vietnam and time to declare the goal of eventual withdrawal to the American people.

Many of those who answered my questions asked about Nixon's position. What had he intended to say in the March 31 speech? And what would he say to the convention? I was vague in my replies, for the mood of the country had changed a great deal since the spring, more than Nixon's thinking had changed. He had both protected and immobilized himself with his moratorium. His statement to the platform committee had to take account of shifting public opinion and, if possible, begin to lead it.

I knew better than to suppose Nixon would step out of character and suddenly choose daring over caution. But I had an opportunity to influence his choice by presenting him with a venturesome position. If he rejected it out of hand, somebody would have to devise an alternative. More likely, in keeping with his character, he would try to inject caution into the statement, which might change details but would leave the basic position intact. In drafting and re-drafting the paper, I realized that I was no longer writing to satisfy Nixon's political requirements. I was writing to satisfy myself. On Friday afternoon, in the cab on the way to the hotel, I was still sharpening the attack on Johnson, the opponent whom Nixon had so carefully avoided.

The other staff members were at work in rooms on the fourth floor. Nixon came in, asked for the Vietnam statement, flipped through it, and handed it back to me. Obviously he was impatient to leave for the White House but unwilling simply to walk through the room. He stood and talked for a few moments, making the gesture of asking us what questions he should raise with Johnson — as though he had not been planning the conversation for several days. "Ask him about the bombing," I said — "and when he's going to stop it." Nixon, moving toward the door, half turned and smiled. I went downstairs to the manager's office and used that all-important instrument of modern politics, the Xerox machine. I wanted my colleagues to read and agree on the paper before Nixon returned.

These were the most important sections of the statement:

. . . I would rather not be nominated and elected than owe the Presidency to false promises. The wreckage of broken promises now forms a deadly barrier of distrust between the American people and the present administration. Only the power of truth can pull down this wall and reunite our nation . . .

The truth, as I see it, is that the present administration has tragically wasted the lives of our fighting men, the resources of the nation, and the all-important will of the American people by making an open-ended commitment to fight the *wrong* kind of war in the *wrong* way . . . The whole indictment of the present administration's misconduct of the war can be summed up, it seems to me, in a single, deeply tragic sentence: it has failed so disastrously that many Americans, rather than suffer more of the same, are prepared to embrace more or less disguised defeat . . .

The tragedy of the Vietnam war has been permitted to go too far for any honest man to promise a swift and painless "plan" for ending the war. Such schemes, when set forth in detail, invariably fail the test of reality and responsibility. I shall set forth at this time only tentative guidelines of my approach . . . subject to revision as the result of the fundamental reappraisal of the war which my administration will conduct immediately after taking office. We shall accept nothing on faith, reputation or statistics. We shall approach the war with a fresh eye and act with a free hand.

The first guideline: America's overriding objectives in Vietnam are political, not military, and these cannot be obtained by reliance on military power, even on a massive scale . . .

The second: America cannot successfully wage a new and unconventional war with an official attitude of "business-as-usual" . . .

(Several paragraphs followed describing how the sleepwalking civilian and military bureaucracies had turned war-making into a futile routine. Material drawn from the March 31 text proposed a shift in military tactics away from large-unit sweeps and toward small-unit police operations to protect the civilian population, all of which would permit "a steady transfer of responsibility from American to South Vietnamese forces." Whether or not such tactics would actually succeed, I made the new American objective explicit.)

The final guiding principle, which is most important of all: The next administration will reverse the fundamental error of the present one and reduce the military and political involvement of Americans in the war. I declare this aim of "de-Americanizing" the war without reservation or qualification, for it is basic to the search for peace.

It is a cruel irony that the American effort to safeguard the independence of South Vietnam has produced ever-increasing dependency in our ally. The present administration has too often treated the status quo in Saigon as though it were sacred . . . Anything less than a total and unstinting commitment on the part of the South Vietnamese, extending not only to military operations but also to overdue political and economic reforms, will be regarded as a legitimate basis for reappraising America's own heavy commitment . . . Our South Vietnamese ally must be strong enough to assume a place at the peace table and to survive the uncertain conditions of the eventual settlement . . .

(If we sincerely believed that the war could be ended only through negotiation, we were under an obligation, it seemed to me, to say something about the shape of a future political settlement. Again I drew on the March 31 speech for passages suggesting Soviet and even Chinese Communist participation. "The conference table must be wide enough, and the issues placed on it broad enough, to accommodate as many as possible of the powers and interests involved." This provided a context for a sentence implying a considerable degree of flexibility.)

Our aim would be to offer generous terms of reconciliation to all those political groups and elements in South Vietnam which have renounced the use of force and are willing to abide by the freely expressed will of the people.

I have carefully avoided a promise of "victory" in Vietnam, for the ordeal inflicted on the nation by the present administration has drained that word of most of its meaning. My desire centers on achieving an outcome which not only leaves South Vietnam free to decide its fate, but also one which reunites our divided nation and restores to us all a sense of common purpose. For after the war in Vietnam ends, as end it shall in my term as President, America must continue.

Early that evening, we boarded the Convair at National Airport. The others had read the paper, and with few qualifications they accepted it. Whether they did so because they agreed with it, or because they thought it was what Nixon wanted, or because they had no alternatives to propose, the fact was that they endorsed the position. Ellsworth was especially enthusiastic about making a "strong" statement. The indictment of the Johnson administration would arouse Republicans for a fighting campaign, and the promise to get American troops out of Vietnam would intensify the divisions within the Democratic party.

Nixon came directly from the White House. As soon as he was seated near the front of the plane, the Convair took off and headed east in the dusk toward New York. Haldeman brought him a bowl of soup and crackers. As Nixon ate, he slowly read the statement, then reread it. The rest of us were seated side by side across the aisle facing him. Finally he turned and asked: "Well, what do all of you think of it?"

As the others, led by Ellsworth, spoke, I watched Nixon's expression. An overhead light shadowed his deep-set eyes. Was it my imagination or was he avoiding my gaze? His expression seemed hooded and wary. The talk was punctuated by long silences. Nixon appeared to be waiting for someone to speak against the position, but he heard only recommendations for minor changes. The scene was both sad and amusing: sad because Nixon said nothing about his own reaction or what had passed between him and Johnson, amusing because we who usually served as buffers, protecting him from press queries on Vietnam, now confronted him on the issue.

When my turn came to speak, I summarized the argument for challenging the administration. The American people knew they had been lied to. In this situation, the best politics was to tell the truth. Nixon listened impassively. *I might as well be talking to Humphrey*, I thought to myself. *Nixon looks just the way Humphrey must look when his people tell him to break with Johnson.*

By the time the plane arrived over New York, I saw that I had succeeded — so far. Nixon had not rejected the statement. Instead he told Price and me to "soften" the language and show him a new draft the following day. After the plane landed, a couple of those present, interpreting Nixon's instructions as approval, congratulated me. But Nixon had not yet bought the statement — he had merely bought time to think about it. Price and I went to headquarters and until after midnight our typewriters echoed down the dark, empty corridors.

The two of us worked closely as technicians, but without the intimacy of comradeship. Our bond was professionalism. Price was painfully shy, and he would blush beet red at his secretary's teasing banter. As the house liberal, he stood ready to debate at the drop of a declarative sentence, but he did so with determined dispassion. At the first sign that his emotions were engaged, he seemed to catch himself. Out would come his pipe and down would come the curtain of silence. For several months we had been rivals, although we carefully avoided noticing it. Now our rivalry for the status of number one writer was drawing to a close. Price would continue to satisfy Nixon's requirements without inner misgivings (so far as anyone could detect), but I could not.

Early Saturday afternoon, Price, Buchanan, and I went to the Nixon apartment and spent more than two hours going over the new draft. Nixon had decided to attempt to extend his moratorium in modified form: he said he would not discuss any question concerning Vietnam that might "undercut" the U.S. negotiators in Paris. And so long as the talks continued with some hope of progress, with the Johnson administration committed to "an honorable settlement," he would promise to refrain from "partisan interference." He contributed a clever, cold-blooded line to the redrafting: "The pursuit of peace is too important for politics-as-usual." Of course, though it sounded like a pledge of patriotic self-denial, that sentence actually sought the opposite. Nixon would be pleased to see the democratic process of debate and decision halted and the most urgent issue before the country shelved for the duration of the campaign.

Even with the moratorium semirestored, however, the statement retained its original thrust. Once again, Nixon wished to be persuaded into the text, and he sat listening to our arguments and counterarguments. His inclination toward slogans was evident. The U.S., I had written, was not being *outfought* in Vietnam but *outthought*, a formulation Nixon liked. But he disliked being concrete. I had written: "The B-52 is an extremely costly and irrelevant weapon against the Vietcong terrorist armed with a knife." This was, in part, a concession to Price's theories on counterinsurgency and in greater part a criticism of our dependence on brute military power in a political war. The U.S. had already dropped more bombs on South Vietnam than on all of Western Europe during the Second World War. Fully one third of the U.S. personnel in Vietnam, according to Pentagon informants, were engaged in moving, storing, and guarding vast quantities of munitions. All this firepower was destroying the country we were trying to defend, while the enemy hung on in the devastated jungle. Nixon had a narrow concern. Wouldn't the description of the B–52 be interpreted as a slap at the Air Force? The line was taken out.

At the end of the session, the language of the statement had been toned down and the challenge to the administration muted, but the central promise remained — to "de-Americanize" the war.

On Sunday afternoon, Price was summoned uptown while I stayed behind at headquarters with Buchanan, a sign that Nixon had heard as much as he cared to hear from my side. As the hot afternoon faded into evening, I decided to do the sensible thing and go home. I telephoned Rose Mary Woods and told her I would be catching the last shuttle to Washington. The most devoted of Nixon's servants sounded worried. Hadn't I been told to stand by? I hadn't been told anything, I said.

When I arrived home that night, a call came from Anderson in Miami Beach. He was full of good news: the final preconvention Gallup poll to be published in the next morning's Miami *Herald* showed that Nixon alone among Republicans could comfortably defeat Humphrey and McCarthy. The best that Rockefeller could manage after his multimillion-dollar advertising campaign was a tie with Humphrey and a slim margin over McCarthy. That seemed to remove the last shadow of doubt that Nixon would be nominated — and it also removed his incentive to do anything even slightly risky.

I expected the telephone to ring again, and within five minutes it did. Price, after repeating the news from Gallup, said that Nixon wanted to take another look at the Vietnam statement in the morning. The Boss wasn't sure about using the code word "de-Americanize."

I no longer cared about the words that had so little substance behind them. "I know you'll take care of it, Ray," I said. "I'll see you at the convention."

XI

1. At his apartment on Saturday, Nixon asked me to assist Ellsworth in working with the Nixon backers on the platform committee in Miami Beach. A week earlier, Mitchell had sent out a mimeographed form letter to the staff members assigned to the convention. It was stern on matters of punctuality, decorum, and diligence, and predictably concerned with money ("For practical financial reasons, you will not be permitted to charge meals in your room"). But the taskmaster's manner concealed a scoutmaster's solicitude. In the midst of the commands came a piece of sound advice: "Be prepared for warm weather outside and cold air conditioning inside."

Outside the Hilton, Nixon's convention headquarters, a hired man dressed in an Uncle Sam costume walked about on stilts. A hired brass band blared away, and a gaggle of Nixonettes, amateurs lured by the prospect of being noticed, pranced and cheered. The neatly dressed crowd at the entrance raised limp hurrahs, but mostly they gawked at the perspiring musicians, the stilt-walker, and the inevitable baby elephant.

Thereby hung a tale known to Nixon insiders. During the 1960 campaign, an elephant had relieved itself in front of the platform from which vice-presidential candidate Henry Cabot Lodge was to speak. The crowd, standing downwind, thinned quickly, leaving Lodge puzzled and upset. Then his patrician nostrils twitched, and he too fled. The episode prompted a contingency plan. Now the advance men in Nixon campaigns, following instructions in their manual, gave every prop-elephant a precautionary enema. I crossed this beast's path without mishap and entered the Hilton.

Mitchell was right: it was cold inside. The chill came from regimentation as well as refrigeration. With the sea on one side and an inlet on the other, Miami Beach was a natural fortress. Road access could be pinched off by closing a couple of causeways. Yet, as I received "credentials" — a plastic badge bearing my photograph and mysterious numbers and markings — I saw that the Hilton itself had been fortified against the intrusion of reality.

The corridors and stairways were patrolled by private guards from the Wackenhut Corporation in powder blue uniforms and snappy, Air Force–type hats. We at once dubbed them "the Wackenhut SS," which wasn't quite fair. Many of them were college students and all were unfailingly courteous. Indeed, they were a bit embarrassed to be jumping up and challenging us at every turn. (Soon, girls on the staff began fraternizing and passing soft drinks and sandwiches to the guards stationed on the sweltering stairwells, and our working environment became less "secure" but more human.)

The enormous Nixon staff had taken over three floors in the Hilton (the overflow was scattered among smaller hotels), and we were carefully sorted, filed, and labeled. My room was on the seventeenth floor, reserved for Nixon's personal staff, and a large sign over the door bore my name. (This proved to be a great convenience in the early-morning hours as we returned, unsorted and unfiled, from the nightly round of un-Republican parties.) There were several telephones in the room, variously connected to the hotel switchboard, the "secure" Nixon switchboard in the eighteenth floor solarium, the research-and-writing command post, and others on the Nixon staff. The only difficulty was that the telephones all rang in the same tone. Answering became a zestful shell-and-pea gamble. Would I find the ringing instrument before the caller gave up? In the corner lay a large brown paper bag, which I took to be a laundry bag. I was about to stuff my wilted shirt in it when Anderson stopped me. "No," he said, "that's the 'Burn' bag."

Each day, a Wackenhut guard accompanied the maid on her
rounds and took away our discarded secrets to a tight-security in-
cinerator. Rather than disappoint the guard, I stuffed discarded
newspapers into the bag each day and sealed it.

Nixon had gone into seclusion in Montauk, there to walk the
beach, inhale the salt air he loved, and compose his acceptance
speech. Each of the writers had been asked to contribute material
toward the speech, but Nixon intended to assemble it unassisted.
(When reporters asked what the candidate was doing, Buchanan
said that the Boss was fine. "He called this morning, said 'Send
over more yellow pads,' and hung up.") At the Miami Beach end
of the operation, Mitchell had matters well in hand. When Nixon
called him one morning to ask if there was anything he should
know, Mitchell answered without hesitation, "No."

The design of the organizational machinery called for a politician and an issues man to collaborate in presenting Nixon's views to
our allies within the platform committee. Each day Ellsworth and I
received a statement on an issue — Vietnam was the first — by
Telex from New York. Together, we showed it to the pro-Nixon
caucus that met in Senator John Tower's suite. Discussion was not
forbidden, but neither was it encouraged. With considerable skill,
Ellsworth guided the assembled hands, all proud officeholders, in
grasping the rubber stamp and applying it. At one session, Alaska's
governor Walter Hickel asked sensibly why the group should bother
reading the statements at all when they were bound to approve
them. Tower, though he changed scarcely a word, insisted on don-
ning his half-moon glasses, asserting his senatorial prerogative, and
reading each statement aloud while the others sipped drinks and
whispered like schoolboys. In the final version of the Vietnam
statement, some of the original language survived, but Nixon now
called for "phasing out" American troops. Ironically, the platform
committee proved bolder and opted to call for "de-Americanizing"
the war. Even in its watered-down form, the Nixon statement delighted the very dovish Tom Wicker, whose column in the *New York
Times* on August 6 praised the Nixon campaign as "masterful . . .

imaginative, forceful, and flexible," an extraordinary mouthful for a man whose heart belonged to McCarthy. This was the only published case of sunstroke at the convention. Within a couple of days Wicker, fully recovered, was blasting away at "the same old Nixon."

The Nixon machinery's efficiency was achieved at some human cost. Ellsworth laid down the law to me as it had obviously been laid down to him: We could not change so much as a comma in the statements we received. At that point Nixon's statement on the economy arrived. Buchanan, in rewriting my long paper, produced a version that Greenspan pronounced factually wrong. To issue the statement as written would make Nixon look foolish. Assuming that the machinery would tolerate minor disobedience rather than stupidity, I began penciling in changes. Ellsworth turned pale.

"I told you not to touch a word," he said.

Why should he and I be afraid to use common sense in this situation? I ignored him and continued to write. Jeannette Lerner, Ellsworth's devotedly loyal secretary, put her hand to her mouth, as though sure we were about to come to blows. Greenspan edged away. Anderson stood silently near the door. Ellsworth repeated his command, demanding: "Didn't you hear what I told you?"

"Yes, Bob," I said, "and you shouldn't have told me that."

I finished revising the statement and gave it to Greenspan, who approved it. Ellsworth stared at us for a long moment, then broke into a smile.

"Goddamit, Dick, all right. But I hope you didn't change it *too much*."

This confrontation, at once real and ludicrous, troubled me afterward. The conflict was not personal — Ellsworth and I shook hands at the door. The conflict was between the campaign we had waged together and the campaign in which we were separate moving parts. What made the scene ridiculous was the fact that the words meant essentially nothing. Nothing stood behind them and nothing would come of them. We had allowed ourselves to be reduced to automatons in a cause completely without substance.

The next day, Anderson closely inspected my badge and informed me that I had been demoted. "You're not allowed to go on the eighteenth floor" — where Nixon would be staying. More clearly than I, Anderson understood the importance of rank and place as we were herded into the mold of Organization. "You'd better get that fixed," he said. "There are guys from the law firm running around here with four stars who've never spent a minute with Nixon. Go see John Ehrlichman."

Ehrlichman, whose name was unknown to me, was in charge of convention arrangements and would be the campaign tour director. (Later I learned that he was Haldeman's UCLA roommate and close friend, and like him a risen advance man. The advance men were the technicians controlling the organizational machinery and formed the close-knit elite corps of the campaign.) Ehrlichman was a stocky, balding fellow in his forties with a brusque manner and an annoying smirk. I stated my business; he said he would check into it and asked me to return the next day.

When I returned the next morning, Ehrlichman told me that there had been no mistake. He had gone to the trouble of calling Haldeman in Montauk, and my credentials were in order. If I was needed on the eighteenth floor, he said, I would be sent for and issued a pass. He returned to his paperwork, indicating that the interview was over.

When I did not leave, Ehrlichman looked up. "Just who the hell are you?" I asked. "I've never laid eyes on you or heard your name mentioned. And I'll be damned if I'm going to take orders from you." "Look," he said, his own temper rising, "I've been with Nixon a long time, and I've seen writer and researcher types like you come and go. You'll go where *I* say you go." "Fuck you," I said, walking out.

The wounding reference to "writer and researcher types" hurt precisely because I knew it was true. The issues men who had put their brains and pens at Nixon's disposal in former years had indeed come and gone without a trace. I decided to stand my ground.

I had addressed Ehrlichman as though he were the architect of the grim mini–police state fastened on the Nixon staff. As my anger faded, I realized that he, like the rest of us, was only a functionary, a part in the machinery designed to serve and protect Nixon. If he and I faced each other as hostile strangers, rather than allies, it was because Nixon put people into slots, as separate individuals, and did not wish to concern himself with coordinating and connecting them — or even introducing them.

Nixon followed a survival-of-the-fittest personnel-relations policy. He did not much care what his subordinates did to each other as long as he was spared the sight of blood. Indeed, he went to some lengths to insulate himself. When Haldeman came aboard unannounced as the candidate's personal chief of staff in the spring, I had asked Nixon pointblank if I should now report to him. No, Nixon said, you, Price, and Buchanan will continue to report to me. "Just call me on the telephone." As a practical matter, we reported both to Haldeman and Nixon, depending on our assignments. Why, I wondered, did Nixon recoil from giving direct orders to implement the organizational structure he desired?

In another example of his aversion to personally setting his people straight, Nixon had recruited James Keogh, a sympathetic biographer and my former colleague on *Time* magazine, to take over as head of the research and writing staff after the convention. Keogh was a seasoned professional and a senior Nixon loyalist entitled to such recognition, but instead of informing us of Keogh's arrival and endorsing his authority, Nixon let the word trickle out, which was unfair and confusing to everyone. His evident wish not to be personally involved suggested the strategy I should follow.

I reported my exchange with Ehrlichman to Ellsworth and Garment, implying that I would take the matter up directly with Nixon the following day. They assured me that Ehrlichman must have misunderstood Haldeman — I was sure that he hadn't — and they offered to intercede "upstairs," presumably with Mitchell. Within an hour, the word came down: my credentials were to be changed, admitting me to the holy of holies on the eighteenth floor. As a bonus, I was told to pick up the insignia the Secret Service issued to members of the traveling staff so that they would be recognized in crowds.

With Nixon's nomination certain, only the details of the ritual remained. In an apparent gesture to the moderates, Nixon had chosen Maryland's governor Spiro T. Agnew for the highly visible honor of nominating him. (The gesture backfired among Rockefeller supporters, who regarded Agnew as an opportunist and renegade.) Once the platform had been completed, I was assigned to oversee the preparation of the nominating speech.

Three members of the governor's staff turned up with a draft of his remarks written in longhand on lined yellow legal paper. Agnew's chief speech-writer, Cynthia Rosenwald, was a pert blond Baltimore housewife. She realized that the draft needed more work, she said, and went off to revise it. The new draft she produced, unhappily, was not much improved.

That day, Nixon arrived in Miami Beach and asked through Haldeman how the nominating speech was coming along. That query prompted me to write a draft, which Cynthia returned full of praise and regrets. It was a fine speech, she explained, but the governor wasn't comfortable with it — "it has too many long sentences." I enlisted Price's assistance, and he quickly wrote a draft. Cynthia returned bearing the same apologetic message. It wasn't quite Agnew's style, and he was worried about muffing his big moment on network television. Time was running out. We could, if necessary, impose a text on Agnew, but that would only cause bad feeling and guarantee a poor performance.

Buchanan came to the rescue. "Let me have those papers," he said, scooping up the drafts and disappearing into his room. For an hour, his typewriter rattled like a machine gun and the prose came out in short, simple bursts. This draft, sped to the governor, came back approved. Confident that we would shortly see and hear the last of Agnew, we turned to the only source of excitement at this cut-and-dried convention, Nixon's choice of his running mate.

2.   Weeks earlier, letters had gone out over Nixon's signature to hundreds of party officials asking their advice on the vice presidency. Everyone who remotely mattered thus was given the satisfying but misleading impression that he was in on the decision. Similar ego-inflating techniques were used by Nixon in face-to-face meetings at Miami Beach. The advice from the professionals counted for little (their letters stacked up unread at headquarters). The polls counted heavily, but these showed an oddity peculiar to Nixon's centrism: he ran less well with *any* running mate, liberal or conservative, than he did by himself. His ideal Veep should be an invisible man.

Even before Nixon went to Montauk to meditate, we knew that he had ruled out such "glamour boys" as Reagan and Lindsay. Assurances were given to the Southerners that Nixon would not pick a "divisive" figure. Important as the Southern votes were, there was another, deeper reason. The glamorous candidates were too tall to pass through the doorway that fit Nixon comfortably. He would have to be followed by a man indisputably shorter and unfailingly grateful for the honor of being chosen. The veto power imputed to Goldwater and Thurmond was readily ceded by Nixon because their supposed pressures "pushed" him toward the inoffensive choice he wanted to make anyway. High on Nixon's mental list, we learned, was Massachusetts' governor John Volpe. An Italian Catholic with appeal rarely found in a Republican among urban ethnic groups, he was also a Northeasterner whom Southern and Western conservatives found acceptable. When we were introduced at a meeting, Volpe gripped my hand as though I were a voter. He knew he was in the running.

A milling, gossiping convention crowd, its members incessantly asking each other *What do you hear?*, has an infinite capacity for make-believe. Men see mirages and convince others that thin air has weight. Sheer boredom inspires fantasizing. It was easy for a half dozen of us to conceive the notion that Nixon hadn't made up his mind about the Veep and that he might yet be persuaded to

choose a moderate and dove. We convinced ourselves that the man
of the hour ought to be Oregon's senator Mark Hatfield.

For a day and a half, we busied ourselves with a Hatfield boom-
let. We used the elaborate (and mostly idle) communications facili-
ties linking Miami Beach, New York, and Washington to assemble
a supporting dossier. It included the texts of his 1960 speech nominating Nixon and his 1964 convention keynote address, his statements as a party loyalist in the Goldwater episode, and an analysis
of his early and restrained criticism of America's involvement in
Southeast Asia. He was, all things considered, an unusually attractive and articulate regular Republican. With Anderson, I wrote a
memo to Nixon, which others on the staff signed, urging Hatfield as
a symbolic choice: his presence on the ticket would indicate the future direction of Vietnam policy even as Nixon refrained from spelling it out in detail. Hatfield could campaign in areas where Nixon
was weakest — in the Northeast, in urban areas, among the young
and the liberals — and also hold the safe, secondary areas while
Nixon concentrated as planned on the decisive "battleground"
states. We discovered that Hatfield, a prominent Protestant layman, had an important friend in the Reverend Billy Graham, and
the material we prepared formed the background for the evange-
list's plea to Nixon on Hatfield's behalf. The Hatfield gambit
looked plausible on paper. Mitchell, who read our document, saw
in it confirmation of his suspicions — the research and writing staff
harbored a nest of covert liberals.

Hatfield, as a declared dove and Nixon supporter, was among
those chosen to second Nixon's nomination. He submitted a text of
his speech in which he attempted to reconcile his position on the
war and his support of the party's certain nominee. To the nervous
Haldeman, the result looked dangerously like a dovish commitment
by proxy. At one point Hatfield insisted that his speech be compared with Nixon's platform statement on Vietnam and drew from
Ellsworth the admission that the two were in apparent agreement.
But the senator's cause was hopeless. Even if he had been willing to
toe whatever line the Nixon men drew, he faced the veto of the

Goldwater-Thurmond axis, which equated reasoned opposition to the war with antipatriotism. In the end, Hatfield's main deficiency was that he wouldn't fit through the doorway.

Although Nixon's nomination realized a universal human dream — the dream of a second chance — the balloting itself had as much drama as the working of an adding machine. A bit of bogus suspense grew out of the last-minute restlessness of the Southerners who hankered for Reagan, but they fell into line behind Nixon's Dixie champion, Thurmond. The hope of Rockefeller and Reagan supporters that Nixon would fall short of the 667 votes required on the first ballot, producing switches and a deadlock, proved to be forlorn. So ample was Nixon's cushion that his floor managers released some secretly committed delegates, being held in reserve, to vote as local pressures dictated.

Agnew spoke adequately, the seconders filed past in blurred procession, and the "spontaneous demonstrations" dragged on. It was after one o'clock in the morning when the roll call of the states began. My wife Joan had flown down to Miami Beach for the climactic moment, and she and I sat in a far corner of the hall with tally sheets and pencils. I envied her excitement as each state's vote was announced. The votes for Nixon's majority waited to be counted and the only question was whether victory would come sooner rather than later. The break came when the shakily led New Jersey delegation split, yielding ten more votes than expected for Nixon. Wisconsin, the next to the last state in the roll call, was bound to give Nixon the thirty votes he had won in the April primary. The crowd held its breath as Governor Warren P. Knowles took the microphone. After drawing out the inevitable, he declared the winner. The crowd cheered, the band played, and balloons cascaded from the ceiling. Richard Milhous Nixon, the man given up for dead politically, once again was the Republican party's nominee for President of the United States.

Joan and I pushed through the crowd and returned to the Hilton after 2 A.M. Victory parties were in progress, but the late hour and long anticipation made for rather subdued celebration. As we came out of Anderson's room, Garment hurried past. He was on his way to Nixon's suite and a meeting on the vice presidency and told me to come along. I had no desire to go. Hatfield was definitely out, Volpe seemed definitely in. (The meeting lasted only forty-five minutes and ended, predictably, with nothing decided.) Meanwhile, Joan and I went to our room, ordered a fine supper with champagne, and hung out a "Do Not Disturb" sign. On the eighteenth floor, through what remained of the night, the kingmakers came and went.

Just before one o'clock the next afternoon, Buchanan and I met at the door of the ballroom where Nixon was to announce his choice of a running mate. He winked and said, "We have a Pope." Before he could whisper the name, Secret Service men stepped between us and ordered the aisles cleared. Thinking the Pope was probably the Bay State Italian, I took a seat next to novelist Allen Drury and Clark Mollenhoff of the Cowles papers in Des Moines. Nixon strode past, smiling and waving. He stood on the low stage at the front of the room, faced the hundreds of reporters and the television cameras, and spoke the incredible name — *Governor Agnew of Maryland.* Gasps of disbelief went up across the room. Drury, Mollenhoff, and I looked at each other. *Agnew?* Nixon left without answering questions, and Agnew, looking stunned, followed. He groped his way through a brief press conference, closing with the wish, soon to be fulfilled, that his would become "a household name." Afterward, as the audience rose unsteadily, shock still registering on many faces, Joan took my arm. Too upset to speak, we broke away from Mollenhoff and fled to the hotel's coffee shop.

Agnew was absurdly unqualified. As unknown to Republicans as to the country at large, he had only one apparent virtue: he stood at the point where opposing forces, in Nixon's view, spent themselves. That point of seeming safety was the "center." Yet this calculation based on negatives, on whom Agnew would *not* offend, was mistaken. Many conservatives, including the Southerners whom Nixon had thought to appease, were incensed at the mediocre choice. They correctly guessed the troubles awaiting them as they tried to convince the press and the public of Agnew's fitness for the office and, possibly, for the presidency.

Since the spring, Nixon had talked a few times with Agnew in New York, a courtship that seemed no more serious than his wooing of other disappointed Rockefeller supporters. Agnew, in due course, had endorsed Nixon, pointedly complimenting his decisiveness. Early in May, Nixon had dispatched Anderson and me to Annapolis to hear the views of the governor and his advisers on urban problems. At the last minute I was unable to make the trip and Anderson went alone. He came from the meeting shaking his head, alarmed by some of the talk he had heard. The men around Agnew were political innocents born yesterday who had just encountered the issues of race and class and civil order. With chilling sincerity, they trusted policy-making to their glands and instincts. They were men of the sort John Stuart Mill had in mind when he described the conservatives of his day as "the Stupid Party," decent but ignorant men full of a sense of their righteousness.

Following Martin Luther King's death, Baltimore had erupted in racial rioting, and Agnew, the former executive of suburban Baltimore County, had erupted in anger. Upset by their apparent retreat before black extremists, Agnew had assembled and tongue-lashed about a hundred Negro leaders, most of whom stalked out as he spoke. It was a sincere outburst on the part of a man who regarded himself as a racial moderate, but it was a disaster in terms of politics and policy, for the black moderates were put on the spot publicly and driven toward the extremists or into silence. Nevertheless, the episode made headlines and helped persuade Nixon that Agnew, whose commanding physical presence he admired, was a very tough and knowing fellow on the "gut" issue in this long hot summer of fear.

Nixon believed Agnew was a credible President-in-waiting and remarked: "This guy has it." But the wan, dejected expressions of the faithful reflected their contrary estimate. In the span of twelve hours between his nomination and the disclosure of his running mate, Nixon "peaked." The confidence and optimism he had produced in the party by his masterful stalking of the nomination were dissipated by his first act of judgment. Without ever going on the offensive as it expected, the party was now thrown on the defensive.

A worried-looking Garment spotted me. "Let's go see Mitchell," he said. In Mitchell's office-suite, Agnew sat on a sofa opposite Nixon's manager. As the governor sipped a cup of coffee, his hand trembled and the saucer shook. After talk about whether Agnew's teen-aged children should be rounded up and flown to the convention, Mitchell got down to cases. It had been decided that Maryland congressman Rogers Morton, Nixon's floor manager and one of those considered in the final round of the vice-presidential sweepstakes, would make the speech nominating Agnew. I had been summoned to assist Morton. The seconding speeches should represent the full spectrum of Republican views, said Mitchell, puffing his pipe, and it would be a good idea if John Lindsay were among the seconders. Casually, he suggested that Agnew place a call to "John." (At that moment, as Mitchell knew, would-be rebels against Agnew were trying to enlist the New York mayor as their standard-bearer. Caught between his desire to please the media and the prospect of certain defeat, Lindsay needed a way out, such as a call to party duty and regularity enabling him to fight again another day.) Agnew spoke with Lindsay and somewhat hesitantly asked him to second his nomination. Much to Agnew's surprise, Lindsay at once accepted the invitation. We might not owe Lindsay a favor, I thought, but we did owe him a certain respect for playing by the rules.

What could be said about "Ted" Agnew, as we were now enjoined to call him? After their first encounter with the press, Buchanan and Garment hastily wrote a memorandum, addressed to "RN et. al.," which had the flavor of a communiqué from the battlefront. The authors had determined that the best strategy was to put a brave, bold front on the awkward facts, and they outlined an aggressive rationale for choosing the governor. "Strength of character . . . Experience at the working levels of government . . . Extremely bright and able man — with the intellectual capacity to become President — the major consideration . . . A standup guy. The kind of man willing to take tremendous heat and pressure — which a Vice President in the next administration is certain to have to do." After we left Mitchell and Agnew, Garment supplemented this brief with a sales talk. I jotted notes: "A really tough, *heroic*, and nonexpedient decision on RN's part. Agnew is a man of the center — the man RN (*not* the bosses) wanted. This choice takes into account *all* sections and factions."

I was forced to admire the *chutzpah* of the argument, and I told Garment as much. But it wouldn't wash. A more heroic choice would have been Reagan or Hatfield, implying a commitment, I said, rather than a man nobody knew, whose selection implied nothing. Garment, the chief litigator of the Nixon law firm, was interested in making the case. I had been asked to provide technical assistance, not an unwanted reminder of the facts.

When I called on Rogers Morton, he said that he would draft his own speech, which gave me a short-lived sense of relief. Then I saw that the amiable Morton, clad in shirt-sleeves, intended to dictate his text while greeting a stream of guests, taking calls, and commiserating over freely flowing bourbon with his brother, former senator and party chairman Thruston "Thrus" Morton, a Rockefeller supporter. It looked like a convivial but unproductive afternoon, and I excused myself to prepare a fail-safe draft. There was nothing to say about Agnew, and so I entertained myself by writing a parody of the traditional nominating speech, including every cliché that occurred to me. When I returned to Rogers Morton's room about six o'clock, my hunch was confirmed. He had dictated only a single paragraph, extolling Maryland's beauty and diversity.

The small element of seriousness in the situation — a man was to be nominated for the vice presidency of the United States — now dissolved, leaving a Marx Brothers farce. Morton, apologizing for his oversight, accepted my text without reading it. Like most politicians, he refused to wear glasses in front of a television camera. The speech would have to be typed on a large-print typewriter and, if possible, put on the teleprompter at the convention hall as well.

But the only such typewriter in the Hilton, I discovered, was being used by Rose Mary Woods to prepare Nixon's acceptance speech. While I was tracking down and unsuccessfully negotiating for that machine, word came that the evening convention program had been moved up an hour, to attract more of the prime-time viewing audience.

Sensing an imminent emergency, "Thrus" Morton straightened his tie and hurried off to the convention. Within a few minutes, the television set in Rogers Morton's suite showed the face of convention chairman Gerry Ford, gravely intoning the chair's recognition of the gentleman from Maryland, whom the chairman said was advancing to the podium for the purpose of making a nominating speech. But the gentleman from Maryland was still standing in his shirt-sleeves, his speech untyped. While Rogers frantically demanded a copy of his remarks, his brother appeared at the podium and on the screen and proceeded to kill some prime time telling family jokes. Meanwhile, back at the Hilton, Rogers Morton threw on his coat, took my ill-typed manuscript, and vanished into an elevator. A police car, siren wailing, sped him to the convention site. I watched the remainder of the televised brother act. Thrus smoothly introduced Rogers. He, in turn, without glasses or noticeable squinting from his six-foot-six height, managed to read the speech nominating the man already becoming known in American households as Spiro *Who?* Soon afterward, in his acceptance speech, Agnew struck just the right note: "I stand here with a deep sense of the improbability of this moment."

Then came the evening's highlight — Nixon's acceptance speech. The product of more than two weeks of solitary labor, held secret even from his writers, this was for Nixon the most important address of the campaign. These would be Nixon's words, expressing his personal thoughts and emotions. He had the opportunity to declare himself, his ideals, and his vision of America before a nationwide audience.

The speech proved to be, line after line, the same one Nixon had given in the primary campaigns. I recognized Price's words, Bu-

chanan's, and my own — "the forgotten American" was praised at
length. All the tried-and-proved "cheer lines" were there — the
Pueblo, the Supreme Court, the pledge to appoint a new Attorney
General. (In this strangely derivative speech, some of the borrowings were credited to the wrong accounts. Reporters who
thought they detected echoes of Martin Luther King's "I Have a
Dream" speech were mistaken. This passage of Nixon's text came
from material contributed by a young conservative writer named
William Gavin.)

The only part of the speech that bore Nixon's unmistakably personal stamp came toward the end. He spoke of a child who "hears
the train go by," dreaming a seemingly impossible dream, who
overcame adversity and at last succeeded in "his chosen profession
of politics." Tonight, Nixon declaimed, "he stands before you nominated for President of the United States. You can see why I believe
so deeply in the American Dream."

XII

1. FROM MIAMI, the Republican nominees, their entourages, and the press flew to Southern California and a resort called Mission Bay near San Diego. There was a brief stop in San Antonio while Nixon and Agnew went by helicopter to the LBJ Ranch and received a presidential briefing on foreign policy developments. At the San Diego airport, the band, balloons, and crowd waited to greet the victorious favorite son. The chief greeter, Dr. Gaylord Parkinson, showed no sign that he recalled being purged by Nixon less than a year earlier. After telling the crowd how wonderful it felt to be coming home, Nixon led a motorcade to the Mission Bay Inn, still a transient on his native ground.

The announced purpose of Nixon's weeklong stay in California was to plan the forthcoming campaign. In fact, the operational plans were well advanced. The actual purpose was to yield the spotlight to the Democrats and the inevitable civil war at their approaching convention in Chicago. In contrast, Nixon intended to project an image of calm, order, and unity as Republicans of every ideological stripe came to pay him homage.

Within a day of our arrival, it was evident that the organizers, led by Haldeman and Ehrlichman, were firmly in the saddle. When the research and writing staff met with Haldeman, I reminded him of our mid-July request for security clearances so that we could receive classified briefings from the White House, the Pentagon, and the State Department. By sharing the same fund of information as Nixon, we could better serve him. Haldeman had agreed, writing: "We will make sure to initiate formal clearance procedures immediately after the convention." Now, however, he withdrew that promise. As a member of the California Board of Regents, he said, *he* had security clearances and that would be quite sufficient.

Next I asked when the writers would meet with Nixon. Most of us had not seen him privately for two weeks. (The extent of my communication had been Nixon's hurried remark at a victory party: "Did you see that I used some of your lines in the acceptance speech?" I said that I had, trying to look pleased.) Now it seemed necessary that he meet with us to discuss and assign the major speeches he would be making during the next ten weeks. "Put the request in writing," said Haldeman. Meeting adjourned.

A single night on the premises drove Nixon to seek refuge in a borrowed home nearby. On that first morning, he threw open the curtains of his picture window overlooking the bay and found himself staring at a clump of tourists pointing fingers and cameras in his direction. The curtains were quickly drawn shut. Later, Chapin went downstairs, checked to see that the coast was clear, and wigwagged to Nixon, who cautiously opened the curtains halfway. That afternoon, he left.

With the meetings of the schedulers, arrangers, and organizers closed to the writers, we were left to occupy ourselves as we deemed best. I decided that our first priority should be getting to know more about Spiro T. Agnew, and I invited the governor's staff for a chat. The results were depressing. In recounting the events leading up to Agnew's tongue-lashing of the Negro leaders in Baltimore, the staff men disagreed to the point of shouting each other down. If these were to be the vice-presidential candidate's escorts and advisers on the tour, disaster was certain. (In the end, Sears would be assigned to ride shotgun on the Agnew Special through Election Day.)

The kind of planning being done at Mission Bay indicated beyond a doubt that the campaign would continue to duck the issues and would rely on merchandising the "new" Nixon. One morning, Garment, Robert Finch, and I sat for the better part of two hours contemplating a pair of advertising layouts. The headline on one paste-up read: THIS TIME, VOTE AS IF YOUR WHOLE WORLD DEPENDS ON IT. On the other, ad-English was used: THIS TIME, VOTE LIKE . . . The weighty subject of our debate was whether Nixon should be sold like a cigaret. I objected to the use of the transparently slick "like," but Garment had the advertising agency's market research, showing that a majority of those polled preferred "like" — they thought "as if" sounded wishy-washy. Finch had the last word. No matter how you said it, the message was true: "With Agnew on the ticket, this time your whole world damned well *does* depend on Nixon."

(I had planned to drive up to Los Angeles that evening and have dinner with a friend, the novelist Joan Didion Dunne, but Mitchell, playing the stern headmaster, had decreed a curfew. When I spoke to Joan on the telephone and reported on my day's work, she remarked in her tiny but stiletto-edged voice: "Oh, is *that* what you're doing with Nixon? Well, I'm glad you stood up for what was *right*.")

I was ashamed of what I was doing. I was ashamed of being in the company of mediocre merchandisers behind a façade concealing a sad mixture of cynicism, apprehension, suspicion, and fear — especially fear. Fear of the next man higher up, fear of being found out by the encircling press. Ambition kept worried and discouraged staff members in line. However, my world did not depend on going to the White House with Nixon. The absence of a desire for a job, a title, and a mite of personal power freed me to leave the winner's cheerless camp.

Over dinner later that evening, several of us talked about two worrisome meetings scheduled for later in the week. Purely image-making productions, they presented hazards the organizers ignored. One meeting would assemble Republican mayors, whom the press would observe "advising" the candidate on urban problems. The cast of Republican mayors was rather small, and so it had been

padded by inviting such luminaries as the former mayor of Pom-
pano Beach. Conspicuously *not* invited was New York City's mayor
John Lindsay, whose exclusion would surely backfire in the press.
The other meeting was potentially even more damaging. It would
parade before the press Nixon's "national security advisory panel,"
a letterhead outfit made up of retired senior military men. The
thought of Admiral Arthur Radford briefing reporters on Nixon's
Vietnam policy, as he understood it, was disquieting, to say the
least. (Admiral Arleigh Burke, sensitive to the dangers of the mission, called from Washington and asked, "Why does Nixon want
the old poops' squad out there?")

The man with all the answers, Mitchell, had dined that evening
at another table in the Mission Bay.Inn, and he now came over to
greet us. His manner was deceptively hearty, and I ventured to
raise the subject of our conversation. Wouldn't it be a good idea to
invite Lindsay? And wouldn't it be safer to put the retired brass on
display another time? Mitchell's smile vanished and his face
clouded. "You goddamned liberals are always worried about Lindsay," he said with surprising vehemence, his speech a bit thick.
Why, he and the state party people were going to carry New York
for Nixon without Lindsay. As for the generals and admirals, perhaps, said Mitchell with heavy sarcasm, you think they should be
coming out here to see *you.*

Other diners, including some reporters, pricked up their ears at
the sound of Mitchell's voice. But he went ahead beating down
what he evidently regarded as insubordination. Finally, he broke
off and lumbered away. (I was soon proved at least half right — the
meeting with the retired military was canceled.)

Afterward, I recalled what Nixon had said in our first conversation about the kind of staff he wanted and his subsequent praise of
his young men for their independence. "You can't go with just
good people," he continued to tell reporters. "You have to go with
the best, really first-raters." The treatment we had received since
the convention was more indicative than Nixon's words. We were

under the heel of men basically unsure of themselves, second-raters playing over their heads and fiercely resentful of anyone who dared approach them at eye level. Nixon's own insecurity caused him to need the protection of men willing to do whatever he wished. In return they wielded unmeasured influence. By controlling the environment in which he moved, screening every person, paper, and choice presented to him, they exercised power beyond argument or appeal. If I remained, I would no longer work for Nixon, but for these men whom I did not respect. Yet they were only incidental foes. The true conflict was between my desire to serve and Nixon's inability to accept service on terms that were not humiliating to the servant.

At breakfast the next morning, after Garment had shared the latest Agnew joke, I told him that I had decided to resign and go home. Thoughts of resignation were part of the cloud of gloom hanging over the Nixon staff, and he showed no surprise. After our session with the advertising layouts the previous day, I had protested that we were wasting our time — let the ad men do the job. "At least it's work," Garment had replied, tacitly admitting that it was all the work there was to be done. The issues men were now superfluous. "The trouble with you, Dick, is that you care too much," said Garment as we shook hands. "You're really a Jew."

I wrote two letters of resignation, addressed to Nixon and Mitchell, and left them with Rose Mary Woods's assistant, Shelley Scarney. Anderson was waiting to drive me to the airport. Like a pair of daylight burglars, we stealthily emerged from the side door of the motel, each carrying a suitcase, and made our way across the parking lot. Mitchell had given orders that no one could leave without written permission, and we wondered whether the Secret Service men lounging in the shade would enforce the headmaster's edict. They nodded as we passed.

"Hey, where are you guys going?"

It was Haldeman, calling from the third-floor balcony.

"Don't worry, Bob," I called back. "I'll write."

2.   Within hours of my departure, Haldeman summoned the writers and researchers to a meeting with Nixon, as though their usefulness had been rediscovered. The aim of the session, of course, was to smoke out other would-be defectors. Finding none, Haldeman ushered the writers back into limbo. For the rest of the campaign, they rarely, if ever, saw Nixon alone. Haldeman was totally in charge, as his handling of my letter of resignation showed. Although the envelope was addressed to Nixon and marked "personal," Haldeman opened it and intercepted the letter. He did not pass it on to Nixon, but read him the "gist," a display of high-handedness my friends found shocking. What they failed to realize was that Nixon did not wish to read my letter. Haldeman was there to shield him and to spare him difficult personal encounters.

Misled by the meeting with Nixon, several of my colleagues called during the next couple of days, urging me to return. "We've won," said one of them. "No, you haven't won," I said. How could anyone bargain with the candidate to run a campaign other than the one he wanted to run? By chance, I threw a scare into the high command, for I picked up the telephone at home and Bob Novak, who was making a social call to a campaign widow, showed his keen reporter's instinct. "What the hell are you doing there, Dick?" he asked. I explained that my daughter was ill and that I had taken a furlough from the campaign. Novak laughed. The next day, the Evans-Novak column bore the headline: NIXON WHIZ KID WALKS OUT.

That shook up the sun-bathers at Mission Bay, including the reporters who had been filing accounts of the placid comings and goings of Republican politicians. The press had a vested interest in the young men around Nixon, having built up our supposed importance, and they reacted in alarm to the outbreak of dissension literally under their noses. Semple of the *Times*, among others, used every ploy to find out why I had left, but I had no desire to harass Nixon through the newspapers. "What does this man really stand for?" I asked when Semple called and let it go at that.

I had written to Nixon — had Haldeman read that part? — that I joined him to serve a cause, and that I would continue to serve it. I hoped, not for revenge but for some unlikely indication that Nixon sought the presidency for principled purpose. When Otto Friedrich asked to publish my campaign diary in *The Saturday Evening Post*, I declined. And when Max Kampelman, Hubert Humphrey's friend-of-all-work, proposed a cozy luncheon, I also declined. Whether or not I owed Nixon anything, I owed a period of silence to my remaining hopes for what I believed in.

3.   Hundreds of chroniclers accompanied Nixon on the climactic leg of his journey to the presidency. My vantage point was that of a distant yet privileged private citizen, who saw and heard much that the Nixon staff took pains to conceal from the traveling press.

"There will be blood all over the convention floor," Nixon said privately of the Democrats, but even he was surprised at the literal accuracy of his prediction. The televised chaos in Chicago, which left Hubert Humphrey in command of a mutinous, rudderless hulk seemingly sure to sink, created a euphoria in the Nixon camp. After his return from Chicago, where he had gone on his own initiative, Buchanan reflected this mood of superoptimism in a memorandum that circulated within the organization. Nixon's success in unifying the Republican party, he wrote, "speaks millions of words about [his] capacity as a unifier of diverse political elements and interests. It is a hopeful sign that Nixon may be the one man truly qualified to unify a divided nation."

As propaganda to bolster the faithful, this was a barely passable claim. As political analysis, it was not to be taken seriously. The Republican party, far from being a microcosm of the divided electorate, was an exclusive, homogeneous, and basically unrepresentative minority. Moreover, its leaders from Nixon down were not really dissatisfied with the party's composition and minority status. The memorandum disclosed once again the insularity of the Nixon strategists and their unwillingness to venture outside the familiar context of Republican politics in which they had been successful. It was this inertia, as much as the Democrats' misfortunes and Nixon's widening lead in the polls, that encouraged a stand-pat, play-safe approach to the fall campaign and the continued playing of the same worn-out themes used throughout the primaries.

The myopic view of the Republican party as a cross section of America, and therefore a ready alternative to the fractured Democratic party, was more than a rationalization for complacency. It served to gloss over the fact that the candidate of the party of the risen and prosperous could talk *about* "forgotten Americans," but he had very little to say directly *to* them. The unrepresentative nature of the G.O.P. did not, as liberal journalists supposed, stem from the evident scarcity of Republican blacks and young people. It stemmed from the relative weakness of the party among the American majority, made up of middle- and working-class whites whose allegiance to the Democrats had weakened to the point where they might be attracted by a campaign aggressively aimed at them. This would not be a "racist" campaign. Rather, it would be one specifically relevant to the needs, interests, and concerns of middling Americans. By imagining that the sloganeering Nixon campaign already met that requirement, Republican strategists missed opportunities and stored up rude surprises.

The Nixon men underestimated, as did most observers, the impact on Middle America of the televised disorders in the streets of Chicago. The demonstrators outside the Hilton were right when they shouted: "The whole world is watching!" But what each viewer saw on the television screen depended entirely on his values and attitudes. Television commentators, network and magazine executives, and editors of the *New York Times* saw savage brutality on the part of those sworn to preserve civilized order. They saw, as Wicker wrote, *their* children — the offspring of the educated upper-middle class — being gassed and beaten. But millions of others not so well educated, not so affluent, saw a spectacle they wholly approved. They saw spoiled rich children throw a tantrum and get the spanking they deserved from the police, who were the children of the lower-middle class.

Two weeks after the Democratic Convention, the pollster Oliver Quayle sampled fifty households in Warren, Michigan, a suburb with homes in the $15,000–$25,000 class. Many of those who lived there were members of the United Auto Workers. (The UAW estimates that it has more than 150,000 members who earn more than $15,000 a year.) Quayle asked this question: How do you feel about the way the police handled the demonstrators in Chicago? Only two of those who responded thought the police were "too tough." Twenty-six said "about right." Twenty-two said the police were "not tough enough." Significantly, no one checked the box marked "don't know."

These fifty blue-collar suburbanites in Michigan were in favor of the police and against the demonstrators regardless of the presidential candidate they preferred when they were polled. Most of them later supported Humphrey as the unions beat the drums for his pocketbook liberalism. But they had been accessible to Nixon — if only he had had something to say to such voters.

As early as mid-July, Jeffrey Bell, a young member of the Nixon research staff, prepared a prescient and perceptive warning against the specter of 1948, when a complacent Thomas E. Dewey had snatched defeat from the jaws of victory. "The RN campaign has been run on a strategy of not taking chances — and it has failed to catch fire," wrote Bell. He urged a strong appeal to "the heart of the middle class: Americans who make $6000 to $15,000 a year — what the Democrats call the Gut Vote." To attract these voters, he recommended "more specificity, more visibility, more controversy, more chance-taking, and above all a New Candor that — in the words of Robert Kennedy — 'tells it like it is,' the hard answers as well as the easy ones, the bad with the good . . . I think that by going after the Gut Voter with honesty and realism, we can . . . win this election going away."

In a memorandum to Mitchell dated August 22, Ellsworth sought to dispel complacency and get the candidate to come down to earth among skeptical Democrats and Independents. During the preceding few weeks, he wrote, issues had been neglected "because of the importance (as well as the fascination) of playing inside convention and party politics. Now, however, it is important to begin projecting Nixon's views on the basic popular issues" — almost a word-for-word echo of Anderson's plea two months earlier, which Nixon had endorsed in principle but ignored in practice. Ellsworth listed some questions that "the general public" was basically interested in — "Will my boy get hurt in Vietnam? When will it ever be safe to walk around my neighborhood at night? Is the value of my house going to hold up over the next few years?" — and urged that "all of us begin projecting Nixon's views on the fundamental public policy issues . . ."

Like all such advice, this fell on deaf ears. At New York headquarters and in the forward compartment of the *Tricia,* the flagship of Nixon's fleet of three chartered Boeing 727 jets, confidence soared to giddy heights — *Why, we're on our way to a landslide.* By late September, Nixon had opened a fifteen-point lead in the polls over Humphrey, 45 percent to an almost incredible 30 percent. To be sure, Wallace was flying surprisingly high, too — 21 percent in the polls — but these voters were assumed to be Democrats lost to Humphrey and they received only sporadic attention.

The aim of the Nixon campaign was entirely defensive: run in place and protect his lead until Election Day. This strategy yielded the initiative to Humphrey, who sooner or later would have to shift away from the administration's Vietnam policy. It relied on hitting him hard for his "inconsistency" when he finally made that desperate move. Another Buchanan memo spelled out the line to be taken: "If HHH shifts on Vietnam now, then he has spent four years deceiving the American people and he is unfit for any job in public life, let alone the Presidency." In this mechanistic view, which mirrored Nixon's, slamming an opponent, like punching a button, would have a predictable effect.

When Humphrey finally moved a half-step to the left in a speech in Salt Lake City, declaring that he would halt the bombing of North Vietnam under certain conditions, Nixon unleashed his long-prepared knockout blow, piously declaring: "I hope that Vice Pres-

ident Humphrey would clarify his position and not pull the rug out
from under the negotiators . . ." But the war-weary voters were
less concerned with consistency than they were with peace. Humphrey not only remained on his feet but, his bonds to Johnson broken, he was at last free to run. As Humphrey's old supporters and
contributors stopped sulking and came around, and as the AFL-
CIO's unprecedented drive to register and mobilize blue-collar voters took hold, confidence began to ebb from the Nixon organization
like air from a slowly leaking balloon. Columnist Joseph Alsop,
who had praised "the quite wonderfully smooth, quite wonderfully
professional" Nixon campaign in mid-September, took another look
a month later. He noted what worried every Nixon man sensitive
to the voters' mood — the curious absence of a "warm, intense feeling of direct communication between the [Republican] candidate
and his hearers." It seemed impossible that Humphrey could over-
take Nixon at this late stage of the campaign, but Alsop saw omens
reminiscent of 1948.

By late October, the portents were full-blown. Nixon was stalled,
Wallace sinking, and Humphrey climbing. An important factor in
his rebound was the unequal contest for second place, in which the
inexperienced, unaware, and ill-advised Agnew fell steadily behind
Senator Edmund Muskie, at one point trailing him by seventeen
points in the polls. Some of the bad advice Agnew received came
straight from Nixon. When Agnew accused the Democratic nominee of being "squishy soft" on Communism, innocent of the origins
of such rhetoric, he was carrying out his orders from Nixon — to
"take on" Humphrey. In spite of the presence of Sears and other
Nixon men, the Agnew staff succeeded in returning to the happy,
hip-shooting days in Annapolis. After they ousted a pair of unwanted speech-writers from the plane, one of the Agnewites summed up the spirit animating this near-disastrous adventure, crow-
ing: "At last we've liberated the governor from prepared material."
When the Humphrey forces finally rounded up enough money to
launch their media campaign, a main theme sprang from the same

inspiration as Finch's quip — the frightening possibility of world peace depending on a President named Spiro T. Agnew.

The Wallace slippage was in part due to his gross error in taking retired Air Force general Curtis LeMay as his running mate, which gave the liberal media the Goldwater–nuclear stick with which to beat him. But at least equally effective in cutting Wallace down was organized labor's all-out assault, which depicted him as an enemy of the unionized workingman on his record as governor of Alabama. Ironically, on orders from hypercautious Mitchell, Nixon men were simultaneously rebuffing overtures from union leaders who had written off Humphrey. For example, in Pennsylvania, which Nixon would unexpectedly lose, Mitchell forbade the candidate's open association with union chieftains prepared to endorse him. The Republican pitch to the wavering Wallace supporters was slick, abstract, and mechanical, barren of warmth and empathy, and blue-collar Democrats reacted as though invited to join a nearly bankrupt country club where they had never been welcome before. Meanwhile, the sweaty, scrambling Democrats welcomed the Gut Voters with open arms and straight New-Fair Deal pocketbook liberalism. "What has Richard Nixon ever done for workingmen?" cried Humphrey. His fast-growing crowds roared: *Nothing!*

A blizzard of paper from the Nixon organization — statements, instant books on the "issues" — and a torrent of money committed to radio and television advertising failed to produce the missing spark. In the rigorously programmed and automated Nixon campaign, designed to travel a predetermined, undeviating course, the possibility of a spark of imagination had been eliminated at the outset as intolerably risky. "For the last two weeks of the campaign," an insider recalled afterward with a shudder, "Nixon did nothing because he had nothing left. We marched straight ahead."

Straight into the last-minute ambush laid by Lyndon Johnson. On October 31 he announced a total halt to the bombing of North Vietnam and the start of peace talks expanded to include the Saigon government and the National Liberation Front in Paris the day after the presidential election. Nixon, thrown off balance by Johnson's dramatic move, recovered when Saigon announced it wouldn't come to the peace table. The real point of this eleventh-hour maneuvering, however it may have affected the fortunes of Nixon and Humphrey, was that the politicians continued to the very end to deal with the overriding issue of Vietnam on the same petty level as they had throughout the campaign. In a little-noticed statement in September, Senator Hatfield said: "In the democratic process, voters should not be forced to go to the polls with their fingers crossed; they should not be forced to rely on blind faith that the men they vote for will share their views on the most important issue of the election." Yet that was precisely the way the American electorate went to the polls on November 5, 1968.

4.   Climaxing the most spectacular political comeback in modern American history, Richard Milhous Nixon won the presidency of the United States narrowly yet solidly. His almost microscopic margin of victory in the popular vote — 31,770,237 (43.4 percent) to Humphrey's 31,270,533 (42.7 percent), for a plurality of 499,704 — widened considerably in the electoral vote, which he won 302 to 191. His broadly based support yielded thirty-three more electoral votes than were necessary to prevent a constitutional crisis and keep the presidential election out of the cloakrooms of the House of Representatives. Wallace, whose aim had been to bring about such a stalemate and bargaining situation, thus failed, but in failing he amassed just under 10 million votes and 13.5 percent of the total national vote.

Nixon's victory fell far short of the expectations of his senior lieutenants. His plurality was barely one-tenth as large as Mitchell's public prediction, and right up to Election Day, Haldeman counted New York in Nixon's column. The loss of Pennsylvania and Texas, once considered reasonably safe, shocked those who waited and watched with Nixon through the night in the Waldorf Towers. But

California, with its rich harvest of conservative votes from the bull-dozed orange groves and tract housing developments in southern suburbs like Yorba Linda, came through, forty electoral votes strong, and that elected him.

Satisfying as it was, Nixon's personal triumph could not obscure the Republican party's continuing weakness. The party gained five seats in the liberal U.S. Senate, but only four in the more conservative House, leaving the G.O.P. in the minority in both chambers. Nixon was the first President elected in this century without gaining control of at least one house of the Congress.

Conservative analysts made much of the combined Nixon-Wallace total of the popular vote, 56.9 percent, which they correctly described as a stunning turnaround from the Democratic landslide in 1964. But they ventured onto treacherous ground when they claimed a right-of-center governing majority. These voters had repudiated the consequences of the particular brand of liberalism personified by Lyndon Johnson, yet that did not translate into sympathy for old-fashioned conservatism. The antiliberal majority represented by the combined Nixon-Wallace vote existed on paper only, and it did not guarantee the inevitability of a new era of Republican ascendancy. Although the number of voters had grown by some 5 million between 1960 and 1968, 2.4 million *fewer* persons voted for Nixon in victory than had voted for him in defeat eight years earlier. Almost half of the Wallace vote came from outside the Old South, and in the two-party regions of the country the protest inspiring this insurgency was open to competitive appeasement by both major parties. All the talk of a Republican "Southern strategy" deflected attention and analysis from Humphrey's late success in holding the lower-middle-class and working-class Democratic constituency in the pivotal battleground states. His ability to roll up lopsided majorities (59 percent to 33 percent nationally) among the critically important Catholic vote, the core of the "forgotten Americans," was a warning to Republicans that shifting ethnic and religious blocs were not automatically moving their way.

They might as easily shift back toward a Democratic party cleansed of elitist liberalism and attuned to the new populism.

In short, the "historic opportunity" that some of us had seen and Nixon had talked about was not seized in 1968, but remained a possibility shimmering over the horizon. To seize it as the spokesman of the Out party, however, would have been infinitely easier than trying to forge a mandate and a majority with the encumbrance of the presidency. For the common denominator of protest against the status quo would disappear the moment Nixon entered the White House, assuming the inescapable responsibilities and burdens of the In party. As it was, he declared a rhetorical objective, which he borrowed from my all-but-forgotten NAM text of almost a year earlier — "America needs to hear the voices of the broad and vital center" — but he had no idea how to achieve it, and even less concern with building an expanded and stronger Republican party to undergird the endangered center.

5. Two weeks after the election, a highly placed friend in the Nixon organization telephoned and asked: "What do you hear?"

"Don't ask me," I said. "You're supposed to be on the inside."

Over dinner, he poured out a tale of personal and organizational uncertainty. In spite of his position, he had not seen Nixon since the morning after the election — "at a small champagne breakfast for one hundred and seventy-five people." He had received thanks for his valuable assistance, but not the slightest clue as to what he was expected to do next. He had received neither an assignment nor a commitment, as though Nixon were not even thinking about staffing the upper echelons of the administration he would form in a matter of weeks. Nor was this an isolated instance of neglect — most of Nixon's personal staff members were sitting around aimlessly, waiting for the telephone to ring. Like Price, some became impatient and disgusted and went off on vacation. The whole enterprise had stopped on Election Day.

I was still puzzled by Nixon's behavior. Why, I asked, didn't he show more trust toward the men who served him loyally and well? The response of my companion came from a depth beyond hurt and disillusionment. "How can he believe in us when he doesn't believe in himself?"

A few days later, my guest at lunch was Garment. He, too, was without a job in the administration, but he at least knew (or thought he did) Nixon's wishes. The President-elect had told him that he could have "any position he wanted," yet it was Nixon's hope that he would remain a free-ranging talent scout and idea man in the private sector. So Garment would come to Washington as a senior partner in the old Nixon law firm, at a hefty raise in salary. His first foray had been a huge success: he had bagged an eager Pat Moynihan ("He almost drank me under the table"). Moynihan's appointment involved risks, Garment admitted. "But you need at least one high-risk appointee in a visible position."

Our talk inevitably came around to the effect of my resignation ("They were afraid. One of the buffers had broken ranks") and to Nixon's strange dependency on Haldeman and Ehrlichman. "They see that he has to deal with only a few people, rather than having a great many people barge in and out," said Garment. "Nixon can't handle that." Why had this pair of protectors come on the scene when they did, as they did? "If Nixon had put them in their slots six months earlier, he would never have gotten off the ground. Price and maybe Buchanan would have done what you did. But, coming in when they did, to take over and control the going machinery, they were very necessary. In fact, considering the way Nixon squeaked in, they were probably essential. Without them, he might have fallen apart."

So much for the making of the President. What of the Nixon administration?

"A lot of things simply haven't been decided," said Garment, "and there's a lot of scurrying around. I doubt that anyone is aware of all that's going on."

That turned out to be an understatement.

6.   In the weeks before and after the Inaugural, the Nixon campaign organization worked, but not *too* hard, at becoming a government.

In the spring of 1968, Nixon set the example by appointing a stranger recommended by a business friend as his "assistant for manpower development," in charge of recruiting for the Nixon administration. Then he completely ignored him. The stranger, a brisk, bespectacled academic named Dr. Glenn Olds (he was insistent on that *Dr.*), spent six months gathering names, assembling dossiers, and showing a select few his grand organizational chart. In the early fall of 1968, Olds paid a visit to Henry Kissinger at Harvard. Although Kissinger was still a disappointed Rockefeller man, he felt obliged to report to an acquaintance at Nixon headquarters: "I must tell you — that man Olds is *crazy.*"

It was not until after the election that anyone bothered to check on Olds. The "manpower" files proved to be quite worthless — some of the people named were prominent liberals who would rather have gone to the penitentiary than into a Nixon regime. More important, time had been wasted. But there was no desperate sense of urgency, and there were no hard feelings toward Dr. Olds. In due course, he was rewarded with a job at the UN bearing the title of ambassador, which he at once learned to listen for.

To renew the talent search (and cover their embarrassment), the Nixon men proposed, and the President-elect approved, a supergimmick. They set out to query — so they claimed — all 64,988 listees in *Who's Who* for their recommendations on how to fill 2000 government policy-making positions. "As you may know," said the letter signed by Nixon, "I have pledged to bring into this Administration men and women who by their qualities of youthfulness, judgment, intelligence, and creativity can make significant contributions to our country. I seek the best minds in America to meet the challenges of this rapidly changing world. To find them, I ask your active participation and assistance."

The idea of throwing the new administration's doors open to the nation's meritocracy was a stroke of public-relations genius — and an acute political embarrassment. The Nixon men were saying, in effect, that they didn't know many smart people, and that they had no particular use for the power awaiting them. They were also telling deserving Republicans and their sponsors in the party and the Congress that they had jobs for the friends of *Who's Who* listees, but not for them.

When Republican professionals reassured each other through the years that Nixon at least would bring a *real* Republican administration to Washington, they meant that he, being one of them, would understand the importance to the party of federal patronage and would do a better job of taking care of his friends than the uninterested Eisenhower. The pros, to their dismay, soon discovered they were wrong. The Nixon patronage operation was a disaster — in part because Mitchell, busier settling a score than staffing a government, sabotaged it.

Nixon had assigned John Sears to act as the political liaison between the White House and the Republican National Committee and state and local party leaders. Because he knew only too well the lavish promises made on Nixon's behalf, Sears asked for, and was granted, the right to monitor the flow of patronage, ensuring that Nixon people got it. While Nixon went on to more cosmic concerns, Mitchell set up his own patronage mechanism and put Harry Flemming, a pliable novice, in charge. He was determined to cut down Sears, whom he considered an upstart, and in that he and others succeeded within the administration's first year. The failure to fill key government jobs with Nixon Republicans was still producing harmful effects in the administration's fourth year.

Not surprisingly, the making of the Nixon administration degenerated into a me-and-thee proposition: if loyalty to RN was the sole criterion for appointment, the exemplary Nixonites were the hyperloyalists around him, and they were pleased to reproduce themselves.* So it was that the once prestigious title of "Special Assistant to the President" was bestowed wholesale on ex-advance men who had proved their fitness to govern by releasing the balloons precisely at the moment the candidate's arms shot skyward in a V. They were sober, industrious, efficient, and almost completely unaware of a wider world and a larger politics than they had known. The ascendancy of these narrowly skilled technicians reflected the triumph of the one-dimensional spot-and-slogan politics of the media age. To govern was merely to extend the campaign and to continue attempting to manipulate those remote, statistically defined populations in that collection of market areas, the U.S.

The contrast with the last interparty transfer of presidential power, from Eisenhower to Kennedy, could not have been more striking. During the fall and winter of 1960–1961, intellectual politicians from institutions along the Charles River met frequently to plan in detail the Kennedy administration's takeover of the foreign policy and national security agencies. Some of those involved were not especially keen on JFK, but their politics mattered less than their expertise. While the Eisenhower-Kennedy political transition went forward rather haphazardly, as usual, the intellectual transition — the substitution of radically different attitudes and policy ideas — was thorough and effective. Fully a decade later, these ideas still determined U.S. policy, sometimes against the will of Republicans who inherited them. But they were powerless to command a change in course. Their party's negligence, in the parlance of the Kennedy era, had foreclosed their options.

To be sure, Nixon *talked* about sweeping change, but the lack of advance planning and preparation for his administration made it impossible. "Right after the Inaugural, over lunch," a member of

---

* The composition of the loyalty review board was not without irony. Haldeman and Ehrlichman had delayed making a firm commitment to Nixon and had not joined the staff until after he won the Oregon primary, which assured his nomination. Young Flemming and his father, Arthur Flemming, Eisenhower's Secretary of HEW, also proceeded cautiously. In a mid-April 1968 memorandum to Nixon, one of his assistants wrote: "Arthur Flemming's son, Harry, informs me that his father is strongly pro-RN, but that he would rather not publicly endorse him at this time because he thinks he could be more effective in convincing other people from an uncommitted posture." He was also, of course, safer.

the campaign staff later recalled wistfully, "Nixon laid down the law on the agencies. 'Clean 'em out,' he said. Everybody nodded and did nothing. The agencies weren't cleaned out and now they can't be."

In mid-July 1970 Senator Barry Goldwater, who as much as any Republican was responsible for Nixon's being President, asked, in effect, what had happened to the party's victory of 1968. Not only were the Democratic "gnomes of Washington" still in charge of the federal bureaucracy, the kind of Republicans who were appointed also tended distressingly toward the liberal side. The philosophy that the electorate had repudiated still held sway, said Goldwater sorrowfully. "I am not completely sure that the President and his advisers understand the necessity for placing at the middle management level men and women firmly devoted to the Nixon administration's philosophy of government and its attitude toward the burning issues of the day." Instead of bellowing his wrath, as he had every right to, the spokesman for the Republican conservatives all but apologized for even this muted criticism of the White House. It was no wonder that the self-styled pragmatists and Ripon Society liberals on the President's staff were contemptuous of conservatives.

The failure of conservative Republicans to ask and if necessary demand due representation within the administration gave maximum scope for enforcing the muddled concept of centrism, which Haldeman translated into a cult of presidential personality. "We started out," said Haldeman in a rare interview, "trying to keep political coloration as much as possible out of policy and hiring matters. However, we realize that these things make for variety in decision-making, and so within reasonable limits we have tried to keep a spread of opinion on the staff, so that no one is to the left of the President at his most liberal or to the right of the President at his most conservative . . . Ehrlichman, Kissinger, and I do our best to make sure that all points of view are placed before the President. We do act as a screen, because there is a real danger of some advocate of an idea rushing in to the President or some other decision-maker, if the person is allowed to do so, and actually managing to convince them in a burst of emotion or argument . . ." *

Long after it was too late, a high-ranking member of the Nixon administration surveyed the consequences of the sway of the hyper-loyalists. "The men around RN can't distinguish friends from enemies. They have no way of judging a substantive issue or anyone's professional competence. All they can ask is: Is he *loyal?* That's very sad. The Democrats were much smarter. The politicians and the experts weren't held to the same standard, for the obvious reason that they had different jobs. Here, *everything's* political — and yet there's no sense of politics. That's why the insiders are like a band of brothers, always embattled. They don't know the limits of what to expect from outsiders. Therefore, nobody outside the brotherhood is to be trusted, and nobody outside can make a contribution. It's very sad."

In the end, the Nixon men tacitly gave up the task of trying to take over the sprawling federal establishment and left it in the hands of the permanent, semi-invisible government consisting of entrenched civil servants, careerists in the downtown bureaucracies, and committee staff veterans on Capitol Hill. The dawning realization among the holdover Democrats that the "new crowd" wasn't really serious had a predictable result. "For a month or so," Anderson, then deputy to Counselor Arthur Burns, recalled, "the bureaucrats were scared to death. Then, when nothing happened, they went ahead with business as usual. After a while, they had so much contempt for us, they didn't even bother to return our calls."

The Nixon men settled for clearing a beachhead in Washington's alien jungle, occupying the White House and sending lightly armed skirmishing parties into the Cabinet departments. (These were one-way missions. After a year, a junior aide dispatched to the Internal Revenue Service, perhaps the most sensitive political choke-point in the government, raised a lament typical of the lonely and abandoned: "I'm the only damned Nixon Republican in the place.")

Within the iron fence surrounding the White House arose a mini-

* Quoted by Allen Drury in "Inside the White House 1971," *Look*, October 19, 1971.

government the Nixonites could call their own. As though attempting to duplicate what lay outside, the staff of the Office of the President swiftly grew to be the largest, costliest, and most elaborately
bureaucratic in history. At the center stood the man who remembered listening as a boy to the train whistle blowing in the California night. On Election Day, Nixon had reached his destination but
there the tracks had stopped. Now he began his improvised presidency.

PART TWO

In Power
A Critical Perspective

XIII

1.   NIXON BROUGHT to the presidency a rather dated sense of
priorities. "I've always thought this country could run itself domestically, without a President," he told an interviewer in the fall of
1967 — just as some of us were trying to engineer Nixon's re-entry
into the turbulent domestic scene that disproved what he had "always" thought. "All you need is a competent Cabinet to run the
country at home," he continued. "You need a President for foreign
policy." *

Nixon's illusion that he would be able to turn the country over to
the Cabinet faded during the administration's first days in office, as
much from his aloofness as from the group's doubtful competence to
reverse the modern concentration of power in the presidency. Attorney General Mitchell stood at a distance from the rest of the
Cabinet and the President's other advisers. He was number one,
tied to the White House by a direct telephone line, the uniquely intimate counselor to whom Nixon turned on every subject from
minor political matters to Supreme Court appointments.

Mitchell, who had never served a day in government, was reluctant to give up his comfortable private life. But he came to appreciate the satisfactions of public service and showed undisguised delight at the uses of power. "The liberals want to run me out of
town," he told a small dinner party one evening late in 1969, smiling. "But I'm going to stay and fight." If the Attorney General in

* Theodore H. White, *The Making of the President 1968* (New York: Atheneum, 1969), p. 147.

his official statements laid down a hard line on law and order, especially campus protests, his private sentiments, as quoted by his outspoken wife Martha, a formidable blond belle from a small town in
Arkansas, embarrassed Republicans and chilled Democrats. "As
my husband has said many times," the Attorney General's wife told
an interviewer, "some of the liberals in this country, he'd like to
take them and change them for Russian Communists."

But even when his advice to the President was disastrously bad,
as in the nominees he recommended for the Supreme Court whom
the Senate rejected, Mitchell could do no wrong in Nixon's eyes.
The dour, pipe-puffing "A.G.," who sat with the National Security
Council and the Urban Affairs Council, continued to be the President's psychic prop.

Authority over domestic policy-making was totally confused,
causing what insiders frankly described as "chaos." Confusion was
inherent in Nixon's division of domestic policy-making responsibility between the liberal Daniel Patrick Moynihan and the conservative Arthur Burns, who approached the President from irreconcilably opposed points of view. A no man's land soon opened where the
administration's domestic program ought to have been.

Moynihan, a bold and stylish man of ideas in drab company,
made the most of his opportunity. During the campaign, Nixon
had exploited the voters' longing to be led out of the wilderness of
ever-expanding welfarism, and he promised — without any program behind the slogan — to start "getting people off welfare rolls
and onto payrolls." The only proved method of drawing the mar-
ginally employable (a small part of the overall welfare population)
into the labor force was through inflationary stimulus of the economy, an avenue closed by the raging inflation inherited from the
Johnson administration. Moynihan advanced the striking proposition that what poor people needed most was — *money*. Almost incredibly, in the face of the stern Republican work-ethic and the
President's memories of a life of upward struggle, Moynihan sold
the idea of income-maintenance under the so-called Family Assistance Plan, or FAP. Given the attractive label of "welfare reform,"

FAP actually would subsidize the unemployed *and* those receiving incomes below a federally defined poverty level, with the result that perhaps as many as 15,000,000 *additional* persons would qualify for public assistance. On their backs and those of the overburdened taxpayers would be fastened still another immense layer of bureaucracy. Projections of the fiscal impact of FAP were hazy yet alarming — an estimated $5 billion a year initially and three or four times that enormous sum when the program was full blown.

To this most un-Republican proposal Nixon assigned "top domestic priority." Members of the party who had heard him state his firm opposition to the idea of a guaranteed annual income blinked in disbelief. Politicians from more conservative areas of the country were forced to insist, barefaced, that FAP wasn't the guaranteed annual income it plainly was. The administration, having urged the most radical social innovation in a generation, found itself in the odd position of trying to keep its substance a secret from its supporters.

Early in his brief acquaintance with Nixon, Moynihan discovered the President's susceptibility to novelty and flattery. In well-crafted memoranda and sparkling conversation, he eluded Haldeman's "screen" and caught the President's fancy with a dubious historical parallel. Nixon could be the reincarnated Disraeli, responding to the needs of his time by advancing in conservative guise reforms too daring for liberals even to talk about. The seeming political shrewdness of stealing the other fellow's clothes and preempting his moves intrigued Nixon and his pragmatic advisers. Not everyone, of course, succumbed to the allure of newness — the borrowed clothes, some advisers pointed out, had to fit, especially when a President carried Nixon's reputation for shiftiness. A senior counselor, well respected among Republicans for his realism, recalled his experience in White House domestic policy sessions: "I would sit and listen to the people with the bright ideas — Ehrlichman, Finch, Rumsfeld, and the rest. When they were finished, I'd just tap my forehead and say, 'Tricky Dick, Tricky Dick.' I would tell them: 'You have to get this warning signal into your heads.'

Nixon has a permanent credibility problem. He can't afford to make a mistake or step out of character because his motives always seem to be in doubt."

Even this friend felt a twinge of regret and echoed the refrain of troubled Nixon men: "It got so that I just couldn't make the connection between the things Nixon accepted and proposed and the Nixon I thought I knew."

Through the administration's first year in office, the improvised, inconsistent, and basically weak domestic program carried no immediate penalty. Although foreign policy as a whole no longer held the high place Nixon assigned, the American public established — and the new President recognized — one paramount foreign-policy objective: ending U.S. involvement in the Vietnam war as quickly as possible, on the best terms available short of surrender and humiliation. Nixon was determined to lead a slow, disguised American retreat from Southeast Asia. The disguise came from clouds of misleading rhetoric about the meaning and prospects of "Vietnamization." Nevertheless, if Nixon could execute the retreat without dishonor and collapse abroad and permanent disunity at home, he would earn the nation's gratitude.

2.   The essence of the elusive Nixon Doctrine, derived from a presidential press briefing on Guam in the summer of 1969 and elaborated thereafter, could be simply stated. The U.S. intended to do less overseas, for obvious reasons, while prosperous yet laggard allies were expected to do more. This policy of disengagement and the overdue push for sharing of common burdens recognized the insistent need to align U.S. foreign policy with new domestic attitudes and necessities. Nixon saw, and was responding to, the reality that the post–World War II era of U.S. global hegemony had ended before his presidency began. Nevertheless, he set an ambitious goal. His overriding desire was to be hailed as the architect of a new era, "a full generation of peace," succeeding where his visionary hero and model, Woodrow Wilson, had failed in an earlier time.

The man he chose as his principal foreign-policy assistant, Henry

A. Kissinger, was at once his most surprising and successful staff appointment. What began as a typically Nixonian and strictly functional relationship between strangers matured into a uniquely close and intense collaboration. Kissinger saw the President alone every day — only Haldeman enjoyed such access — and he normally spoke with him several times in the course of a working day that ran between fifteen and twenty hours. When, in January 1971, Kissinger announced that he would not return to the Harvard faculty (and thereby protect his tenured professorship), a grateful Nixon acknowledged their special relationship in a remarkable letter, declaring: "Frankly, I cannot imagine what the government would be without you."

Nixon's admitted dependence on Kissinger worried observers who saw a Svengali emerging in the West Wing of the White House. With disarming candor, the brilliant and power-hungry Kissinger spoke of his "megalomania" to interviewers, and his background briefings encouraged speculation that he was the genius who pulled the strings on the President. In this dull administration, the pudgy, middle-aged Kissinger, without changing his ninety-hour workweek, could play the secret swinger by dating Hollywood starlets. ("Power is the great aphrodisiac," said Kissinger in one of his unabashed advertisements for himself.) The fact was that "Dr. K.," as White House aides called him, exercised more influence over foreign-policy decision-making than any presidential assistant in history. With a staff of some one hundred and ten persons, a budget of $2.2 million (triple Walt W. Rostow's in 1968), and extraordinary personal involvement at the highest levels of diplomacy, as in his secret missions to Peking and the Paris peace talks, Kissinger alone disposed more power than the Department of State.

In an unknowing administration, most of whose highest figures were neither as bright nor as hardworking as he was, Kissinger was bound to stand out. "Henry is the only guy whose mind ticks away — and that shows how my standards have deteriorated," said a high-ranking colleague who was also a former academic. "The rest of these people are unbelievable jerks who can't make the connection between A and B. They want to take up today's problem today and let tomorrow take care of itself."

Kissinger's power stemmed from a fact that he never for a moment forgot — Nixon preferred to deal with one staff man on matters of foreign policy, and he had chosen Kissinger to be that man. So long as his wishes were carried out, Nixon did not care how powerful that intermediary between himself and the foreign-policy establishment became. Those who knew Kissinger's reputation for tyrannizing over his staff, but who did not grasp the basic fact of his relationship with the President, were amazed by his obsequiousness before Nixon. For his part, Nixon enjoyed the deferential attention of this Eastern academic headliner, who once had seemed destined to serve only a President Rockefeller.

Nixon and Kissinger had in common social backgrounds that made them at once competitive and insecure. Heinz Alfred Kissinger, who came to the U.S. before World War II with his German-Jewish refugee parents, was Americanized by being drafted into the army. Afterward he was launched on his spectacular career — he initially aspired to become an accountant — by the GI Bill, which opened the gates of Harvard to his intellect, ambition, and *chutzpah.* Kissinger, like a Sammy Glick of the Cold War, made his way by conniving for foundation support and government-agency consultancies, but the patron — Rockefeller — to whom he tied his hopes of power let him down. Then came Nixon's surprising and swiftly accepted postelection invitation, which enabled him to join forces with another man on the make.

Nixon and Kissinger shared a world-view: they believed a traditional balance-of-power politics could be plied in the nuclear age, based on national interests and geopolitical realities. They recognized a cold and logical world without fated allies or enemies — only interested parties — and they expected foreigners to understand when they dealt with them on these terms.

The collaborators, in spite of their informed, intelligent grasp of the world, did not have, individually or together, a sure sense of the country they served. Kissinger simply did not know (or care to find out), and Nixon minimized conflicts between domestic and foreign policies, assuming for himself and his actions a popular trust in the presidency such as Eisenhower had enjoyed in a less troubled time. Neither man gave the slightest indication that his statecraft was an expression of a coherent personal philosophy or stable set of values. All was maneuver in an amoral universe ordered by *realpolitik.* The Nixon-Kissinger foreign policy, while undeniably daring, had the weakness of being pursued independent of a popular consensus or even much public understanding. It went on above the heads of the American people as though it were a high-wire act involving the fate of the trapeze artists alone.

The American people often stubbornly refused to accommodate themselves to a President's scale of priority. Lyndon Johnson, who had always thought the country needed a strong, domestic-reform President, had tried desperately to keep the Vietnam war's imperatives in the background and protect his dream of the Great Society. He succeeded only in deceiving himself as much as the people. Whether or not Nixon's foreign-policy priority was sound, and it could be argued that the weakening U.S. position in the world made it so, such issues, apart from the war, were on the far periphery of public awareness. The American people, after a generation of being interested in the world, were intensely and anxiously self-interested. They demanded a leader who shared their perception.

Nixon pretended to do so as best he could, but the uncertainty of his grip on the mood of the American people was sometimes apparent, and they repaid pretense with mistrust. The President's weakness for inflated gestures and rhetoric was deep-rooted in his complex and contradictory personality. Nixon's inner defenses against self-disclosure were as formidable as the outer defenses of his privacy. Extremely sensitive about his limitations, he was continually tempted to conceal them. He was tempted, too, to conceal points of vulnerability in his actions by grossly overselling strong points.

Thus when Nixon took a necessary step in Southeast Asia, his tendency to falsify on the margin made the core of the deed suspect. The decision to mount a border raid against the Communist sanctuaries in Cambodia, thereby gaining time for the Vietnamization program and permitting continued withdrawal of U.S. troops, could have been defended on these limited, reasonable grounds, especially against semihysterical opposition. Instead, in his April 30, 1970, announcement, which he wrote unassisted, Nixon pulled out all the stops: "We will not be humiliated. We will not be defeated. If when the chips are down, the U.S. acts like a pitiful, helpless giant, the forces of totalitarianism and anarchy will threaten free nations and free institutions throughout the world . . ."

This apocalyptic tone did nothing to calm the stunned public, whose temper and reaction Nixon had misjudged. His plea for personal sympathy — "I would rather be a one-term President than be a two-term President at the cost of seeing America become a second-rate power," showed him at his most insensitive. In this situation, the fears of Americans were for their sons, not for a politician's future. The "something extra" Nixon felt compelled to inject into his explanation and justification revealed meager resources of empathy in the nation's ranking crisis manager. For a period of several weeks, and especially after the tragic killing of student protesters in Ohio and Mississippi, the country seemed to reel out of control.

Protests erupted within HEW and other departments, but these were less damning than criticism voiced just beyond the Palace Guard. The President was disbelieved by his own second-level aides. "Cambodia isn't black or white — it's shades of gray," said one of them. "Now the administration" — the aide, though part of it, spoke as an outsider — "has turned a psychological corner and retreated into itself. Cambodia's being made a black-or-white, all-or-nothing test of our loyalty to RN. They must think we're awfully dumb or gullible."

3.   The suite of offices occupied by the Vice President of the United States is on the second floor of the Executive Office Building. Through the long, heavily draped windows, beyond the balconies and the window boxes ablaze with tulips in springtime, one can see the West Wing of the White House, perhaps fifty yards

away. The physical proximity is deceptive. Any man condemned to the limbo of the vice presidency, the office perhaps best described by one sufferer as "not worth a bucket of warm spit," is reminded every frustrating day how far he stands from the power of command.

By the summer of 1970, a special estrangement had developed between Spiro T. Agnew and the administration of which he was the strident, slashing partisan. The one-time Rockefeller booster and reputed moderate displays the instinct identifying him as a true-believing, ideological conservative. The word "sincerity" is so debased by the usage it receives in Washington that one recoils from it, but it fits Agnew perfectly. He is sincere in his attacks on media bias, "radiclibs," and campus anarchists, and his sincerity sets aglow like-minded Republicans who form the nucleus of the party's workers, organizers, and fund raisers.

These are the Republicans whose hearts belonged to Goldwater, and who might have eloped with Reagan, but who made a sensible, passionless match with Nixon. Now they and their hero, Spiro, are assailed by doubts. Nixon's selection of Agnew revealed much about his estimate of the presidency; now, the disaffection of the Agnewites reveals much about the party's attitude toward Nixon. Over the past three years, the Nixon administration has behaved like an unfaithful spouse, and the conservatives find the bed they made in Miami Beach cold and uncomfortable.

To the extent that Agnew is committed to the profession of politics, he puts party above ideology. But his commitment, for one sitting only a heartbeat away from the Oval Office, is extraordinarily shallow. He can honestly say that he never expected to be where he is and doesn't expect — or much care — to go higher. "The Veep," a member of his staff told me, "isn't interested in being President. He's interested in making money. He feels that he owes his kids an estate, and that he'd better start making some real dough soon." This eminently Republican ambition reinforces Agnew's status as the authentic common denominator of the G.O.P. What he says from the platform is what other good providers say on commuter trains when their thoughts turn from moneymaking to politics.

The root of Agnew's disillusionment lies in his earlier innocence and credulity, qualities shared with his constituency. Usually the man chosen for the vice presidency is a veteran politician who knows the national scene and harbors no illusions about the emptiness of the office. Such a man consoles himself with the dream of succeeding to the big job some day. Agnew, however, came straight from his freshman term as governor of Maryland, and when Nixon gave him a sales pitch, telling Ted that he would have responsibility for overseeing domestic affairs while the President wound down the war in Vietnam and dealt with the Russians, why, gullible Ted believed him.

Now he knows better. Awareness has come painfully and at the cost of diminished gratitude toward the seeming statesman who lifted him from obscurity to the big leagues. If Agnew were a conventionally ambitious Vice President, he would be restrained by the same inhibitions that made Nixon such an unappealing figure as the leading idolater of Ike. As it is, Agnew is much freer to sound off — and yet more securely bound.

This is easily explained: he is proud of being the man he is, and he values his pledged word and personal honor. Agnew, as a private person, is earnest, intelligent, and likable. He is considerate of his staff, in a warmly personal way, and does not dissemble intimacy with strangers. In his jet compartment, he will dash off an amusing piece of doggerel verse to stem the tears of a young secretary, crying because an exciting campaign is ended. He is prepared to wear the same face before the world today and tomorrow, which is why the Washington *Post* and his White House enemies, for once, agree that he is a menace.

"You wouldn't believe the incredible memos those punks at the White House send over here addressed to the Vice President — you will do this and you will do that, signed by some twenty-five-year-old advance man," said an Agnew aide. "The Veep doesn't pay the slightest attention. The only one he takes orders from is the President, and Nixon hasn't told him to stop doing or saying anything."

Nixon, always indirect, will not do so. He leaves the retooling of the Vice President's image to others. Unfortunately for the President, Agnew, in the phrase of a confidant, feels "tremendous personal hatred" toward the intermediaries who want him to be synthetic. "Agnew knows they regard him as a dolt, and so he ignores them. And the fellows who have milk with Nixon at night take every opportunity to knife Agnew. It's a *lovely* situation."

Nevertheless, Agnew loyally plays the role of Nixon's Nixon. He does not mind acting as the hard face of a sledgehammer politics; indeed, he privately complains: "I think if we were a little more hard-nosed, we'd get more support from the people." As governor, trailed by reporters who became cronies, he fell into the enjoyable habit of hip-shooting for headlines. He loves publicity and naively measures his influence by his clippings.

This would seem to make Agnew the ideal spokesman for the pseudo-conservative tough-cop state, as Herblock and White House strategists alike would have it. But he isn't a cynical demagogue or even a very exciting speaker; after blowing off steam, he remains discontented. "He doesn't get his kicks from the roar of the crowd," a politican who knows him well reflected. "He gets his satisfaction from managing and administering. That's what he liked about being governor — the feeling that he could get something done."

There is nothing to do in the vice presidency, of course, but Agnew's problem goes deeper. There is nothing for him to attach himself to: no administration philosophy, theme, or identity. If Nixon had something genuinely affirmative and constructive to say, Agnew would enthusiastically spread that message. Because Nixon doesn't, Agnew can't.

In September 1970 the Nixon administration prepared intensively for the midterm elections and the first popular verdict on its performance. The stakes were invitingly large: in addition to the State Houses and the House of Representatives, there was the chance that the Senate, with its large Democratic majority thwarting the administration, might be brought under Republican control through a net gain of seven seats. Setting himself that goal, Nixon hand-picked the candidates for the most promising Senate races and drew up the plan of the campaign. In a pair of briefings that brought the President and Vice President face-to-face alone, a rarity in their distant relationship, Nixon handed Agnew a hard-line script: he was to hammer the Democrats anew on the "law-and-order" issue, blaming their permissiveness for everything from drugs to crime to campus protest.

As a politician, Agnew allowed himself to be programmed, a human missile cocked and aimed at the disturbers of the silent majority's peace. Yet, as a sincere man, he realized slogans wouldn't reach or alter much that was disturbing middling Americans.

Almost on the eve of his blastoff into the campaign, Agnew confided his misgivings to friends. His worries were not immediate. The election results would fall short of the extravagant White House predictions, he said, but would be satisfactory. And he believed that Nixon probably would be re-elected in 1972. When Agnew looked further ahead toward 1976, however, the prospect darkened. On that horizon he saw repudiation and defeat for the Republican party.

"We're not doing a goddamned thing about any of the problems that got us elected," said Agnew to a friend. "For that matter, we're not doing a goddamned thing about *anything*."

By 1976, Agnew expected the country would be in such shape that "anybody who's credible, even a Wallace-type," could run the Republicans out of office. "And I'm not sure I want to sit around for six years and wait for that to happen," he told his intimates in the late summer of 1970.

These were not disloyal words, but the words of a despairing man adrift. Where the hope of the Nixon administration's continuity should have been strongest, the official successor testified that it did not exist. A one-shot, perhaps a lucky second, and the Nixon presidency would end, leaving America facing a blank wall or perhaps a barricade.

4.   Republican politicians outside the White House assessed the 1970 election outcome pessimistically. "The administration really overdid it," confided an official of the national committee. "The President sacrificed a lot of his credibility — he looked like the old Nixon."

From the Vice President's men came equally somber judgments. "I guess," said one, "they [the White House] came out O.K., and the Veep came out a little bit on the positive side because of New York and Tennessee" — where Agnew had waged personal vendettas against two especially hated "radiclibs," renegade Republican Charles Goodell and Democrat Albert Gore, respectively. "If we'd lost those two," the aide concluded, "there's no question Spiro would have been made the scapegoat." Through the reactions of the professionals ran a new skepticism concerning the President's astuteness as a practical politician. "Dammit," said an exasperated pro, "they" — again, the distant White House — "sounded like they were still 'out' and the other guys were still 'in.' People aren't listening — they seem to believe less and less about more and more. Now Nixon's responsible for everything, and he ought to realize he can't win it again on promises."

Nixon, for his part, privately and publicly declared himself well pleased with the 1970 election results, saying "the majority has spoken, the real majority in this country." The phrase, significantly, was borrowed from the title of that fall's best-read book around the White House, *The Real Majority*,* by Richard M. Scammon and Ben J. Wattenberg, a pair of social and political analysts steeped in demographic data. (Scammon was John F. Kennedy's Director of the Census Bureau and election oracle; Wattenberg had been a speech-writer for Johnson and worked in Humphrey's successful campaign to recapture his Minnesota Senate seat.) These liberal Democrats, surveying an electorate in which the poor, black, and young would remain minorities, urged new concern for the majority's chief concern — The Social Issue, defined as "a set of public at-

* New York: Cowan-McCann, Inc., 1970.

titudes concerning the more personally frightening aspects of disruptive social change" — crime, drugs, campus radicals, riots, pornography, promiscuity. "Most voters," wrote Scammon and Wattenberg, "felt they gained little from crime, or integration, or wild kids, or new values, or dissent. Of many of the new facets of American life they were downright fearful" — and, given the chance, they would vote against their fear.

White House technicians swallowed that advice whole, as the design of the Agnew campaign showed. If fear would drive voters away from "soft" Democrats and into the arms of "hard" Republicans, then scare-talk was smart politics. The President impulsively changed his plans, jumped into the campaign in mid-October, and stumped the country repeating many of the shrill, frightening things Agnew had been saying since Labor Day. It was a classic instance of Nixon oversell, and the voters, weary of hearing the same slogans, tuned out. Meanwhile, Democratic candidates tuned in to "Social Issue" and responded to gimmickry in kind: they switched their images overnight, putting American flags in their lapels and making speeches praising the misunderstood police. As Bryce Harlow, chief of the White House team traveling with Agnew, later remarked ruefully, the "Social Issue" wasn't much if a hurt opponent could neutralize it so easily.

The Nixon men hadn't paid enough attention to another piece of Scammon-Wattenberg advice: "The ever-potent Economic Issue always holds a high priority." They badly underestimated the effects on the voters of slack in the economy, rising unemployment, and unabated inflation. By November, 5.6 percent of the work force was jobless and consumer prices were climbing at an annual rate of 6 percent. When the Vice President and then the President barnstormed through slump-ridden industrial states, promising to put down unruly college demonstrators, blue-collar and middle-class voters said, Fine — but what will the administration do for *us?* (As Agnew had admitted, the answer was very little.) A few days before the election, antiwar protesters threw rocks and eggs at the President's car in San Jose, much to the delight of his campaign image-makers. The incident provided further evidence of the viciousness of left-wing radicals. But the wife of a jobless aerospace engineer, one of thousands in depressed Southern California, didn't see the threat to Middle America as the image-makers supposed she would. She told a reporter bitterly: "The kids beat us to it."

The stress Nixon laid on the alleged "ideological" content of his claimed victory was curious, coming from so confirmed a pragmatist and one whose New Conservative advisers had either left or been banished to the fringes of the administration. What he had in mind were not social *ideas* and a commitment to fulfill them in programmatic fashion. He had in mind tactical *position,* a stance athwart the technically determined "center" of the electorate. In practice, this amounted to a stand-pat defense of an undisturbed liberal status quo, disguised beneath conservative-sounding rhetoric. But many of the social ills frightening and harming the American majority stemmed from the liberal assumptions of the 1960s, now established in federal programs the Nixonites had inherited and left unchanged.

A theoretician of the new, populist conservatism, Kevin P. Phillips, had crowned his service in the 1968 campaign as Mitchell's voting trends analyst by writing *The Emerging Republican Majority,** the White House best seller of 1969. Nixon professed not to have read the book dedicated to him. Whether or not he had, Phillips believed the President's men had missed the point. Now a columnist increasingly critical of the administration, he restated his thesis in the last days of the 1970 campaign, writing: "The huge middle segment of the U.S. population feels itself under siege from every direction: the erosion of traditional values and respect for authority; the decline of patriotism; the rise of welfarism and the decline of enterprise and craftsmanship; the attack on neighborhoods and schools led by the Ivy League social planner; the lack of elitist (liberal or conservative) concern for the average man's job security or economic well-being. To decisively win the hearts and ballots of middle America, one party or the other must appeal on a new,

---

* New York: Arlington House, 1969.

broad 'socio-economic issue,' and do so with genuine concern."

The last words were especially wounding. Phillips, with the damaging authority of a former insider and a disappointed prophet, was calling the administration's appeal phony. Ehrlichman, Assistant to the President for Domestic Affairs, asked for a chance to plead the cause of centrism. Over lunch Phillips asked him how many administration programs directly benefited Middle Americans.

"Oh," Ehrlichman replied, "fifty or sixty."

"Name one."

"Postal reform."

Phillips, taken aback but inclined to be liberal in this situation, nodded and said, "Name another."

Ehrlichman, after several moments, silently turned to his lunch.

5.   About a month after the 1970 election, a member of the White House staff shared with a visitor an analysis almost as black as the coffee he sipped.

"It's all even for seventy-two, and maybe trending uphill if we don't deliver on the economy and inflation," he said, gesturing toward the charts and tables spread on his desk. "We're in trouble in the ten largest states, and in some of them the situation won't get any better. The ones that really matter are Texas and California. Without them, you can forget it in seventy-two." Like others on the staff, he had written a memo to the President documenting the obstacles to the arithmetic of his re-election.

The telephone buzzed three times — the signal that the Oval Office was calling. A great many members of the huge Nixon staff go for months at a stretch without exchanging a personal word with him, but he does call them occasionally, usually to compliment their work. In this instance, the President also had a piece of news to impart. During the brief, one-sided conversation the aide said almost nothing. His reaction showed in his expression, which changed from surprise to astonishment to utter disbelief. As he put down the receiver, he slowly settled back in his chair.

"The Old Man's decided to do something about the Texas situation," said the staff man, shaking his head. "And you won't believe who he's got to help him do it."

Richard Nixon's sense of privacy is well known. Less well known is the delight he takes, after making a solitary decision, in springing it on the unfailingly appreciative insiders. This gives him a nice, preliminary lift before facing the press and public. On this occasion, he enjoyed a bonus. Earlier on the morning of December 14, 1970, the White House operator had placed a call to the LBJ Ranch. Accustomed to receiving courtesy briefings from Nixon and Kissinger, Lyndon Johnson suspected nothing. After the customary pleasantries, the President said in a casual way that he was calling to introduce his new Secretary of the Treasury — "an old friend of yours." While Johnson waited for the telephone to be passed from hand to hand in Washington, he may have run down a mental list of old friends whose elevation to the Nixon Cabinet would do him no harm at all, none at all. Then he heard the voice of a very old friend indeed, one who had addressed him in every tone from a conspiratorial whisper to an angry bellow over the past thirty years. It was, unbelievably, John Bowden Connally.

Johnson's one-time protégé proceeded to inform him of the way matters had been arranged without his advice and consent, and the very long distance call ended. Several months later, with an ambiguous smile and considerable understatement, Connally recalled: "Johnson was miffed, and I don't really blame him."

By nightfall, the news of Connally's appointment had heads shaking from Wall Street to Zurich to Tokyo. The President-watchers in Washington, who supposed they had Nixon figured for a methodical percentage player, were paralyzed with amazement. Known to the world beyond Texas chiefly as the survivor of Dallas, Connally had none of the credentials expected of a Secretary of the Treasury in a professedly sound-money, inflation-fighting Republican government.

Inevitably, surprise and consternation gave way to the knowing

consensus. The Nixonologists who lunch at Sans Souci, drink on
P Street, and dine at Rive Gauche, seldom encountering a real
live Republican whom they know well enough to talk to, had it
doped out. Connally, three times governor of Texas (his last majority, in 1966, was a resounding 72 percent), boss of the solidly entrenched state Democratic establishment, and presumed owner of
twenty-six critically important electoral votes, had made a deal
with the professional in the White House. Connally received a seat
in the Cabinet, Nixon a clear shot at the state he had to have to be
re-elected, and both men, so the instant analysis ran, saw the logic
of sealing the bargain by getting together on the 1972 Republican
ticket.

Surprisingly, in the unchic places where they tend to eat and
drink when not fleeing to the suburbs, Nixon men were telling a
parallel "inside" story and congratulating themselves on Nixon's
cunning. No one went so far as to say that Agnew, the spearhead of
the fall campaign, was as good as dumped with Connally coming on
board, but the sly winks and smiles suggested it. In any event, the
President had pulled off a beautiful triple play in the eyes of his admirers. He had repaired his relations with a hostile Congress,
gained at least the appearance of bipartisan support for his economic policies and an articulate advocate to promote their success,
and — most important — put Texas within his grasp. "Here's the
President surrounded in the Cabinet by all these former governors,"
said a middle-ranking White House aide impressed by the sheer
practicality of it all, "and nobody seems to be able to deliver his
state in an election. The Boss is willing to make a bargain with
Connally because he may be able to deliver."

On Capitol Hill, a world apart from the Georgetown sophisti-
cates and the Nixon squares, the truly practical pols who run their
own show regardless of the transients in the White House were inclined to credit Nixon's shrewdness. A Texas Democrat spoke with
new respect for the President's ruthlessness. "You have to admit
that Nixon is one mean sonofabitch. The Republicans in Texas
couldn't produce in sixty-eight, and they couldn't produce this time

when they had a good man [Congressman George Bush, defeated in the Senate race by Connally's friend and ally, Lloyd Bentsen] and the President's personal intervention. So he's written them off. If he wants a good Southern conservative, he's decided he has to take a Southern Democrat." Of course, these men who knew Connally allowed the President might have just a little difficulty making the deal stick. "Nixon sees the key to the South," said a Southern Republican congressman, "*if* Connally doesn't betray him." An oddsmaker in the administration rated the chance of a Connally double-cross at about one in five.

The only flaw in the knowing consensus was the assumption that Nixon and Connally had made a deal. They hadn't. Instead, the two men had entered into a subtle, flexible arrangement based on the noncommittal sharing of immediate satisfactions. The most interesting relationship in American politics, and one which could influence the fortunes of both parties in 1972, rested on considerations of power, but at the outset it had not turned these into a mutually rewarding power transaction: yours plus mine equals ours. "There's nothing political about my entry into this administration," Connally insisted when we talked. The meaning thus conveyed was plain: I'm a free agent.

With his selection of Connally, Nixon did much more than fill an important vacancy in his Cabinet. He filled a void in his administration. No one around the President had a sense of politics remotely as acute as Connally's. And no one could so effectively share the responsibilities of domestic policy leadership and advocacy that Nixon wished to shun. The administration had been plodding along in its domestic policies, going nowhere in particular. Now the newcomer's energy and ability brought a feeling of movement, at least in the direction of his own ambitions. All at once, while Agnew languished, Connally vaulted to Nixon's side, an "Assistant President" who looked to many like a 1972 running mate.

Those who underestimated Connally as a hick wheeler-dealer soon had second thoughts in the face of his spectacular acceptance by Congress and the business community and his astonishingly swift rise within the administration's councils. But the gross overestimate of Nixon's bargaining strength was subject to much slower correction, for the myth of presidential leverage in all trading situations dies hard. The reality that Connally had the advantage, and that he joined the Nixon administration much as a receiver joins a bankrupt enterprise, entirely on his own terms, to see what could be done about holding off the creditors and salvaging the business, perhaps for his own account — this reality challenged the conventional awe of the presidency. In truth, it cost Connally next to nothing to come to Nixon's Washington and very little more to command the city's dulled imagination.

XIV

1. THE LONGER observers have been in Washington, the more accustomed they are to the traditional rules and practices of politics and therefore the harder it has been for them to comprehend the strangers who arrived in their midst in January 1969. On the Hill, at the Press Club bar, and in the K Street offices of lawyers and lobbyists, puzzled men exchange bits and pieces of information like CIA agents studying satellite photographs of Siberia. It is not merely the culture shock of Republicanism. (It is a bit startling, though, when Attorney General John Mitchell, at a black-tie gathering in the starchy F Street Club, tells very old stag jokes, while being heckled by wife Martha.) Judged by the standards of the Eisenhower era, this is not a very Republican administration.

No, the puzzlement stems from the way the Nixon men go about their presumed business of governing. From the top down, they seem oddly disinterested in the bureaucratic machinery they nominally control and almost oblivious (when not gratuitously hostile) to the legislative machinery they don't control. The Nixon administration gives outsiders the impression of a four-year sales meeting. Weeks after the President proclaimed "the new American revolution" in his January 1971 State of the Union Address, Congress still awaited proposed legislation to effect some of Nixon's "six great goals." Johnson, to be sure, was also a supersalesman, but the great difference was that he had his foot in the door — and often on a lawmaker's neck — the day after making his pitch. The lack of follow-through on the part of the new people suggests a novel, baffling lack of seriousness. For example, the once urgently important Family Assistance Plan seemed to die of presidential neglect soon after the headlines petered out.

Acknowledging criticism in Congress, Haldeman, in an interview with the sympathetic chronicler Allen Drury, expressed extraordinary indifference: "I don't think Congress is supposed to work with the White House — it is a different organization, and under the Constitution I don't think we should expect agreement."

The curious disinterest of Nixon men in matters of concern to other politicians extends to fellow Republicans. A few months after the 1970 election, Congressman William J. Scherle, a third-term conservative Republican from Iowa, received a letter from the White House. Presidential aide Harry Flemming informed Scherle that, "in view of the large number of highly qualified applicants in comparison to the relatively few positions to be filled, we are unable to offer you encouragement at this time . . . Your file, although inactive, has been placed with a selected group in our talent bank. If in the future your file is activated you will be so notified. Thank you for your interest." Scherle, just re-elected by a comfortable margin and named to the powerful House Appropriations Committee, was not amused. Like an irate depositor attempting to argue with his bank's errant computer, he fired off a reply: "It is incomprehensible that a letter such as this would go out over the signature of a supposedly responsible White House official to a member of Congress . . ." The incident, sadly, is all too typical of the way the Nixon White House regards the world beyond the iron gates.

John Connally belongs to that world, and practices the traditional political art, which calls for deference to members of the House Appropriations Committee. His entry into the highest circles of the Nixon administration thus involved much more than merely crossing party lines. Like a modern Marco Polo, he came upon an inward-looking, walled palace, the Great Within of a most unlikely Kublai Khan.

Many have remarked on the monarchical tendencies of the American presidency. The Nixon White House has brought them to the surface in all their dubious glory, down to the police dressed up in high, visored hats and thickly brocaded Sigmund Romberg uniforms. The Court is organized to perpetuate in the presidency the rigorously controlled environment — almost, it seemed, the soundproof, shock-proof bubble — within which Nixon glided to victory in 1968.

The emperor's environmental engineer, Chief of Staff Haldeman, is one of the most influential and least known White House assistants ever to gain access to presidential power without benefit of election. "I'm basically a perfectionist," Haldeman once told a reporter. With his skintight crewcut, mechanical smile, and brusque manner, he looks the part he plays: absolute disciplinarian of the movement of people and paper between the President's office and the rest of the government. Haldeman has said, rightly, that "every President needs an S.O.B. — and I'm Nixon's." Any man who fills that role, however, needs qualities of restraint that Haldeman does not visibly possess. Early in the administration, an assistant to the President spoke in awe of the totality of Nixon's protection: "Haldeman and Ehrlichman shield the President by monopolizing him. One of them is present at every meeting in the Oval Office — Nixon sees no one alone. Every meeting follows precisely, down to the second, the 'talking paper' prepared in advance. Haldeman sees everything — even the daily news summary is reviewed before it goes in to the Old Man. Nixon's made himself their captive. How can he find out whether his orders are carried out? All the channels flow back to Haldeman." The Chief of Staff continues to be the first man to see Nixon officially each morning and the last to see him each evening. He stands ready to perform any task from fetching a sandwich to firing a Cabinet officer.

No potential danger is more ominous in a free society than the secret leaching away of presidential authority from the man the people choose to the men he chooses. To whom are they responsible? To him and their own consciences, of course, which is the essence of the danger when a President is protected even from the knowledge of what is said and done in his name.

Within the first hundred days, Haldeman drew a virtual siege line — soon called "the Berlin Wall" — at the threshold of the President's office. One morning in the spring of 1969, Arthur Burns emerged after an appointment with the President. As he did, he remembered something the Postmaster General had asked him to mention to Nixon and he turned to re-enter the room. Haldeman blocked the way. "Your appointment is over," he said. Burns explained that he wanted only a moment — he must keep his promise to the Postmaster that he would deliver the message personally. That didn't mean anything, Haldeman said curtly. Loyalty to the President overrode every other consideration. He told Burns to submit a memorandum, which he would place in the President's reading folder. Amazed and at a loss for words, the Counselor to the President walked away.

Other loyal aides of the President have received similarly high-handed treatment. One day, in what seemed a thoughtful gesture, Haldeman sent a dozen roses to Rose Mary Woods. The next day he sent an assistant, Larry Higby, to ask for her office, proposing to move her to more spacious quarters in the Executive Office Building across the street. Miss Woods knew an eviction notice when she saw one. The red-haired secretary, who had begun working for Nixon when the messenger was a toddler, told him to tell his boss that she would not budge from the West Wing. If Haldeman wanted her out of the White House, he would have to carry her — and thanks for the flowers. Miss Woods remained under the same roof as the Boss.

Haldeman has disclaimed any involvement in the substance of policy, in spite of his strategic position and far-ranging, arbitrary authority. It was at his suggestion, however, that domestic policy-making was reorganized and centralized around Ehrlichman, his closest friend, fellow Christian Scientist, and fellow teetotaler. Ehrlichman's elevation as director of the newly created Domestic Council eliminated at a stroke the countervailing influence of such presidential counselors as Moynihan, Burns, and Harlow. "The Germans," as Haldeman and Ehrlichman became known within the White House, and their scurrying squads of close-cropped, but-toned-up ex-advance men took over with Teutonic thoroughness. Even the White House Mess, which in former administrations had been a place of welcome respite from protocol where junior men rubbed elbows with their bosses, became regimented. "The big people," in a junior aide's tart phrase, have their own separate dining room, with nameplates on their reserved tables.*

As though suffocated by the pressure to conform in endless small matters while large issues went ignored, one of the White House aides shoved aside by Haldeman's "Beaver Patrol" said despondently: "They'd rather have control over everything, and let it all fall apart, than share power and accomplish something." As "the Germans" and their underlings see it, the intensely satisfying accomplishment is having control for its own sweet sake.

Anyone who is not inside the White House and subject to its peculiar discipline and ideology of nonideology ("We're for what works for us," said an up-and-coming German) is an outsider, even though he may be a Cabinet member, a would-be supporter in Congress, or a generous campaign contributor. The marketing managers of Nixon, Inc., working in their willed atmosphere of isolation, sometimes reveal almost an adversary attitude toward the rest of the Nixon administration. Presidential vetoes are announced without warning to the heads of affected departments, legislative signals are switched without consulting congressional leaders, and people at every level of the party, who supposed they were part of the game, discover, like Congressman Scherle, that no one inside ever heard of them. "It's a crime," a senior Republican congressman laments, "the number of times important people up here, or out in the country, call the White House and wind up talking with Dwight Chapin." The pleasant, thirty-year-old Chapin is an assist-

* According to former Secret Service agent Rufus Youngblood, who went into early and reluctant retirement in mid-1971, Haldeman barred him from continuing to eat in the White House Mess because he was regarded as excessively loyal to former President Johnson. During the assassination of President Kennedy, Youngblood shielded then Vice President Johnson with his body, a valorous act for which he was decorated. Haldeman and Ehrlichman, Youngblood told the Washington *Post*, try to run the Secret Service "like a Los Angeles advertising agency or Disneyland."

ant to Haldeman and worked for him at J. Walter Thompson in
Los Angeles. In his closed domain, nobody is important unless
Haldeman says so; and Haldeman is too busy to be bothered with
anything but serving a President who doesn't wish to be disturbed.
*"Can you call me back later, Senator? If I'm tied up, my assistant's name
is . . ."*

2. Like the inhabitants of the imperial city of Kaifeng on whom
Marco Polo was the first Westerner to gaze, the Nixon courtiers are
skilled in exotic crafts that their opponents imitate badly or not at
all. But they are themselves innocent of the ways of the Great Outside: pressing flesh, hearing petty concerns patiently, conferring,
consulting, cajoling, and persuading — the whole art of reaching
out, man-to-man, eyeball-to-eyeball, for sympathy, support, and
votes. Happily, these are the ways of John Connally, the stranger
from the West, and his mastery inspires wonder among his new colleagues.

John Connally's confirmation hearing before the Senate Committee on Finance was something to write home about — and, in
fact, more than one marked-up copy of the *Congressional Record* was
forwarded to Lyndon Johnson. The elders behind the elevated,
curved desk in the high-ceilinged chamber were not Connally's inquisitors, but his friendly interlocutors, concerned with helping
their fellow Democrat make a properly impressive entrance. Chairman Russell B. Long frankly expressed his intense curiosity as to
where, precisely, Connally stood, for that would guide his relations
(and those of other Democrats) with the new Secretary and the administration. He brushed aside the customary question of financial
conflict and raised the intriguing question of "potential political
conflict."

Recalling that he and Connally had campaigned for the Ken-
nedy-Johnson ticket in 1960, Long drawled: "I think if you and I
had stayed home, President Nixon might have been in the presidency eight years sooner. How do you explain being here under the
present circumstances?" Connally drawled in reply that the Presi-

dent "convinced me . . . that I could contribute something to his administration and thus to the welfare of this country . . . And I suppose I was vain enough to believe it and silly enough to try it." The printed record does not show that the chairman and the witness exchanged winks, but they might as well. It was a well-played exchange, the kind that makes the Congress the best theater in Washington. Long had what he was after: the assurance that Connally was public-spirited, vain, and still a Democrat.

Georgia's senator Herman E. Talmadge, another Democratic grandee, asked, in effect, if his friend knew what he was getting into. He had heard some disturbing reports on the way matters were organized at the other end of Pennsylvania Avenue, and he offered some advice. "It would be demeaning to the stature of your office as Secretary of the Treasury to report to a staff member in the White House rather than directly to the President," said Talmadge with the air of a man who knew whereof he spoke. "As Secretary of the Treasury, I hope you will undertake to fulfill your responsibilities in accordance with the duties of your office and not in accordance with the dictates of a White House staff member, and I hope that the flow of power will be down from the President rather than up from the staff."

Connally, with a sure instinct for diplomacy, responded to the cautionary counsel by declaring himself "new in this town, at least on this visit" and therefore unable to confirm what the senator told him. After expressing his desire to cooperate with everyone, he put Talmadge at ease and the White House staff and any other trespassers on notice. "I think, without in any sense appearing to be arrogant, Senator Talmadge, that you can be sure that so long as I am Secretary of the Treasury, I shall be Secretary of the Treasury . . ."

Not long afterward, the first test of strength occurred. Connally had addressed a memorandum to the President and was astounded to find it back on his desk, undelivered and accompanied by a note. One of the paper-controllers at the White House wanted to know why the Secretary wished to raise this particular subject with the

President. Connally's predecessor, the self-effacing Chicago banker David M. Kennedy, would have dutifully explained himself, perhaps apologizing for the inconvenience he had caused. Connally just stared at the paper. By all accounts, he does not have a bad temper — he has a *magnificently* bad temper. Now, having contemplated the offending document and the presumption behind it, he flew into a splendid rage. When he had worked up a suitable head of steaming indignation, he composed a memorandum to the White House aide, demanding a written explanation for this intolerable interference in his personal communications with the President. The following day, he had it, complete with an apology. Nixon's reply came swiftly. His courtiers, used to dismissing Cabinet officers, had met a titled gentleman sure of his ground and fiercely determined to defend it.

(A Treasury official, delighted with his boss's style, mused on the difference between amateurs and professionals: "I really believe that Connally had a long talk with the President about how the game would be played, and that the two of them laid down the rules. Some Cabinet members came into this administration without attaching any strings or laying down any rules. They were amateurs, and they had their tongues hanging out for the big jobs and titles." Such men, like most men, did not want the substance of power, only the ego-inflating appearance. They wanted, not the fact of command authority, but the prerogatives of office, however empty. "Nixon could say to them: 'Go and see the staff,' " the Treasury man continued. "They were shocked. They were naive enough to assume that they would automatically see the President. You can be damned sure that Connally isn't naive." Just as sure was his perception of the uncertainty masked by arrogant presumption: presidential staff men did not know what private understanding the Boss had reached with a pro like Connally, and he knew that *they* knew they challenged him at their peril.)

With Connally's arrival, the ascendancy of the giddily risen advance men halted where he was concerned, and as the ambit of that concern expanded, at presidential direction, their control weak-

ened. Nixon, who shuns so many would-be companions and counselors, seeks Connally's company and advice. He calls him frequently, summons him to play host at White House breakfast and
dinner briefings, and shows open delight at his winning way with
outsiders. With only slight exaggeration, an observer high up in the
Treasury assesses Connally's position, gained with astonishing ease.
"There's nobody around town, with the possible exception of John
Mitchell, in whom the President has so much trust and whose wisdom he so respects." Another President-watcher, closer to the
White House, confirms the apparent linkage of Connally and Mitchell in Nixon's mind and offers an explanation: "Connally is the
kind of physically impressive and commanding guy who inspires a
certain awe in Nixon. He sees great *strength* in him, the same as he
does in Mitchell." What Nixon may see in these self-assured men is
the strength of success: both have taken the world as they found it
and bent it their way.

Such tributes to Connally are doubtless merited, yet they recall
the sovereignty of the one-eyed man in the land of the blind. So out
of place is a poised, gifted politician in the upper reaches of Nixon's
Washington that even the formerly wary join the chorus of praise.
At the Federal Reserve Board, which viewed with apprehension the
takeover of the Treasury by a cheap-money Texas Populist, an
official declares: "He's a big, bright star in a dreary setting." Even
within the White House, where the effect of Connally's presence is
to reduce the power of the jealous insiders, a kind of dazzled gratitude prevails. A presidential aide speaks of Connally's "great understanding of what motivates people" as though describing a miraculous quality rather than a commonplace attribute of a winning
politician. The first outsider admitted all the way inside the Nixon
sanctuary, Connally, like the thirteenth-century Venetian in
Cathay, astonishes simply by being himself. To those who toil inside
the bubble, untouched and untouching, his access to reality, his intimate familiarity with the men shaping it — *he calls them by their first
names* — seems almost magical. *Why, he can call Wilbur Mills "Wilbur."*

The admiration is mutual. Connally, in the words of a Treasury staff member, is "the strongest Nixon admirer I've found down here," which says a great deal about Republican morale. The President, Connally told me in a conversation in the spring of 1971, sounding rather like Jack Valenti used to sound on the subject of Lyndon Johnson, "is a man who fully understands some of the very basic problems of this country. He's a man willing to risk his political fortunes on proposals that aren't necessarily inviting. I've found in Nixon a surprising kindness toward individuals. But he also has undaunted courage to make the tough decisions. His ideas in foreign policy reflect an unusual awareness of the uses of power in the broadest sense . . ."

Where had I heard *that* before? Why, from someone quoting Nixon on Connally. The President was said to include Connally in a very select company, "one of the few men in this country who understands the uses of power" — by which Nixon means *national* power. With his shrewd sense of what motivates people, so impressive to Nixon men, Connally grasps Nixon's tremendous desire to be proved right in his international moves. From his own visceral conservatism, Connally lends psychological support to an embattled President.

Although Nixon is by nature a solitary reader and a consumer of yellow legal pads, he enjoys the kind of agreeable company and conversation Connally provides. For Nixon is the born second-stringer who captains the varsity by hard-plugging, self-discipline, and perseverance, and he is attracted to the graceful superstars. Connally is not just another fawning courtier, another yes man whose murmur of approval is taken for granted. For the round-shouldered, palm-rubbing President to hear his views echoed and his courage praised by this strapping, handsome Texan is like standing on tiptoe and seeing an unexpectedly pleasing image in the mirror.

Connally has positioned himself at Richard Nixon's right hand and serves him as counselor, companion, clever lobbyist, generalissimo to the worried captains of industry, and, above all, upright advocate of whatever Nixon currently favors: the salesman's salesman. "You know," Connally remarked to me in our spring 1971 interview, smiling expansively in the manner of a man well pleased with himself, "I thought I would be putting myself in a difficult position coming here. But I'm not finding it difficult at all." As he strolled from his office, he took a piece of candy from a jar on his secretary's desk and rolled it over his tongue. "I'm in the fortunate position of having been asked."

Connally had reason for self-satisfaction. He had done all that he was invited to do as a politician. But he could do nothing to repair the administration's deeper, intellectual bankruptcy.

3. In the summer of 1971, the President stunned the world with a pair of announcements a month apart, each marking a momentous turn in U.S. policy. The first, prepared in deepest secrecy, was the announcement of Nixon's plan to visit Peking, ending in the most dramatic fashion imaginable a generation of American self-isolation from mainland China. The reversal of U.S. policy and his own former position concerned Nixon not at all — in fact, it made for much of his evident delight with himself. For here he was embarked on a high adventure after his Wilsonian model, acting the role of foreign-policy President and architect of a new era of peace to which he gave first priority. The flood of approving publicity, however, was not matched by much enthusiasm or even interest among ordinary Americans. The reaction in the opinion polls, which Nixon watched intently, amounted to a shrug. The people, absorbed in their economic worries, would wait and see what came of their monarch's journey to the Court of Chairman Mao.

The second announcement, in mid-August, ironically met with overwhelming popular approval and lifted the President's standing overnight, yet he could take no satisfaction from it. Once again, after secret deliberation, he executed a spectacular reversal of course and announced a far-ranging new domestic and foreign economic policy: a freeze on wages and prices, suspension of the U.S. guarantee to redeem dollars in foreign hands at the rate of $35 per ounce of gold, imposition of a 10 percent surtax on most U.S. imports, and an array of tax measures designed to stimulate consumer spending, investment, and employment. In the phrase of a participant in the meetings at Camp David preceding the President's announcement, the New Economic Policy "came together like a great thunderclap." Indeed it did. Until almost the last moment, Nixon men had insisted that the economic skies were clearing, that the President definitely would *not* do what he finally did, and that the watchword was, "Steady as she goes." The man up front as the administration's spokesman, earnestly forecasting sunshine and then just as earnestly unfurling an umbrella, was Secretary Connally, the partisan of the present policy, whatever it might be.

For more than a year before the thunderclap over Camp David, Arthur Burns, the resolutely outspoken chairman of the Federal Reserve Board, assumed the more hazardous role of partisan of what he believed to be the *necessary* policy. Seeing in the administration's course a steady drift toward disaster, he had urged his long-time friend Nixon to take direct measures against a worsening inflation. For a man as committed to free-market economic principles as Burns, such advice was hard to give, but he gave it nonetheless. In an increasingly politicized economy, which made market forces ineffective and doctrines based on their operation obsolete, he saw no alternative to presidential intervention serving the broad public interest. His advice was unwelcome and went unheeded.

Late in July 1971, in testimony before the Joint Economic Committee of Congress, Burns spoke the plain but unadmitted truth: "The rules of economics are not working in quite the way they used to." The key sentences of his lengthy, courageous presentation were these: "I wish I could report that we are making substantial progress in dampening the inflationary spiral. I cannot do so. Neither the behavior of prices nor the pattern of wage increases as yet provides evidence of any significant moderation in the advance of costs and prices." Privately, Burns amended that statement, omitting the softening adjective "significant." He saw, bleakly, no moderation at all, but instead the grim possibility of a quickening of the pace of inflation. He also spoke of the atmosphere of the White House Court: "Everybody wants to make the King happy. I wish that *I* could make him happy. But the evidence isn't there."

For the high political crime of committing truth in public, Burns was subjected to crude personal attack by petty White House barons reacting to their sovereign's displeasure. Word was leaked to the press that Burns, who wanted an "incomes policy" for others, was seeking a raise in salary for himself — which was utterly false. In fact, Burns had specifically told the President and his aides that any increase in the salary of the Federal Reserve Board chairman should take effect *after* he left the position. The anonymous character assassins went on to tell reporters that the President was so incensed he would seek to expand the Fed's Board — that is, to "pack" it with supporters of his policies. When the stories reporting these alleged presidential intentions appeared, the reaction in financial circles at home and overseas was just the opposite of the effect intended by the malicious insiders. Those who respected Burns's integrity and judgment, and who saw the truth of the U.S. economic situation as clearly as he did, were thoroughly alarmed. In spite of the President's attempts to repair the damage at a hastily called news conference, in which he disowned the charges against Burns and went out of his way to praise him highly, the weakness of the U.S. position abroad, plus the attacks on the honest, realistic critic, brought the crisis to a head.

"We have awakened forces that nobody is at all familiar with," said Connally after the President announced his new policy. The sudden disclosure of a 180-degree turn in policy guaranteed that the attention of the media and the public would focus on the newly adopted course rather than the one so long defended and so abruptly abandoned without a backward look. A former White House assistant, seeing a familiar pattern, said: "Nixon doesn't edge into a new position the way most politicians do. He jumps all at once. That's where he gets his support. Then he begins to hedge that position and ease away from it. That's where he gets his distrust."

Nixon had leaped into the dark, a gambler for the highest stakes, and all those whose fortunes he carried could only pray for a safe landing. His overture to Peking, made without consulting Tokyo, risked already weakened U.S. relations with Japan, our closest ally in Asia and an economic superpower. His decision to impose unprecedented peacetime wage and price controls on the U.S. economy assumed the nation's ability to retrace its steps and recover the free market after the inflationary emergency abated. His sudden torpedoing of the world monetary and trading system assumed that the non-Communist nations, without accustomed U.S. leadership, could agree on new long-term arrangements. To hasten the coming of his heralded "era of negotiation," Nixon announced plans to visit Moscow — another dramatic presidential "first." He hoped to crown his exercise in summitry with the long-delayed U.S.–Soviet treaty limiting strategic arms, and his domestic political needs gave the Soviets added bargaining leverage to obtain U.S. concessions.

Through the President's maneuvers ("churning" was a word often heard) ran his transparent personal motives. To improve his chances of re-election, he would pre-empt any position the Democrats might take in the 1972 campaign, as he had done by adopting their program for the economy. To deny them ground to stand on, of course, he was obliged to shift his own. For example, on the question of Peking's admission to the United Nations at the price of Taiwan's ouster, Nixon over the years had been adamant. With Henry Kissinger in Peking as the vote on China's UN seat was taken, however, many delegates thought they saw the U.S.'s true intentions toward Taiwan plainly. Telling Ambassador George Bush polite lies about how they would vote up to the last minute, they did the cynical deed while a silent Nixon looked the other way.

As Nixon abandoned pledged positions, a gulf opened between the administration and the silent majority of Republicans. By the fall of 1971, the President had exhausted the affection and patience of the conservatives. A dozen representatives of conservative organizations and publications, led by William F. Buckley, Jr., publicly announced that they had "suspended" support of the Nixon administration. Soon, Representative John Ashbrook of Ohio came forward to oppose Nixon in the New Hampshire and Florida primary elections. The editors of *National Review* and *Human Events,* and officers of Young Americans for Freedom, the American Conservative Union, and the New York State Conservative party, had little political "clout," and it was easy for Ehrlichman to dismiss them as "the knee-jerk right." Moreover, their former champions — Goldwater, Reagan, Tower, and Thurmond — turned out to be practical-minded Nixon loyalists and apologists. Nevertheless, these right-wingers expressed a disillusionment running deep among moderate, rank-and-file Republicans. The conservatives closed their July 1971 manifesto on a wistful note: "We consider that our defection is an act of loyalty to the Nixon we supported in 1968." Many Republicans remember that Nixon and wonder what in the world has become of him in the White House.

The newest Nixon allows his conservative instincts to show only in private company ("Why, he sent for coffee, put his feet up, and gave the liberals hell," runs a visitor's typical report). In public, the salesman in the Oval Office evidently believes that he must position himself well to the left of his party because the "center" of the electorate appears to be there. White House strategists assume that unhappy Republicans have nowhere else to go while Nixon courts left-of-center voters. Those voters, it is assumed, will decide that the President ought to be re-elected, not on the basis of promises fulfilled, but on the basis of policies he has expediently adopted. "Seldom in Western politics," said the *New York Times* in a half-admiring editorial in early 1972, ". . . has a national leader so completely turned his back on a lifetime of beliefs to adopt those of his political opponents."

Nixon is both the impulsive gambler of 1971–1972 and the play-safe strategist of the 1968 campaign. He has made the cautious judgment, amounting to a self-fulfilling prophecy, that the Republicans will remain an electoral minority through his presidency. Instead of attempting to build a Republican majority based squarely on a new populist conservatism and specific programs for Middle

America, Nixon's sights this year are set on the same goal as in 1968: an ad hoc, one-shot plurality.

It is too late for an administration without design, theme, or direction to have any other goal. The President and his men did not arrive in Washington with the intention of restoring Great Society liberalism. But they arrived empty-handed, which makes their intentions (beyond protecting incumbency) the hostage of their circumstances. Under the pressure of the program and budget cycle, the Nixon men have been forced to make wholesale borrowings from the Democrats. But too many of their "new" ideas are novel only to them and a Republican setting. Some G.O.P. dogmas were outmoded and impractical, to be sure, but these uncritical — even unwanted ("How do we kill Model Cities?" demanded a perplexed Nixonite) — borrowings are no better. Moynihan's parting praise of the President for preserving faith in the system by maintaining continuity with the Johnson administration attempted to make helpless default appear to be an act of deliberate choice.

Those conservative intellectuals who now oppose the administration bear some responsibility for its incoherence. "We touch only lightly on the failure of Mr. Nixon's administration domestically," declared William Buckley and the others in their 1971 statement. "These domestic considerations, important as they are, pale into insignificance alongside the tendencies of the administration in foreign policy." But the voters have put America's homely problems first, no matter how much Republican intellectuals may yearn for the priorities of the Cold War era, and that fact cannot be argued.

The Republican failure — not Nixon's alone — is a failure of perception and vision. Too few Republicans see the opportunity for our party to lead culturally as well as politically. The Republican party traditionally has been indifferent to social ideas, and the Nixon image-makers, in their search for a quick, easy way to exploit the plight of the "forgotten Americans," merely behaved as Republicans usually behave.

Partly as a result, the popular political discontent and distrust of politicians goes very deep. At the height of his strength in 1968,

George Wallace was the preferred candidate of one voter out of five. At his peak, Wallace would have received 20 million votes — only 11 million less than Nixon. His base was impressively broad. He had the support of close to one third of the young workers (aged 21–29), who far outnumber the campus population. Here was a quite different wave of the future from the student and black "revolts" dominating the media. Regardless of what happens to Wallace in 1972, the angry white lower-middle-class constituency will persist, for the simple reason that their grievances are not being removed — indeed, under economic pressure, they have become more intense. The system remains unresponsive and the pace of threatening social change quickens.

One of the best descriptions of the Wallace voters was provided in October 1968 by Senator Edward Kennedy, who recognized these voters as disaffected Democrats. Most Wallace people, he said, "are not motivated by racial hostility or prejudice. They are decent, respectable citizens who feel that their needs and their problems have been passed over by the tide of recent events. They bear the burden of the unfair system of Selective Service. They lose out because higher education costs so much. They are the ones who feel most threatened in the security of their jobs, the safety of their families, the value of their property and the burden of their taxes. They feel that the established system has not been sympathetic to them and their problems of everyday life — *and in large measure they are right* . . . We cannot expect our citizens to pay taxes to solve other people's problems in our country — as they will have to — when their own problems are not being met. *Government programs must no longer be directed to one race or one class,* but to all Americans." *

As Kennedy declared, the Wallace supporters are largely justified in their sense of injury, but our society's established arbiters of political morality, the liberal intellectuals, stubbornly deny the legitimacy of white lower-middle-class protest.

In an interview published in the *New York Times* during a confer-

* Kennedy's statement was quoted in Andrew Knight's article, "Remembering George Wallace — The Anatomy of a Campaign," *Interplay*, January 1969.

ence at Princeton University in December 1968, political scientist Zbigniew Brzezinski described the liberals' self-made social dilemma. "A great deal of what we, the liberal establishment, but also the upper-middle class — which we are and which we hate to admit — really advocate is social revolution at the expense of the white lower-middle class. [The hostility between their class and mine] is not due to the racial prejudice of the lower-middle class alone. If they all had incomes of $25,000 a year, they would be as liberal as we are. The fact is that they live in marginal environments, and the fact is that I — and I'll speak for myself here, for I feel strongly about this issue — I do not really have to make many sacrifices on behalf of social revolution. The nature of our system is such that I can preach it, I can advocate it . . . but I don't pay very much for it, and I don't have any solution."

Nixon Republicans saw the stake in 1968 and 1970 as winning elections only, rather than seeking as well to replace the intellectual-cultural establishment Professor Brzezinski described. They tried to harness the anger of the white lower-middle class without extending genuine compassion or making reasoned arguments. But ordinary people realized that their lives and values were threatened on the field of ideas and that they needed to be defended there by men of ideas who could claim genuine moral authority for their views. The marketing men of Nixon, Inc., were unable to synthesize such authority, and neither hard-hats nor liberal intellectuals were much impressed by the administration's performance.

In his book *The Middle Americans,* psychiatrist Robert Coles talked with people who did not fit the stereotypes of the administration. A twenty-five-year-old welder, though an admirer of the Vice President, saw less than the leader he wanted. "You know, I hate snobs," he told Coles, "but you've got to be honest and ask yourself if that man has what it takes up in the head to be President. I don't want a guy there just because he sounds like me shouting my head off over my lunch box."

In his December 1970 farewell address to the President, Cabinet, and White House staff, Moynihan said: "The people in the nation who take . . . matters seriously have never been required to take us seriously. Time and again the President would put forth an often-times devastating critique precisely of their performance. But his initial thrusts were rarely followed up with a sustained, reasoned, reliable second and third order or advocacy."

Moynihan, an intellectual and a convinced liberal in spite of his sojourn among the Republicans, might well wonder why the lesser advocates were so few and timid in this administration. *He* was eager to defend *his* ideas. But his colleagues were strangers on that ground; more important, the ideas needing advocacy were not their own. Men will stand up for what they believe, not for what they borrow.

The all-important fact shaping the future of American politics is public *awareness* on a mass scale never before seen in any human society. Television has all but replaced the traditional political party as the aggregating force in our politics. As a result of this awareness, the strongest, fastest-growing political body in America is not the Democrats and certainly not the Republicans — it is the Independents, those people who are more and more likely to value a personality and life-style above a promise.

Superficially, Republicans would appear to have an advantage in such competition, not because of Nixon's personality, surely, but because we are a fairly homogeneous social minority. We are united around clear-cut cultural values underlying the new American majority way of life in the green suburbs. But the Independents, particularly the younger ones, tend to be like the welder quoted earlier. They are aware of the difference between first-rate and third-rate; they are not easily fooled. In egalitarian America, ironically, the mass of citizens are aware of aristocratic standards and expect to see them acted upon in high places. They have taken to heart what they understand to be part of John F. Kennedy's legacy. Presidential leadership, they believe, should be marked by the appreciation and pursuit of excellence.

In January 1969, at a post-Inaugural banquet given by friends in Annapolis, Vice President Agnew informally defined the new administration's position on the political-cultural battleground, declaring: "We're all middlebrows here." The great majority of Americans are middlebrows at best, but they do not necessarily want to be led by men who are no better than they are.

When Nebraska's senator Roman Hruska defended the nomination of Judge G. Harrold Carswell to the Supreme Court on the remarkable ground that the mediocre, too, deserve to be represented, he inadvertently exposed the basic defect of Nixon Republicanism. It sincerely believes that mediocrity, dressed up in the trappings of power, is good enough.

5.   Before John Sears finally was forced out of the White House in October 1969 — with their usual subtlety, his enemies applied pressure by such tactics as omitting his name from the staff list distributed to the press, later claiming clerical oversight — we talked one evening until very late. As we had during the campaign, we talked not only of politics, but of what politics was supposed to accomplish. "We joined up with the Old Man" — he still referred to Nixon that way — "to do something for the future, something that would continue. This won't. We're losing ground instead of consolidating it. The way our institutions are going and the way people are losing belief in even the possibility of hope from politicians, this country could be in terrible shape by seventy-six."

I resisted that bleak conclusion as late as February 1970. In a letter to the President, the last I wrote, I recalled our first conversation, which looked beyond immediate political objectives to others in the sphere of cultural and intellectual influence. Though unrelated to immediate political necessities, these were, I believed, crucial for the politics of the future.

"In the long run, ideas are the decisive force in a free society," said the letter. "It may take a generation or two, but ideas, effectively argued, change attitudes, capture institutions, and channel political energies in new directions. The survival of our system through the end of this century may depend on the struggle presently being waged in the mass communications media, the publishing industry, and the academic-foundation complex — especially the last. For it is there that social ideas originate, and it is there that the ideology of 'revolution' is gaining the ascendancy.

"Talk is cheap, but all revolutions begin with talk, and they flourish if those in power seem to have no philosophy, no ideas, nothing to say beyond campaign slogans. Unfortunately there is no specifically 'political' response to cultural and intellectual insurgency: it must be countered in its own terms, on the battleground of ideas. If we lose the war there, as we are losing it largely by default, our victories at the polls go for nothing.

"Our side is woefully short of the institutional resources necessary to complement and consolidate our present political strength. We lack, not talented and committed people, but the apparatus of argument and persuasion: sympathetic foundations, well-staffed and well-financed research centers, publications appealing to a younger, increasingly well-educated population, strategically placed communications outlets, publishing houses, and review media — the list can be extended. It reflects almost two generations of one-party, one-philosophy dominance, during which an establishment arose to enforce intellectual conformity. Now that establishment is collapsing and the vacuum invites the rush of 'revolutionary' ideas to fill it.

"On our side there is no Ford Foundation, no Brookings Institution, no Kennedy Institute; and yet we have intelligent, resourceful men, instinctively aware of the deficiency, who need only inspiration, leadership, and a strategy to do what is required. You are in the best of all possible positions to provide such inspiration and leadership . . .

"In recent weeks, several of us — Martin Anderson, Alan Greenspan, Pat Buchanan, and others — have begun talking informally about the main outlines of a strategy. I am told that Bryce Harlow shares our enthusiasm and sense of urgency . . ."

The letter reached Nixon's desk, was read, and went into his briefcase. For six weeks, it traveled with him back and forth across the country. Friends within the administration whose similar urgings had been blocked reported on its progress. Finally, one of them passed on Nixon's response.

"Tell Dick to proceed discreetly."

XV

MEMORANDUM

TO: RN

FROM: RJW

I don't suppose Bob Haldeman has put a copy of George Reedy's *Twilight of the Presidency* beside your Night Reading File — the title does sound rather depressing. Nevertheless, it is a book that deserves your attention as much as the cables marked "Top Secret" because it describes what is happening, not in Moscow, Peking, or Saigon, but inside your White House.

Like every other occupant of the modern, monarchical presidency, you are now a King and you live in a splendid Court, surrounded by an aura of majesty. The entire structure, Reedy writes, is designed "for one purpose and one purpose only — to serve the material needs and desires of a single man." You are that man. You are completely protected and insulated, your every wish and whim is anticipated. Every moment of every day, you are compensated in ways large and small for the hard knocks and disappointments you encountered on the road to the White House.

Unfortunately, there is a flaw in this otherwise perfect environment. It is the absence of tenure. The American monarchy rests on the shifting sands of democratic sovereignty. Should the people turn against their would-be King, all pretensions will come tumbling down with terrible swiftness.

In spite of the panoply of the presidency, as you seek re-election this year you resume the role in which I served you in 1967–1968, that of petitioner for popular favor. Then, you were simply "RN" and you sought plain-spoken counsel, for you wanted very badly to win and were prepared to say and do whatever seemed necessary. It was your extraordinary good fortune — or so it seemed then — that the Democrats, in their suicidal divisions, spared you the necessity of spelling out your views in detail.

Even so, we Republicans, exercising the prerogative of the Outs, made a great many generalized promises. In sum, these amounted to the pledge that you would bring to Washington a different kind of government, one that would pursue a different course at home and abroad. The electorate received essentially this message: the Nixon administration will tell you the truth of America's situation and will act resolutely to set it right.

In your present circumstances, should you ask your subordinates whether that promise has been kept, you will surely receive an affirmative answer. Courtiers never speak unless spoken to first, and when they are addressed, they seek to please you. Quite humanly, they fear your power to shut out unpleasantness and banish the bearers of unwelcome news. So they tell you the part of the truth which, like the rest of the White House structure, serves your need and desire for reassurance. *Yes, there is progress.* And the flip charts in the Cabinet Room unfold the glad tidings.

What the yea-sayers and your "realistic" Republican apologists do not dwell upon is the direction of much of this progress. It is *away* from the goals you proclaimed in the 1968 campaign. The difference between what your administration has done and proposed to do, and what a Humphrey administration would have done, is not very significant. What *is* sadly significant is that a liberal Democratic administration would have acted out of mistaken conviction. Your administration's slithering to the left — to borrow a phrase from our common political hero, Churchill — is prompted by mistaken calculation.

In the course of the 1969 campaign, you declared: *I seek the Presidency, not because it offers me a chance to be somebody, but because it offers me a chance to do something.* I believed then that you sincerely meant that, and so did others around you. In June 1968, you may recall, you confided to a visitor that you expected to be a one-term President, for a pair of reasons. First, you would have to make many hard and unpopular decisions. Second, the physical and emotional demands of the world's most responsible office would drain your energies.

Somewhere in the transition from citizen to monarch, your principled determination truly to govern, rather than merely reign, faltered. For that reason, I am bound to say, the chance that you will be a one-term President is perhaps greater than you realize.

Apparently, each would-be King must discover for himself that the American people, though sometimes fooled, aren't fools. They know what their real needs and interests are. They are mature enough to face harsh facts, whether these relate to our position in Southeast Asia, our growing strategic weakness vis-à-vis the Soviet Union, or our approaching fiscal-financial crisis arising from the uncontrolled expansion of the federal budget. They are intelligent enough to distinguish between straightforward government and political gimmickry. They are prepared to follow a steadfast leader who does not hesitate to invoke a spirit of genuine national sacrifice in dealing with America's trials.

To be believed, you must act on what you believe. As it is, your administration does not appear to have any settled beliefs. On the eve of the first hundred days, an unidentified but clearly authoritative White House aide set the tone, telling the *New York Times:* "There is no ideology, no central commitment, no fixed body of thought."

Not long afterward, John Ehrlichman stated your position on a proposed domestic program and a highly placed member of your official family challenged him, saying the statement contradicted what he knew of your philosophy. Ehrlichman informed the stunned questioner that you didn't have any philosophy — that you did what was feasible and tactically shrewd. "Ehrlichman didn't realize what he was saying," the official later told me. "*I* know Nixon has values and a philosophy, but why doesn't Ehrlichman? And why does Nixon rely on a man like that?"

I, too, know that you have a philosophy, to which you once privately gave the name "conservative." Publicly, however, you give your government the label "centrist," which shifts meaning so frequently as to be meaningless. An authentic liberal or conservative government has an inner steadiness and confidence that a "centrist" government lacks. The latter is never sure of its identity as it tries to be liberal today, radical tomorrow, and conservative the day after. It confronts the electorate from an equivocal crouch, scarcely a posture to inspire popular trust.

If you could have trusted your convictions and declared your course forthrightly, you would have been a convincing leader. But you relied on calculated, synthetic gestures. Of course, there was a risk of rejection involved in declaring yourself. Every President of the first rank has braved that risk; and every mediocre President has shied away from it.

But time and opportunity have run out. The silence of the great silent majority can no longer be plausibly advertised as assent. Now the silence may signify only indifference toward government that has made little positive difference in the lives of ordinary citizens. Among your most enthusiastic supporters of four years ago, the people who did not need to be rounded up by Ehrlichman's advance men, rising disaffection is evident. You might ignore these people who nominated and did so much to elect you if "centrism" were attracting others to replace them. But where are the new Nixon enthusiasts?

Not long ago, one of your more thoughtful assistants spoke to me in a tone of discouragement, almost despair, that probably did not reach your ears. "You do have to be committed to ideas, values, a direction," he said. "In here" — he gestured toward the White House walls as though imprisoned — "we're just coping day to day.

And I can see circumstances in which it could all come apart very suddenly."

It is hard, even for those within your administration, to tell what the consequences of your tenure will be for the nation and our party. Liberals as well as conservatives are uncertain, and in conversation they often refer to the campaign four years ago, as though trying to determine where the sense of direction was lost. It is sad when men of Cabinet rank, who presumably counsel you now, ask me, in effect, if I recall what it was that we set out to accomplish behind your leadership. Would I mind sharing the memoranda I then wrote? In this book I have done so, in spite of your last advice to me — "proceed discreetly."

What I saw in 1967–1968, I see today, for the American situation is essentially unchanged.

We Republicans believe in setting limits on government power and authority, as our opponents generally do not. We believe in the integrity and worth of the individual — which is the underlying demand in every rebellious sector of our society. We know that middle-class Americans, regardless of their politics, try to order their lives around values that can only be called conservative. Moreover, these people who make up the great majority of Americans sensibly recognize the effective limits of politics and sensibly resist their government's impulse to politicize every human problem and concern. Our opportunity in 1968 was clear. If we had honestly defined what was worth conserving and set about it, if we had done everything possible to turn power back toward the people (instead of merely talking about it), if we had performed the tasks government can perform well, showing respect for the integrity of individuals, communities, and smaller nations — if we had done these things and more, we might have rallied a cultural majority and made it an effective new political majority.

Our peril was also clear, and we have succumbed to it. We Republicans, while temporarily enjoying governing power, have contented ourselves with overseeing a government we do not truly control, one that is moving by blind momentum further and further away from our party's distinctive beliefs. Without intending it, we have replaced the meddlesome philosopher-king of the liberal state with the repressive policeman-king of the pseudo-conservative state. Instead of doing everything possible to revive the decisive force for civilized order, the confidence of the people in themselves and their freely chosen codes, we have hastened the transformation of a free citizenry into a "protected" and controlled subject mass. In the process, we have undermined our party's reason for existence.

The alternatives, then, were to govern or reign. You have reigned.

An explanation is in order for the title of this book. One morning in November 1969, after you had spoken to the nation on Vietnam the previous evening and called on "the silent majority" to rally behind you, your aides found in their in boxes small American flag lapel pins. Obediently, they put on the new "team" emblem. It must have seemed a stroke of genius to the hucksters in the White House. Of all the symbols of American belief, unity, and sacrifice, the flag is easily the most compelling.

But this resort to gimmickry, like similar calculations, proved unsuccessful. I am less offended by the street guerrillas' burning of the flag, despicable as the act is, than by the attempt to convert it into a partisan, divisive insignia — and I know that I am not the only Republican who feels this way. We Republicans owe our loyalty, not to the device worn by temporarily powerful men in Washington, but to the enduring ideals of individual freedom and limited, responsive government the flag represents.

The flag, as symbol of these ideals, is falling, and I have written to hasten the arrival of the courageous leadership needed to catch and raise it.

APPENDIX

Richard M. Nixon's Speech Scheduled for Delivery on March 31, 1968

Viet 3rd Redraft 3/30

TONIGHT, I would like to discuss with you a problem that absorbs and concerns every American — the war in Viet Nam.

Both in Viet Nam and here at home, we are still feeling the shock waves touched off by the Communist Tet offensive. The policymakers in Washington, we are told, are subjecting our entire strategy to a far-reaching and fundamental reappraisal. Whatever the final results of this reappraisal, the fact that it has been necessary is clear evidence of failure.

There is still time to correct this failure. But time is running out. Unless a start is made soon in a new direction, the United States will confront a grim choice between the massive risks of a larger and more brutal war, and the disastrous consequences of defeat.

The answer to failure is not simply more of the same. The continuing debate over military escalation versus military de-escalation misses a fundamental point: that this is more than a military war. Its progress depends on the way it is waged on all fronts — military, economic, political, diplomatic, psychological — and even in military terms, the direction of our effort can be as important as the level of our effort.

The answer to our present troubles is to be found neither in the quantity of arms, nor in the number of men, nor in the geographical boundaries of their use.

There was a time — in the war's earlier stages — when the massive weight of American arms, applied swiftly and sharply in a decisive blow, might have brought the war to an end. But by following its misguided policy of *gradual* escalation, this Administration has

wasted its military options. In the present situation, the first need is
not to do *more* of what we have been doing militarily, but to shift
priorities and change directions.

We need a new approach and a new policy, but first we must
speak with a new candor and clarity.

We must begin with two things: first, we must view the war itself
as the kind of war it is; and second, we must face up to the key role
in Viet Nam, and necessarily in the settlement of the war, that is
played by the world's other great super-power, the Soviet Union.

There are many changes of policy that must be made. But it is to
these two matters that I wish to address myself tonight.

In Viet Nam itself, the fundamental failure has been a failure of
understanding — a failure by our leaders in Washington to understand the complex nature of revolutionary warfare as practiced by
Ho Chi Minh and Mao Tse-tung, by General Giap and Marshal
Lin Piao.

If nuclear war is "total war" in the sense that it threatens total
destruction, these guerrilla wars are total wars in the sense that they
involve every aspect of the life of the nation in which they are being
fought. They are more than battlefield wars. In a guerrilla war,
the price of rice is a weapon; the education of the children is a
weapon; the promise of land is a weapon. And above all, effective
appeals to the loyalty of the people are weapons. Central to any
hope of success is the degree of faith the people have not only in
their own government, but in the whole structure of political, economic, social, military and police power with which they live.

In Viet Nam, we have been failing in large part because the
Johnson Administration has tried to counter the sophisticated techniques of revolutionary warfare with means appropriate to the two
World Wars and the Korean War, but wholly inadequate to the
new kind of war we now are engaged in. And it has acted without
any organized comprehension of the history, the psychology, and
even the language of the people of Viet Nam.

In this new kind of aggression the enemy's target is only secondarily the opponent in the field. His primary targets are the peasant in the hamlet, the people in the cities, and the structure of authority that supports the government. To succeed, the new aggression depends on winning the support of the people — whether that support is given voluntarily or exacted by violence and terror. If it wins that support, there is little that conventional military forces can do to thwart it. If it fails to win that support, then — as Mao himself acknowledges — it cannot win its objectives.

This, then, is a war not for territory, not for battlefield victories, but for the people of South Viet Nam.

It follows that the measure of progress is not the weekly body count of enemy dead. We should never forget that the Viet Cong *are* South Vietnamese — and what finally matters is not the number of Viet Cong killed, but the number of South Vietnamese won over to the cause of building and defending their own country.

Winning the commitment of the South Vietnamese to this cause is a many-pronged task, involving a full array of efforts at political and economic development, administrative reform, the employment of advanced techniques of psychological warfare — but the first requirement is providing protection. This means protection from our own weapons as well as the enemy's.

When we inflict casualties on South Vietnamese civilians equal to or greater than the casualties we inflict on enemy soldiers in the same engagement, we can hardly expect to gain their support — or indeed anything but their bitter hostility.

Beyond this, it means protection by night as well as by day. It means the guarantee that protection provided this month will not be withdrawn next month. And, therefore, in terms of military tactics, it means a shift of emphasis away from search-and-destroy missions, and toward clear-and-hold operations — or what might better be called protect-and-expand operations.

Far more than in a conventional war, in this kind of guerrilla war military tactics must be viewed as part of an *overall* strategy focused on the fundamental political and psychological objectives on which, in turn, success or failure will ultimately turn. Whatever the purely military arguments for search-and-destroy, the larger objectives of this kind of war dictate a different set of priorities.

Protect-and-expand does *not* mean a retreat into enclaves, which would be dangerously vulnerable and would represent a wholly untenable posture of static defense. Rather, it begins with the securing of large populated areas, and then keeps enlarging the secured area. In protect-and-expand, what our side takes, it keeps. As the area is cleared, policed and protected, the boundaries of protection are constantly extended. As the number of protected people grows, the momentum is built that can shift the balance. The dominant *military* objective must be to protect the South Vietnamese so that they can develop the will and the capacity to defend themselves, and so that the wide-ranging reforms needed to build a stable nation can proceed in safety.

Just as a narrow, traditional military framework does not fit the reality of Viet Nam, neither does our equally narrow view of Viet Nam as an isolated trial, a war in a vacuum.

So much is said and written about the scene of the war, about a small and tormented country in a remote corner of Asia, that the rest of the world — and, therefore, the wider context in which the struggle occurs — is too often obscured.

Beneath the struggle among Vietnamese lies the larger, continuing struggle between those nations that want order and those that want disorder; between those that want peace, and those that seek domination.

It is this larger conflict which gives the war in Viet Nam its importance far beyond Southeast Asia.

There is one factor, too frequently unmentioned, we must recognize if we are to restore a realistic perspective on the war in Viet Nam. This is the deep and direct involvement of the Soviet Union. The Kremlin's support of Hanoi profoundly affects the whole nature of the conflict.

The war in Viet Nam has long been explained as an effort to contain the expansive force of Communist China. And so it is — it remains the principal testing-ground for Mao's "wars of national liberation," and is being watched as such in Asia, Africa and Latin America. But in terms of aid and political support, Peking is no longer the senior partner that it once was in North Viet Nam's aggression. It has now become a very junior partner to Moscow.

Today, the Soviet Union and the Communist states of Eastern Europe are providing fully 85 per cent of the sophisticated weapons for North Viet Nam and 100 per cent of the oil. It is Soviet SAMS and Soviet anti-aircraft guns that are shooting down American planes. It is Soviet artillery that is pounding the Marine fortress at Khe Sanh. Without Soviet military assistance, the North Vietnamese war machine would grind to a halt.

The Johnson Administration has made a fundamental error in basing its policies toward the Soviet Union on the wishful assumption that the Soviets want an early end to the war in Viet Nam. Not the small, primitive state of North Viet Nam, but its great Soviet ally and protector inhibits the full exercise of America's military power. Not even the proximity of Red China's massive armies is as powerful a deterrent to U.S. actions as the presence of Soviet freighters in the port of Haiphong. North Viet Nam can hold out stubbornly for total victory because it believes it has total Soviet backing. Yet Washington's desire for a broad political accommodation with the Soviet Union — for *détente* — arouses a will to ignore or to minimize that backing.

Hanoi is not Moscow's puppet, but it must remain a respectful client in order to keep Soviet aid flowing and to balance the influence of nearby Peking. If the Soviets were disposed to see the war ended and a compromise settlement negotiated, they have the means to move Ho Chi Minh to the conference table. The Soviets are not so disposed and, in terms of their *immediate* self-interest, it is hard to see why they should be.

The Soviets enjoy a position of extraordinary advantage in Viet Nam. They hold what could be decisive influence over the duration of the war, and yet they escape the normal hazards — and more important, the responsibilities — of involvement.

Also, they enjoy immense strategic advantages. While the United States is tied down in Viet Nam, the Soviets are loose in the world — free to challenge us in the Mediterranean, free to move into the vacuum left by retreating colonial powers in the Middle East and along the vast rimland of the Indian Ocean. Soviet aid to North Viet Nam has now reached about $5 billion a year — but this compares with our annual expenditure of $30 billion. Just as they did in Korea and Cuba and other encounters, the Soviets have intervened in Viet Nam without committing their own troops, and virtually without casualties. As of the middle of this month, the Viet Nam war had claimed more than 140,000 American casualties — more than we suffered during the entire Korean War. The war bitterly divides the people of the United States, and separates us from our allies.

Yet the Soviet contribution to American frustration costs them nothing in terms of our direct relations. Far from suffering economically or politically because of their sponsorship of aggression, they have received lavish offers of expanded trade and easy credit from the Johnson Administration, which has asked — and gotten — nothing in return. Surely, this is the greatest political and strategic bargain the Kremlin has ever stumbled upon.

The Soviets have reason to be satisfied with the status quo in Viet Nam. Not only is the United States frustrated by the flow of Soviet-supplied arms and inhibited from striking a decisive blow by the Soviet presence, the war also gives the Soviets a position of key political influence in a corner of the Communist world that their Chinese rival would like to consider its own.

The Soviets have no present incentive to see the war ended on a basis satisfactory to the United States, because nothing in the situation seems to offer any immediate threat to their vital world interests — and much appears to enhance those interests.

At every point along the borders of the Communist and non-Communist spheres, the interests of the super-powers are engaged, usually silently and invisibly, but sometimes, as in Viet Nam, openly and directly. Where this is the case, the real centers of decision are Washington and Moscow. To gloss over this fact of international life in our time is to close our eyes to the real world in which the war rages and peace must be made.

In the course of the past generation, the world has changed dramatically — and so has the contest between the super-powers. The cold war of two decades ago, ten years ago, even five years ago, is not the contest of today. The steps toward liberalization of Soviet life, the stirrings of national independence in Eastern Europe, the deep and bitter split between Moscow and Peking, for example, all have had far-reaching consequences. Yet, in our eagerness to see hopeful change occur, we often have based our policy and strategy on overly optimistic judgments. We should not delude ourselves that the Soviets want an early settlement of the war in Viet Nam. The evidence indicates all too clearly that they do not. In their support of Hanoi, the Soviets have encouraged violent disorder rather than peaceful stability.

And yet, while the situation in Viet Nam is obviously bad for the United States, it also is dangerous for the Soviet Union. By accident, by the grim momentum of events, the super-powers could be hurled together in a stark confrontation, ending perhaps with a catastrophic war that neither side wants. The longer the war in Viet Nam goes on, the greater this danger becomes. In view of the risks plainly in sight, the war has already gone on too long.

The easiest way to end the war quickly would be for the United States to surrender on terms designed to conceal the fact. Senator Robert Kennedy probably could end the war quickly — but if his impassioned rhetoric is to be believed, he would do so in a way sure to lose the peace. The silence of defeat that would descend over the Viet Nam battlefield would soon be shattered by the roar of guns elsewhere. Not only the hard-liners in Peking, but also the hard-line doctrinaire faction in the Kremlin, which has recently recovered prestige and influence, would be greatly encouraged to support bolder and more dangerous adventures. Inevitably, the challenge to our power, interests and security would bring a clash, the possible consequences of which are too easily imagined.

For its part, the Johnson Administration has shown that it does not understand either the political nature of revolutionary war, the uses and limits of military power, or how to cope with the Soviet involvement.

The drive for broad understanding with the Soviets — for *détente* — has now faltered and come virtually to a halt. We can and must recover this lost momentum — resolving not only the war in Viet Nam but also many other of the questions which divide the two super-powers that have the destiny of the world in their hands. But the pursuit of peace will require a rebuilding of American strength and a restoration of American purpose. It will require a renewal of intelligence and flexibility at the top of our government, an openness to new ideas and fresh initiatives. It will require careful and deliberate preparation, a full orchestration of the political, economic and diplomatic resources of the United States on a world scale.

Unless there is a sharp change in policy, it must be concluded that the present Administration cannot end the war. It has committed too much power and prestige to fundamentally mistaken policies. It has given too many hostages to the past.

We need a new policy that will awaken the Soviet Union to the perils of the course it has taken in Viet Nam. This should be done, not through belligerent threats, but through candid, tough-minded, face-to-face diplomacy cast in the language of realism that the Soviets understand. The Soviets are unable to comprehend an adversary who confuses the military and political aspects of warfare. Worse, they cannot respect him or take him seriously. And when this erosion of respect undermines the credibility of American will and strength, when the unsure American grasp of the realities of power inspires contempt, the danger to the world grows enormously.

President John F. Kennedy was a realist: he had to be. He learned the hard lessons of power and of the responsibility for exercising power during those anxious nights of the Cuban missile crisis in October, 1962. But, like the people he led, he was also an idealist who believed that men and nations must find a way to live in peace on this small planet. We must recover this essential balance of realism and idealism, and make a fresh start on the difficult road to peace.

The Glassboro summit was a perfect example of how a summit conference should *not* be conducted. It was thrown together hastily and without preparation; the groundwork had not been laid for meaningful discussion and decisions. The conference ended with nothing changed, for the simple reason that the forces that could produce change had not been brought into play.

When the leaders of the super-powers again meet at the summit, as I believe they must and shall, the situation and the atmosphere should be entirely different. We should be certain of our strength and clear about our purpose. We should be ready to advance sound, relevant, and concrete proposals — *not* in the form of unilateral concessions made from weakness and self-doubt, but in the form of offers for mutually advantageous cooperation, made in a spirit of fairness to our adversary and respect for ourselves. And when we go to the summit, we must keep constantly before us an awareness that we represent not only ourselves but the two score nations with which we are allied and whose vital national interests we hold in our trust.

The agenda at the summit should include not only Viet Nam, but also other points of pressure and tension, such as the Middle East, where the Soviets are underwriting aggression, and Castro's Cuba, which is attempting to export subversion throughout the Western Hemisphere.

It would necessarily include the question of the eventual place of Communist China in the community of nations, recognizing that nearly a billion of the world's most dynamic people cannot be allowed to live forever in angry isolation, there to brandish their weapons and threaten their neighbors.

We would offer the Soviets, in the most specific ways possible, as much friendship as they were willing to reciprocate. We would be guided by a recognition that if the dangers of the present are to be

surmounted and the promise of the future achieved, the first necessity is that the two super-powers must find their way to a new beginning.

If the Soviet involvement in Viet Nam causes us frustration and
magnifies the hazards of that war, it also increases the chances of
finding a way· *around* the deadlock in Viet Nam, rather than
through it.

What seems insoluble in a narrow context often becomes soluble
in a larger one. The larger the table, the more can be placed on it,
and the more traders there are, the greater the range of possible
combinations. Precisely because both American and Soviet interests in Viet Nam extend beyond Viet Nam itself, the two super-
powers can discuss the problem in a broader perspective. Bargaining counters that would be irrelevant in the narrow context of Viet
Nam itself, or even of Southeast Asia, become usable when the discussions are global in nature. New levers can be brought into play
to give new leverage. Imaginative diplomacy would find ways of
enlisting those levers controlled by our West European allies, for
example, rather than bemoaning a lack of support in Europe that
stems from a failure of persuasion by the Johnson Administration.
And prudent diplomacy would reserve further economic concessions
to the Soviets for use as bargaining assets.

I am not suggesting that a U.S.–Soviet understanding should be
pursued to the exclusion of other possible avenues. Certainly Hanoi
has its own interests, which do not entirely parallel those of Moscow
— and we should persist in our effort, by both force and diplomacy,
to persuade Hanoi itself that the war is not worth the cost. Beyond
this, we should move swiftly to involve the rest of the world's leaders
in a realistic joint effort to see the war settled — and by this I mean
neither sterile UN resolutions nor pious exhortations to the combat-
ants to stop fighting. Our central objective, after all, is the establishment of conditions in which *other* nations can be secure, and especially the other nations of non-Communist Asia. We should insist
on the translation of that shared stake into a shared responsibility
for defining and achieving a satisfactory solution, consistent with

our own special obligation to the people of Viet Nam and to the long-term cause of peace.

To restore the effectiveness of our diplomacy, we must restore the credibility of our policies and our leadership. This will require a change on the home front. Millions of Americans no longer believe their government. The President has shown incredibly bad judgment in overplaying the good news about Viet Nam and withholding the bad, in portraying victory as just around the corner, and in treating the delicate diplomacy of a search for peace as an exercise in public relations.

The American people are being asked to fight and to pay for the war in Viet Nam, and their future is deeply involved in its outcome. An Administration that lacks faith in the people cannot expect faith from the people; an Administration unwilling to take the people into its confidence cannot expect the people to give it their confidence. Only if we re-establish the credibility of our leadership at home can we begin to re-establish the credibility of our determination where it matters most — in Moscow, Peking and Hanoi.

The American people are not divided between those who want "war" and those who want "peace." Every American wants an end to the war *and* progress toward lasting peace.

The peace we seek cannot be won by surrender, whether outright or camouflaged. It can be neither the illusory peace of scuttle-and-run, nor the fragile peace of retreating into barricaded enclaves, nor the silent peace of the apocalypse. We must seek a just peace, and a durable peace — a peace that neither encourages a new aggression by its weakness, nor sows the seed of explosive resentment by its harshness.

All who see the struggle in Viet Nam clearly, and who recognize its cruel and almost infinite complexity, recognize that there are no swift and simple "solutions," no push-button answers, no gimmicks, no neat or concise "plans" to assure the success of our dual objectives.

But those objectives can be achieved. Of this I am convinced, and to this I am committed.

This evening I have indicated some aspects of the new approach I believe should be taken toward achieving these objectives — toward ending the war in Viet Nam, and winning peace in the world. These mark, I believe, the beginning of realism about the war and about its larger context. There is far more to be done — and in the weeks and months ahead I will be explaining in greater detail my views on other aspects of the effort needed. But the first needs are those I have spoken of tonight.

We are now approaching what perhaps is the decisive test of our national maturity, in which our immense strength will be measured against our courage and intelligence in applying it. I believe we can and will pass this test, and I believe we can move not only tiny Viet Nam, but the whole world in the direction of genuine and lasting peace.

INDEX

Index

Abernathy, Reverend Ralph D., 163–164

ABM (antiballistic missile), 3–4, 25, 63; RJW memos on, 63–65, 72–74

Abplanalp, Robert, 150

Agnew, Spiro T., 125–126, 198, 205, 212, 240–241; speech nominating Nixon at convention, 198, 201; selected as RN's running mate, 202–203; nominating speech for, 204, 205–206, briefed (with Nixon) by LBJ on foreign policy developments, 208; and Nixon's campaign staff, 209, 210; in opinion polls, 218; estrangement from administration, 241–244; role for 1970 elections, 244–247; and 1972 elections, 250, 251; and the "middlebrows," 272

Allen, Anne, viii

Allen, George, viii

Allen, Richard, 178

Alsop, Joseph, 218

American Conservative Union, 267

Americans for Democratic Action, 38

American Society of Newspaper Editors, 152–153, 158; format of meeting, 154–155; Nixon's preparation for appearance at, 155; success of Nixon appearance at meeting of, 157

Anderson, Admiral George, 31–32

Anderson, Dr. Martin, 22–23, 36, 153, 183, 190, 203, 212, 217, 273; his testimonial for Nixon, 55; and Nixon's choice of running mate, 179–180, 200; at July 14 strategy meeting, 181; at Miami convention, 193, 195, 196, 200, 202; on staffing of RN administration, 228

Arlington, Virginia, 162

Ashbrook, John, 267

"Asia After Vietnam," Nixon article in *Foreign Affairs*, 21

Associated Press, 96

Backlash, white, 45–46, 174. *See also* Middle class, white

Baltimore, 203, 209

Baroody, William, Jr., 17

Bay of Pigs, 137

Beaufre, André, 93

Bell, Jeffrey, 216

Bellmon, Henry, 19

Benigna, Mother, 9, 10

Bentsen, Lloyd, 250

Bethesda, 162

Big business, 13, 50–51

Birch (John) Society, 14, 40, 41, 169

"Black capitalism" concept, 158
Blacks, 6, 7, 37–45 *passim*, 145–146,
151–152, 163–164; and Nixon's
"politics of stability," 45; and
backlash, 45–47; "open society"
concept, 159–162; Nixon needs
support of, 174
Bohemian Grove, Nixon speech at,
4, 25, 28, 68–69
Bradley, General Omar, 32, 136–
137
Brinkley, David, 104
Brown, Sam, 90–91
Brownell, Herbert, 91
Brzezinski, Zbigniew, 270
Buchanan, Patrick J., 23–24, 30,
36, 65, 69, 80, 152, 197, 223, 273;
and Nixon's Vietnam position
statements, 33, 134, 135, 141–
142, 189; and Nixon's domestic
peace-keeping stance, 38; as acting press secretary, 52; stressing
of "issues," 57; view of television
exposure, 61–62; and New
Hampshire campaign, 79, 80, 84,
89; and Rockefeller's withdrawal,
127; reaction to Nixon speech
before American Society of Newspaper Editors, 157; and Mitchell,
167; and Nixon's response to
Wallace phenomenon, 174–175,
177–178; at July 14 strategy
meeting, 181; at convention, 194,
195, 202; and Agnew, 198, 204–
205; and Nixon's acceptance
speech, 207; report on the Democratic convention, 214; memos
to RN on Humphrey, 217
Buckley, William F., Jr., 39, 266–
267, 268
Burke, Admiral Arleigh, 10, 68, 211
Burns, Arthur, 156, 228, 256; and
domestic policy, 234, 256; character assassination of, 264–265
Burns, James MacGregor, 109–110

Bush, George, 250, 266
Business, *see* Big business

California, 14, 17, 36, 173; as
pivotal state, 174, 182; black
vote in, 174–175; Nixon plans
campaign in, 208; Nixon carries,
220–221; and 1972 election, 248
Callaway, Howard (Bo), 68, 71
Cambodia, 239–240
Campaign funding, 156–157
Campus radicals, 41
Carmichael, Stokely, 147
Carswell, G. Harrold, 272
CBS, 102
Center for Strategic and Inter-
national Studies, Georgetown
University, 10; Young Presidents
Organization meeting at, 66–71
Chamberlain, John, 46
Chapin, Dwight, 68, 209, 258
Chicago, 146, 208, 214; riots, 215–
216. *See also* Democratic National
convention
Chicago *Tribune*, 101
China, 25, 64; and Nixon's Viet-
nam formulations, 131, 132;
Nixon's visit to, 263, 266
Chotiner, Murray, 53
Christian, George, 112
Churchill, Winston, 58
Cities, 37, 38, 39, 155–156; in RN's
National Industrial Conference
Board speech, 49; Rockefeller's
proposal for, 157; RJW memo
on, 158–162. *See also* Urban
problems
Citizens Committee for Peace with
Freedom in Vietnam, 32–33,
136–137
Civil disorder, *see* Law and order
Clifford, Clark M., 121–123
Coles, Dr. Robert, his *The Middle
Americans*, 270